teach® yourself

postmodernism

teach yourself ®

postmodernism
glenn ward

The **teach yourself** series does exactly what it says, and it works. For over 60 years, more than 40 million people have learnt over 750 subjects the **teach yourself** way, with impressive results.

be where you want to be
with **teach yourself**

For UK orders: please contact Bookpoint Ltd., 130 Milton Park, Abingdon, Oxon OX14 4SB. Telephone: +44 (0) 1235 827720. Fax: +44 (0) 1235 400454. Lines are open from 09.00–18.00, Monday to Saturday, with a 24-hour message answering service. You can also order through our website www.madaboutbooks.com.

For USA order enquiries: please contact McGraw-Hill Customer Services, PO Box 545, Blacklick, OH 43004-0545, USA. Telephone: 1-800-722-4726. Fax: 1-614-755-5645.

For Canada order enquiries: please contact McGraw-Hill Ryerson Ltd., 300 Water St, Whitby, Ontario L1N 9B6, Canada. Telephone: 905 430 5000. Fax: 905 430 5020.

Long renowned as the authoritative source for self-guided learning – with more than 30 million copies sold worldwide – the *Teach Yourself* series includes over 300 titles in the fields of languages, crafts, hobbies, business and education.

British Library Cataloguing in Publication Data: a catalogue record for this title is available from The British Library

Library of Congress Catalog Card Number: On file

First published in UK 1997 by Hodder Headline Ltd., 338 Euston Road, London, NW1 3BH.

First published in US 1997 by Contemporary Books, a Division of The McGraw-Hill Companies, 1 Prudential Plaza, 130 East Randolph Street, Chicago, IL 60601 USA.

The 'Teach Yourself' name and logo are registered trade marks of Hodder & Stoughton Ltd.

Copyright © 1997, 2003 Glenn Ward

In UK: All rights reserved. No part of this publication may be reproduced or transmitted in any form or by any means, electronic or mechanical, including photocopy, recording, or any information storage and retrieval system, without permission in writing from the publisher or under licence from the Copyright Licensing Agency Limited. Further details of such licences (for reprographic reproduction) may be obtained from the Copyright Licensing Agency Limited, of 90 Tottenham Court Road, London W1T 4LP.

In US: All rights reserved. Except as permitted under the United States Copyright Act of 1976, no part of this publication may be reproduced or distributed in any form or by any means, or stored in a database or retrieval system, without the prior written permission of Contemporary Books.

Typeset by SX Composing DTP, Rayleigh, Essex, UK

Printed in Great Britain for Hodder & Stoughton Educational, a division of Hodder Headline Ltd., 338 Euston Road, London NW1 3BH by Cox & Wyman Ltd., Reading, Berkshire.

Impression number   10 9 8 7 6 5 4 3 2 1

Year   2009 2008 2007 2006 2005 2004 2003

contents

preface

The aims of this book

The fact that you have picked up this book suggests that you have heard of postmodernism, and perhaps that you would like to know what it means. Maybe you already have an idea of the kinds of thing that it refers to, and would like to find out more about it. Or perhaps you find it utterly confusing, and want to be furnished with a definition. Either way, it is hoped that this book will fulfil your needs.

Despite its title, you can't 'teach yourself postmodernism' in the same way as you can teach yourself economics, upholstery or the rules of chess. You don't have to master a specific set of skills in order to be able to 'do' it. Nor are there strict rules and requirements to memorize which will qualify you to be a fully fledged 'postmodernist'. Whatever postmodernism may be, it isn't exactly a discipline, activity, ability or pastime. That is not to say, of course, that there is nothing useful to learn about postmodernism. Far from it. I wrote this book with the conviction that it puts forward a number of ideas and debates which are both stimulating and worthwhile. I hope this will become apparent to you too, as you read the book.

As we will see, one of the difficulties, but also perhaps one of the strengths, of postmodernism is its sense of fluidity and open-endedness. It resists being conveniently summarized in easy 'soundbites' and refuses to lend itself fully to any single cut and dried definition. So this book does not aspire to 'solve' postmodernism. It pretends to be neither definitive nor totally comprehensive. Rather than being an encyclopaedia of post-modernism, it is a guide to the territory which sets out to provide you with useful points of entry and orientation. To that extent, and in order to avoid confusion and congestion in its very limited space, it has to take a selective view. This inevitably means that some aspects are covered in more depth than others, and that there are some things I have decided to leave out completely.

But being necessarily partial is not the same as being narrow. One of the problems with introductory texts in this area is that they often give an account of the 'postmodern condition' from a single angle, or from within the limits of just one academic field. The danger here is that the perspective on postmodernism given by one subject area does not necessarily correspond to or illuminate what it means for another. One outcome of addressing a more specialized audience in this way is that it can seem rigid and insular to the general reader. To avoid that problem I have tried to take a more cross-disciplinary approach. This book therefore introduces as wide a range of ideas, thinkers and views as is possible without losing focus.

Using this book

Chapters have been organized around broad themes and concerns rather than around individual ideologies, schools of thought or art-forms. This should allow you to tailor the subject matter to your own interests and requirements. The book probably makes most sense when read from cover to cover, but individual chapters are designed to be coherent by themselves and can be read in an order of your own choosing. I do not make all of the connections or point out all of the contradictions for you. Indeed, I hope that, in following your own threads, you will find echoes and tensions that I wasn't aware of. The index, glossary, 'taking it further' section and chronology at the end of the book should help you do this.

Some of the theorists discussed here can be a struggle to read. I do not claim that what follows will miraculously transform their writings into works of incredible clarity. They will remain difficult. But this book will give you a grip on many of the key ideas wrapped up in their notions of the postmodern. In that respect you can treat it as a self-sufficient statement in its own right. But my desire is that, having used this book, you will want to go beyond it: I hope that it will have provided a framework of ideas through which to carry out your own investigations.

01

post-modernisms

In this chapter you will learn:

- the significance of the word postmodernism
- the history of the word post-modernism
- some of the different uses of the word postmodernism.

Postmodernism is everywhere

The term postmodernism has been in widespread use for three decades, but the story of its spread through culture is fairly complex. Apart from a number of isolated early sightings of the term (some of which we will discuss later in this chapter), postmodernism started life mainly as an academic category concerned with certain developments in the arts, but soon became a descriptive term for all sorts of proposed shifts and changes in contemporary society and culture. To take just one example, it was argued that the world had lost faith in technological progress. Because faith in technological progress was seen as belonging to a specific 'modernist' historical period, the term 'postmodernist' was thought an apt description of our new period of disillusionment. However, by the mid-1980s, postmodernism had blossomed into what can sometimes seem like a catch-all term for just about anything.

By the middle of that decade, postmodernism in many areas (like architecture, politics or literature) was frequently discussed in late night television 'culture' slots, radio arts programmes, and middlebrow Sunday newspaper supplements. These discussions often consisted of either agonising over what sense could possibly be made of a word like postmodernism, or dismissing it outright as a trendy buzz-word rapidly reaching its sell-by date.

Today, the deluge of books on postmodernism has slowed to a steady drizzle, and heated debate has cooled into sober reassessment. In some quarters (the art world for instance) the word, if not the issues to which it refers, seems to be in the process of being wilfully forgotten. Meanwhile, aspects of postmodern theory have been fully integrated into humanities courses right across the Western world.

So postmodernism persists, to the extent that we might almost say (again with a little exaggeration) that it has become part of everyday speech. This suggests that it might be worth our while to look into exactly what lies behind it. *Teach Yourself Postmodernism* is a guide to doing so.

Multiplying meanings

It is possible to look at the field of psychoanalysis, identify its founding figure as Sigmund Freud, and go on to describe the main conceptual tools behind the psychoanalytic method. With postmodernism it is not quite so easy to do this. Postmodernism is not, strictly speaking, a school of thought. It is not a unified intellectual movement with a definite goal or perspective, and it does not have a single dominant theoretician or spokesperson.

This is because ideas about postmodernism have been adopted by virtually every discipline, from philosophy to cultural studies, from geography to art history. Each area has produced books and periodicals with their own particular angles on the topic, each has defined postmodernism in their own terms. In short, postmodernism has proliferated. Taken on board in so many different fields, where it can refer to so many different things, its meanings have multiplied, and the sheer volume of texts it has generated have tended to obscure, rather than clarify, what on earth it is all about. The problem is that what postmodernism might mean in one discipline is not necessarily compatible with what it might mean in another.

So postmodernism now leads a complicated life. So complicated, in fact, that there are really several postmodernisms in existence, or at least many variations on it. On the one hand it now circulates, however ironically, in popular culture. On the other hand, it remains a controversial subject in academic books and journals. Some areas have become bored with it and are looking for alternatives. Others are only just getting used to having it around. For some, it is now a firmly established shorthand for a range of social and cultural transformations. Still others remain sceptical about its usefulness.

Even in the day to day speech of what are sometimes called the 'chattering classes' postmodernism has more than one application. It can be used, for example, as a vague term for any contemporary artefact that seems in some way ironic. Or it can be used, even more vaguely, as a general name for our particular moment in history. Add to this the fact that its meaning has been argued over in the very areas (such as literary criticism) in which it was born, and it seems the only certain thing is that postmodernism is hard to get to the bottom of.

A flexible term

All of this might make it sound as though postmodernism can be anything you want it to be, and perhaps there is a little truth in this. In ways which this book will demonstrate, postmodernism can be:

- an actual *state of affairs* in society
- the *set of ideas* which tries to define or explain this state of affairs
- an artistic *style*, or an approach to the making of things
- a *word* used in many different contexts to cover many different aspects of all the above.

These are just four of the ways you can think about what postmodernism is. There are probably others. Of course, it is not so easy to separate these approaches in practice. For instance, if there is such a thing as a postmodern artistic *style*, a theorist of postmodernism might look at how that style relates to, or arises from, a postmodern *condition* in society.

Although taking something from all of them, the second approach in the above list is closest to the one adopted by this book. Rather than attempt to offer one all-embracing definition, postmodernism is most fruitfully viewed as a variety of perspectives on our contemporary situation. This means seeing postmodernism not so much as a thing, but more as a set of concepts and debates. We might even go so far as to say that postmodernism can best be defined as that very set of concepts and debates about postmodernism itself.

New times

Despite its great flexibility, postmodernism is not meaningless, and ways into it are not so hard to find. Of course, it still has the connotations of obscurity and elitism that always seem to stick to words with a so-called intellectual origin. But although theories about it are often discussed in very abstract terms, postmodernism can equally be concerned with far more concrete matters.

There are a number of identifiable themes which run consistently through the different versions of postmodernism, and the chapters of this book have on the whole been organized around them. Put as broadly as possible, these themes are to do with what it means to live in our present times, and with how best to go about describing them.

- They propose that society, culture and lifestyle are today significantly different from what they were 100, 50 or even 30 years ago.
- They are concerned with *concrete* subjects like the developments in mass media, the consumer society and information technology.

- They suggest that these kinds of development have an impact on our understanding of more *abstract* matters, like meaning, identity and even reality.
- They claim that old styles of analysis are no longer useful, and that new approaches and new vocabularies need to be created in order to understand the present.

Pre-history

Perhaps the biggest problem with postmodernism is the word itself. The prefix *post-* means *after*, and *modern* can be taken to mean *current* or *up-to-date*. How then is it possible to be *after* the *modern*? How can we get a handle on such a paradoxical notion? One thing we can do is look at some of the word's history.

Although postmodernism's boom time has been in the last two decades, it has actually been around for quite a while. The term did have a number of isolated early incarnations, and these make up a kind of 'pre-history' of postmodernism. Before we go on to look at some of them, it is worth remembering that we should not see such 'pre-historic' examples as definitive. To do so can sometimes lead you up blind alleys, because what post-modernism meant *then* does not always sit comfortably with what it means *now*. Having said that, the six examples given below are worth looking at because they do overlap in some interesting ways with today's varieties of postmodernism. As we will see, they anticipate to a certain extent the terms and debates of the more recent, more fully developed postmodernisms. Attempts by historians to discover the first ever use of the term have so far been inconclusive, but early appearances include:

The 1870s

An English artist called John Watkins Chapman used it to describe painting which he saw as more advanced than that of French Impressionist painters like Claude Monet or Auguste Renoir. The work of the Impressionists had been seen as the most up-to-the minute expression of modern times – in other words as the most *modern* of modern art. In Chapman's usage, postmodernism referred to new (post-Impressionist) art which went further than Impressionism's attempts to capture in paint the fleeting appearances of nature.

1917

The German writer Rudolph Pannwitz spoke of nihilistic, amoral new 'postmodern men' who had broken away from old established values of modern European civilization.

1947

In his summary of British historian Arnold Toynbee's six volumes of *A Study of History* (1947) D C Somervell suggested that Toynbee's focus on history could be called 'post-Modern'. Toynbee then took it up, and in subsequent volumes of his work he put forward the notion of a 'post-Modern age'. This age was the period following on from the Dark to Middle Ages (1075–1475) and the Modern Age (1475–1875). The 'Modern' was regarded by Toynbee as a time of social stability and progress. But since about 1875 Western civilization, with the growth of industrialized cities, had been troubled by social turmoil, anxiety and revolution.

1957

American cultural historian Bernard Rosenberg named as postmodern the new circumstances of life in society at that time. He argued that important social and cultural changes were taking place. These changes included the rise of technological domination and the development of a mass culture of universal 'sameness'.

The work of Rosenberg, Toynbee and others provides a good example of how early uses of the term postmodernism do not always tally with how it is used today. In their work, changes in the values and conditions of society were effectively brought about by the expansion of industry. Their use of the term postmodern to describe this expansion was both specialized and potentially confusing. Specialized, because it was meant to draw attention to the contemporary world's difference from certain political, economic and philosophical aspects of the 'Modern' age. Potentially confusing, because the period of transition from one era to another (roughly the late nineteenth to early twentieth centuries) is more usually known as the period of *modernity*. We will come to describe the features of modernity in more detail in a moment.

1964

Leslie Fiedler described a 'post-' culture which rejected the elitist values of highbrow modern art and literature.

1968

American art critic Leo Steinberg noticed in contemporary visual art (for example, Pop Art) a change in interest from the representation of nature to the 'flat' representation of man-made images. He called this tendency postmodern because whereas older kinds of modern art (from Impressionism onwards) had been concerned with capturing visual or emotional truth, Pop Art was interested in artificiality.

There are two important areas of overlap between these various 'pre-historic' postmodernisms and the meanings of post-modernism today. The first concerns the notion that we have entered a phase in history with its own unique characteristics. The second concerns an important distinction (but also an equally important mingling) between theories of postmodernism in society, and theories of postmodernism in the arts. Both of these aspects are surveyed in the rest of this chapter. Though brief, this survey will provide some orientation for our later explorations.

Modernity and enlightenment

Some of our postmodern forerunners spoke about society entering a new phase. They claimed that we were in a historical period with novel features that distinguished it from any other time in history. In particular, it was to be distinguished from the preceding Modern Age. The exact character of this age, as well as the precise dates of its beginning and end, has been described in different ways by historians, but it is often associated with faith in:

- progress
- optimism
- rationality
- the search for *absolute knowledge* in science, technology, society, and politics
- the idea that gaining knowledge of the *true self* was the only foundation for all other knowledge.

In debates about postmodernism, these kinds of value are often called *Enlightenment Ideals*. In other words, they are associated with the *Age of Reason* (or Enlightenment), which originated in seventeenth and eighteenth century Europe, and which quickly influenced all Western thought. As the above list suggests, early Enlightenment ideals involved rational enquiry as the guiding principle for all knowledge, and the belief that only progress in intellectual method could bring about a world of order, security, social understanding and happiness.

This so-called *enlightment project* or *project of modernity* is not without its own internal disagreements, of course; it involves as many doubts and disputes as any other historical phase. To this degree it may be something of an over-statement to speak of the Modern Age (in Toynbee's sense of the term) as having, or being, a single project. Nevertheless, the general philosophy of the period is often defined in terms of its belief that progress in society could be brought about through the gradual perfection (through increasing self knowledge and rigorous intellectual method) of humanity. Thinkers associated with this tradition include Kant, Hegel and Voltaire. The up side to it was an investment in universal human rights that ultimately led to the French Revolution and the United States' Declaration of Human Rights. The down side to it is that, in believing that their values should be universally applied, Enlightenment thinkers tended arrogantly to see Europe as the most enlightened and advanced part of the world. Europe was seen as more civilized than the rest of the globe, and this led to the dangerous feeling that other countries and races could be colonized, exploited or bettered. As we saw in the case of Arnold Toynbee, some early accounts of a *post*-modernism describe a decline in these values or a radical break from them.

This proposed decline or break also forms an important part of today's debates about postmodernism. It is often argued that today's society has lost sight of these ideals. In direct contrast to the above features of the Modern Age, postmodern society is often negatively associated with:

- exhaustion
- pessimism
- irrationality
- disillusionment with the idea of absolute knowledge.

To confuse matters even further, the Italian novelist and theorist of culture Umberto Eco has seen, as a result of these supposedly widespread features of the present historical moment, a return in our times to attitudes of the middle ages.

On the other hand, many postmodern thinkers, rather than regretting the fall of the Enlightenment, have actively sought to challenge its assumptions or have celebrated its supposed decline. As you will see, this has been the case with most of the thinkers dealt with in this book. Their reasons for doing so will become clear as we go along, but for now we can note the following broad themes:

- an erosion of conventional distinctions between high and low culture (see Chapters 2 and 3)
- fascination with how our lives seem increasingly dominated by visual media (see Chapter 4)
- a questioning of ideas about meaning and communication, and about how signs refer to the world (see Chapter 5)
- a sense that definitions of human identity are changing, or ought to change (see Chapters 6 and 7)
- scepticism about the stories we tell to explain 'the human race', and about the idea of progress (see Chapter 8).

Modernity and modernization

Another name for the Modern Age is *modernity*. Modernity is connected to the idea of modernization. Modernization suggests updating something, or bringing something into line with what are seen as present day fashions and needs. If we talk, for example, of having our kitchen modernized, we mean that we are having it fitted with the latest equipment and decorated in a more 'now' style (of course, having a 'now' style these days might involve having a very 'tomorrow' (futuristic) or 'yesterday' (Olde Worlde) style. Likewise, modernization of the workplace (whether shopfloor, classroom, hospital or office) usually consists of keeping it up to date with current technological innovations and of putting into practice the latest ideas about achieving efficiency and maximum productivity. Similar processes of modernization can be seen in most walks of life, from medicine to town planning to education to tele-communications. It is, of course, an endless process. No sooner is an innovation put into service than it is modified or replaced by a newer, better model. Hence styles in clothes and kitchens will always be going out of fashion, washing powders will forever be 'new and improved', and employers will always find ever-better ways of 'streamlining' their workforce. Such a dynamic of constant and rapid change has been accelerating especially since the turn of the nineteenth and twentieth centuries.

In or after modernity?

These and other factors have all been seen as part and parcel of a unique stage in social history – a period featuring many important differences between traditional and contemporary society. To this extent, the society we live in now can be interpreted as the result, or as the intensification, of the key features of modernity outlined above. It seems clear, for instance, that new ways of communicating are still being developed (the Internet and the mobile phone are two fairly recent examples), that cities are continuing to grow upwards and outwards, and that the updating process is (at least in areas like fashion) as rapid as ever.

For these sorts of reason, some versions of postmodernism (both pro- and anti-) have seen it not as a break, but as an outcome or extension of modernity. Postmodernism in this case is to do with what modernization has so far led to – postmodernism as the latest point in the progress of modernization. For example, we see in the sixth chapter of this book how recent developments in cybernetic technology can be linked to theories of post-modernism. Yet these developments can be seen as the most recent product of the process of endless invention triggered by the Industrial Revolution rather than as part of a unique contemporary historical epoch that at some recent point simply snapped off from the past.

To take another example, television has sometimes been seen almost as a symbol for postmodernism itself. Television today, with its satellite broadcasts, channel surfing, live reports from war zones and so on, can indeed seem like a unique innovation. But it can just as easily be seen as a product of the rise of mass media that began in the final quarter of the nineteenth century. It was at that time, for instance, that Marconi invented telegraphy, and the Lumière brothers developed cinematography out of a whole array of photographic experiments and discoveries. Thus, for all its apparent newness and technological sophistication, television today can be seen as another product of modernity. Some of the aspects of television that have recently attracted the attention of postmodern theorists will be dealt with later in this book, especially in the fourth chapter.

The question of whether postmodernism is a split from an older era, part of an endless cycle of change, or just another aspect of the Modern Age (perhaps with a genuine postmodern period yet to come) has been a focus of considerable debate. Opinions on it depend largely on how the timetables of history are drawn up. They depend on where people draw their lines between and around so-called periods of history. As any theorist of postmodernism would argue, such periods exist more as man-made ways of carving up the past and the present than as real stretches of time with actual, momentous beginnings and endings.

Just as there is no straightforward way of drawing a line between the Middle and the Modern Ages, so there can be no clean, objective, distinction between the modern and the postmodern. We can point to no single date and claim that it marks either a chasm or a point of transition between the two periods.

A distinction

If you look back at our six early uses of the word post-modernism, you will see that it could be divided into two main categories. On the one hand, there was the concern with postmodernism as a *social and economic* event, brought about mainly by the spread of mass industry. On the other hand, there was postmodernism as what we might loosely call a *cultural* matter, a matter of changes in the arts.

In some ways this distinction between the social and the cultural is quite artificial. The two can be said to inform each other to such a degree that, in reality, they cannot be separated. Would you, for example, put television into the cultural or the social category? Again, why should the arts be considered as apart from the social? Despite this, it is a useful distinction to bear in mind when you start looking into postmodernism. For instance, recent novels that have been called postmodernist (novels by, say, John Fowles, Kurt Vonnegut or Don DeLillo) may be named as such because they reflect or express postmodern social conditions or because they have parallels with some postmodern factor found in other art forms. But they may also be called postmodernist because they can be said to come in an important way after literary modernism. Without having to define literary modernism for now (and it is quite a contentious matter), the point to note is that it is not *necessarily* the same as modernity in society at large.

Now, as you will have noticed from the above, a distinction can therefore be made between: postmodern*ism* and postmodern*ity*.

Technically speaking, the first refers to cultural and artistic developments (i.e. in music, literature, art, film, architecture, and so on), while the second has to do with social conditions and the 'mood' that these conditions give rise to.

Sometimes this distinction has been adhered to in postmodern theory, and sometimes it has not. Nowadays, however, postmodernism tends increasingly to be doing service for both sides. For the sake of consistency, I will tend to follow this practice of using postmodern*ism* to describe the two.

Conclusion

So far, we have looked at postmodernism in largely negative terms. We have looked at some of the confusions which continue to surround it despite, or because of, its popularity. We have indicated some of the general trajectory of postmodern theory, and we have made some suggestions about what postmodernism is not. What we have avoided so far is one clear, single definition of what it *is*.

When people ask what postmodernism is, they often seem to be asking for the word to be used as a name for a single, observable thing. That thing may be an object, a human condition, or whatever. Either way, it is something that is assumed simply to exist. The postmodernism label, it is assumed, can then be unquestionably stuck on to it. The thing can be defined, and we can all go home happy, secure in our knowledge of what postmodernism is. However, many theorists of postmodernism would argue that things do not really happen that way. They would argue that unquestionably postmodern things are not just going about the world waiting to have their postmodern credentials objectively identified by you or me. To name something (whether a theory, artwork, or aspect of society) as postmodern is not simply to unearth an objectively existing truth about it. Nothing contains a retrievable 'essence of postmodernism' which you can drag into the light and examine for clues to postmodernism's ultimate nature or genetic code.

Rather, if you call something postmodern, you are placing it in a certain category, or framing it in a certain way. You are bringing an idea *to* it, rather than discovering a quality *in* it. In doing so you are ultimately linking it to a set of ideas about the world and our relationship to the world.

So postmodernism is most usefully thought of as an elastic critical category with a range of applications and potential understandings. It is a kind of 'portable' term which enables us to enter a great many ideas about the specific characteristics of the world today. Some of these ideas have only been hinted at so far, and the rest of this book is devoted to unravelling them.

There are various ways of dividing up these ideas. One is to define postmodernism in terms of the 'deaths' or 'ends' that it has been said to signal:

The end of history. This is to do with postmodernists' scepticism about the idea of progress. It also relates to debates about how histories are written, and to the thought that events lack unity or direction.

The end of 'man'. This is to do with postmodernism's interrogation of 'mankind' as a social and historical invention. It is also connected to the idea that new technologies are moving us into a 'post-human' stage of development.

The death of the real. This is to do with postmodernism's abandonment of the pursuit of absolute truth, and its preference for the temporary, the superficial and the apparent. It is linked to philosophical reflections on the relationship between reality and representation, and to the view that reality is increasingly constructed by *signs*.

These three 'posts' are recurring themes throughout this book.

Further reading

You can find more about the Enlightenment, its ideas, and the postmodern challenges to them in:

Postmodernism: A reader, edited by Thomas Docherty (1993)

The Enlightenment and its Shadows, edited by Peter Hulme and Ludmilla Jordanova (1990).

02

issues in 'high and low' culture: architecture and literature

In this chapter you will learn:

- how and why postmodernist culture challenges traditional distinctions between 'high' culture and 'low' culture
- the role in this challenge of *eclectic*, *pluralist* approaches to style
- the role of self-consciousness and irony in postmodernism.

We will focus on examples from literature and architecture because those two fields were particularly important in the early identification of a postmodern 'turn' in the arts. We will find that what modernism has come to mean for architecture is not quite the same as what it has come to mean for literature, and therefore that these two art forms are not always reacting to exactly the same thing. Their individual 'postmodernisms' will inevitably be geared towards their particular requirements. It is always important to bear this in mind. Nevertheless, many postmodern ideas, practices and debates are shared across the arts, and this allows us to make some generalizations. *Pastiche* and *eclecticism*, for example, have been seen as common artistic strategies within postmodern culture at large. This chapter will look at how such practices participate in a blurring of the high/low culture divide that is often taken as a key feature of life in the postmodern age.

The critic Andreas Huyssen has suggested that modernism in the arts defines itself as necessarily outside of, and superior to, the rest of culture and society. Postmodernism, on the other hand, crosses the great divide that modernist art and criticism once tried to place between themselves and mass culture. For various reasons, that supposed split between high and low has become less and less relevant to many artists and critics since at least the 1960s. For Huyssen, postmodernism represents a rejection of modernism's 'relentless hostility to mass culture', and moves towards a new situation in which 'the pedestal of high art and high culture no longer occupies the privileged space it used to'. This means that while the role of the arts is, for Huyssen, to maintain a critical stance towards contemporary society, they no longer do so from an imagined position of superiority.

Postmodernist arts have their feet more firmly on the ground and recognize that they share the same world with all other aspects of cultural life.

Let's see how this works in practice.

The demolition of modernist architecture

If you have visited a shopping centre built at some point in the last 20 or so years, there is a good chance that it had at least some of the following characteristics:

- a mixture of architectural styles from past times (perhaps you can find echoes of Victorian greenhouse, art deco cinema, Georgian and so on)
- a mixture of styles from different places: American-style diner, Italian-style pizzeria, London pub, Breton crêperie)
- numerous ornamental, decorative or pictorial features (murals, reliefs, pediments, clock towers, columns that don't hold anything up)
- lots of play between different surfaces, materials and colours (marble effects, plexi-glass, mirrors, unconcealed girders, smooth plastics, wood, plastic wood, chrome)
- a high degree of 'fake' (tap any interior column and it is likely to make a hollow sound; examine any flagstone floor and you are unlikely to find it made of real stone)
- a high degree of 'referencing' (as well as referring to the styles of different times and places, the exterior of the building might echo the shapes and materials of the surrounding area).

As you will have guessed, all of these features can be, and often have been, defined as postmodernist. That is to say, they represent a departure from the rules and conventions of modernist architecture. Modernist buildings, generally speaking, are easy to identify. Think of any large grey office block, factory, or housing development constructed between the 1950s and the mid 1970s, and you will probably have in mind a classic example of high modernism at its most depressing. It is likely to feature the following:

- repetition of a simple shape (squares, rectangles, boxes)
- uniformity of design (mostly the same all over)
- complete lack of frills (no ornamentation)
- harsh, industrial looking materials (especially reinforced concrete)
- a flat roof (totally impractical in wet countries)
- dominance over the surrounding environment (very big, towering over older buildings, neighbourhoods were probably flattened to make room for it)
- an imminent demolition order.

The contrast between this and your nearby out-of-town leisure complex is probably quite stark.

Some modernist edifices have been officially preserved as part of our cultural heritage. Others are continually spruced up by local authorities with a lick of paint and the odd façade. In some quarters, high-rise living has even become fashionable, a style choice rather than a necessity. Yet many examples are now being pulled down, associated as they often are with vandalism, 'concrete cancer', and the misery of living in an anonymous box in the sky. One of the first major demolitions of a modernist development was as long ago as 1972, when the Pruitt-Igoe housing project (completed in 1955), was declared uninhabitable and was subsequently dynamited by the city of St. Louis, Missouri. Many of its low-income inhabitants so disliked the prize-winning accommodation they were forced to endure that they repeatedly vandalized it. One postmodern architect, Charles Jencks, has identified this as the day modernism died. We will return to Jencks in a moment.

It can be hard to believe that the modernist style was once considered the future of urban planning. Yet the originators of this style saw themselves as part of a genuinely Utopian impulse. They really believed that they could make the world a better place, that modernism could play a major part in the improvement of human life.

Modernist architecture

Modernism in architecture is generally identified with a small number of European and American architects working early in the twentieth century: Mies van der Rohe, Walter Gropius, Henri Le Corbusier, and Frank Lloyd Wright. Their ideas rapidly spread on a global scale. Many of the techniques, as well as the appearance, of their buildings were adopted by architects all over the world, becoming the familiar *International Style* which we caricatured above. Although there are differences between their ideas, the main thrust was a belief in:

1: Novelty

It is necessary to be 'up to date'. Architects should express the spirit of the modern, industrial age, and not be tied to the past. The new world has its own, dynamic qualities and architecture should both speak of and contribute to this dynamism, unfettered by tradition. It should make maximum use of new building materials and methods.

Engineers are new modern artists. The art of architecture is now a matter of maths, science and function. Buildings should be streamlined, *rational* machines. Being rational means that they should be based on rigorously scientific (as opposed to subjective) reasoning. Housing should be based on the same design principles as factories and automobiles. Modern cities should be designed to accommodate speed.

2: Progress

Humankind can only escape from misery by shedding the past and embracing the age of the machine and mass production. In uniting industry, science and art, rationalizing the organization of urban social spaces and sweeping away the congestion of the old city streets, modern architecture can create Utopia. This will be achieved on an international scale, with no thought for backward-looking, stifling regional traditions. New communities can be quickly built on the basis of cheaper materials and standardized units. Modernity is technological progress; industrial manufacturers and machine designers are engaged in a search for universal harmony and perfection. Architecture should participate in this evolution towards a bright, hygienic, efficient society.

3: Heroism

Modernist architects see themselves as the god-like creators of a brave new world. They have privileged access to the keys to the advancement of civilization, and so they draw the blueprints of the future.

4: Purity

This Utopian vision is to be achieved through the strictest of means. Buildings are to be reduced to their purest forms. Their beauty lies in their function, simplicity, rationality, newness and unity. Beauty is not something tacked on to them in the form of decoration. Ornament is to be rejected as superficial, dishonest and wasteful. Modern building must be 'true to itself'. Frivolous trappings serve only to detract from a building's integrity.

As you can see, this all links directly back to the points we made about the Enlightenment project in the previous chapter. This can be summarized as the belief that the progress of the whole world could be spearheaded by the superior, more rational knowledge possessed by the Western intellect. The rest of the world could be literally civilized by the values that the International Style represented.

So what went wrong?

The modernist architect was uncompromising in his attempt to break with the past and forge a brave a new world of clean, disciplined order. He had principles. He was committed to producing a democratic architecture for all. The problem was that he became authoritarian and dogmatic, presuming to tell the 'masses' what was good for them, and attempting to fit them into abstract, rational systems. Le Corbusier wanted homes to be 'machines for living', but most people don't want to live in machines. Nor do most people live by Mies van der Rohe's dictum that 'less is more'. While modernists loathe 'unnecessary' decoration, many people find decoration entirely necessary. One defence of postmodernism is that it simply tries to accept this. It replaces modernism's functionality, rationality, and purity with a more democratic, less elitist, playfulness.

The big question is whether, and why, modernism 'failed'. Are the infamous architectural 'disasters' an inevitable consequence of modernism's brutal logic, or is something else to blame? In a lecture delivered in 1981 the German scholar Jurgen Habermas asked, 'is the real face of modern architecture revealed in these atrocities, or are they distortions of its true spirit?'

In modernism's defence Habermas pointed out that the forward-looking 'spirit' of modernism is not at fault; the finger should be pointed at big businesses, unscrupulous developers and third-rate planners who don't understand its principles. Market forces and bureaucracy, especially in the urban reconstruction that followed the Second World War, had caused modernism to lose contact with everyday life and the diverse experiences of ordinary people. The standards of factory building should never have been confused with those of house building. Hence the problem lay not in *aesthetic modernism* itself but in its relationship with *capitalist modernization*. Social and political change would enable modernism to fulfil its ambitions; it wasn't over, it was unfinished.

Plural coding

The architect and theorist Charles Jencks has praised post-modernist architecture for its ability to go beyond modernist elitism. Modernist ideas aimed to strip architecture of ambiguity and connotation. They stated that a building should carry no associations outside of its own magnificent declaration of modernity. Jencks calls this aspect of the modernist ideal *univalence*. What he means by this is that buildings were supposed to have a single meaning. For example, the International Style preferred buildings to be structured around the repetition of a simple geometrical formula.

One problem with this was that modernist buildings often failed to give pleasure to their users (the exception being luxury houses commissioned from modernist architects by wealthy patrons for private use). Against this, Jencks proposes that postmodernism is *multivalent* (has many different meanings) or *plural coded*. That is, it is deliberately open to many different interpretations. Instead of imposing a single meaning, formula or presence on anyone, postmodernist buildings are more free-style and allow for the pleasures of finding associations and making connections. They have little respect for whatever might be regarded as architecturally pure or correct, preferring instead to reach out into the wider cultural arena of which they are a part. They therefore try to effect a greater sense of communication.

To take one of the most well-known examples: in the A.T. & T. building in New York, designed by Philip Johnson, a classical broken pediment perches on top of what appears to be a typical case of high international modernism (a rather imposing oblong skyscraper). The building as a whole can be said to refer (at least for those who get the references) to a modernist skyscraper, a particular Italian Renaissance chapel, Chippendale furniture, and even the radiator of a Rolls Royce. Modernist critics will be unlikely to take much of an interest in A.T. &T.'s resemblance to a grandfather clock. Being modernists, they will be keen to study its harmonious orchestration of forms and materials, rather than what these might allude to. The rest of us can take pleasure in resemblance to other things, or in the effect of mixing ancient and modern in a single building.

You can of course find equally good examples in any urban centre today: ironically enough, plurally coded postmodernism has itself become a new sort of international style.

The function of postmodern architecture

So postmodern buildings are collages of different visual styles, languages, or codes. They allude at once to local traditions, popular culture, international modernism, and high-technology, yet refuse to let any one of these elements become dominant. Jencks argues that by mixing and mis-matching in this way, plurally coded architecture opens itself up to a wider audience. It is a form of 'dissonant beauty' which, full of vitality, ambiguity and irony, defines different functions according to the needs, tastes and moods of different social groups. It speaks in many accents in order to engage as many 'readers' as possible, all of whom will be able to read the language of the building in their own terms, relating it to their own knowledge and experience.

In this way postmodern architecture is a democratic 'juxta-position of tastes and world-views' which responds to the fact that we live in what Jencks sees as a *pluralistic*, cosmopolitan 'culture of choice' rather than one of enforced sameness. This theme of cultural diversity occurs frequently within postmodern theory and practice. It will reappear several times in the rest of this book (see, for example, the discussion of Jean-Francois Lyotard in Chapter 8).

Jencks argues against the criticism, sometimes levelled against postmodernism, that it is necessarily a conservative or merely nostalgic tendency. He claims that postmodernism, rather than simply regurgitating tradition, can be seen as a 'radical *eclecticism*' which actively engages in a dialogue between past and present, showing (contrary to the modernist myth of absolute novelty) that each affects our understanding of the other. He also argues that, by colliding different codes, postmodernism highlights the different ways in which buildings can be read into by diverse 'taste cultures'. They show, against modernist ideology, that meanings are never absolute or universal. According to this argument, the idea that there are timeless or universal aesthetic truths which we should all learn to appreciate is the product of a privileged social group (the modernist 'taste culture') with a specific area of knowledge and a particular agenda. Ideas about purity and progress and beauty are far from neutral: they are cover-ups for the social, historical, and political positions of power from which architects draw up their designs.

Some criticisms of postmodern architecture

Some critics have seen postmodernism as a failure of nerve on the part of architects. They have regarded it as a decline in standards, a collapse of the artistic imagination, a conservative appeal to the lowest common denominator. Although postmodernist buildings do embrace the latest construction techniques and materials, their designers have lost their bottle and run out of revolutionary spirit. Swapping their moral and aesthetic responsibilities for easy populism, they no longer see their activity as vital to the creation of a better tomorrow. One reason for this is that architects are married to commerce. Another criticism is that the more progressive postmodernist principles (see below) are mostly applied only to places of business, leisure and/or shopping. Housing design remains as unimaginative as ever. Postmodernism is therefore just a way of trying to get people to spend longer at the shops. Like the literature of the late 1960s (see later in this chapter), this seems to be the architecture of exhaustion. It is therefore regressive rather than progressive, reactionary rather than radical. Distinctions like this are common in debates about postmodernism. Jencks, for example, distinguishes between:

Straight revivalism

Buildings in this category are seen by Jencks as reactionary or conservative. Any building that is new but looks old fits this description. Simply old fashioned, it acts as though modernism never happened. Instead of challenging tradition, it merely repeats it. It is stuck nostalgically in an imagined past that it never questions. This reflects a general tendency in our culture to be simultaneously obsessed with images of the past and forgetful of real history. (Similar criticisms are often made about theme parks, theme pubs, heritage parks and costume dramas).

Radical eclectism

The kind of architecture which Jencks puts into this category mixes up styles and references in an ironic way. By placing different styles together it effectively puts buildings in quotation marks, expressing a more critical attitude both to tradition and to architecture itself.

More recent *deconstructivist* architecture has attempted to pursue this critical spirit. Influenced by the ideas of the philosopher Jacques Derrida, it combines hi-tech materials and methods with postmodernist *pluralism* and a collage-like sense of design. We look at deconstructivism in some detail in Chapter 5.

Another critic, Fredric Jameson, has found a similar two-part categorization within the entire field of postmodern culture. He distinguishes between:

Pastiche

Echoing Jencks' view of 'straight revivalism', Jameson sees postmodernism as an art of *pastiche* that merely mixes references in a hollow, empty spectacle. Pastiche, for Jameson, revels nostalgically in past styles, but shows no understanding of history and no desire to look forward. It pieces old styles together because it can think of nothing better to do. Lacking modernism's Utopian impulse, it just plays with what's already there, but proposes no other options. In this way it is symptomatic of a 'late capitalist' society that has abandoned any possibility of change (he points out that the end of the world can be more easily imagined than the end capitalism). In Jameson's opinion, pastiche is taking over as postmodernism's dominant trait.

Parody

Seen by Jameson as more common to modernism, this is mimicry of old styles again, but unlike mere pastiche it mocks rather than merely plunders from tradition. Like Jencks' 'radical eclecticism', it has a critical edge. Parodying something implies that you want to ask questions about it. Pastiche means showing your 'references' off just for effect.

Jameson and Jencks would not necessarily agree with each other about what constitutes a 'conservative' building and what constitutes a 'radical' one. What looks like empty pastiche to one critic will often look like a daring juxtaposition of codes to the other. Jencks is certainly more optimistic than Jameson about the 'critical' potential of postmodernism.

A query

Is that new shopping mall or multiplex cinema on the outskirts of your home town critical or uncritical? Was that Coen Brothers film or episode of *The Simpsons* an example of parody or pastiche? Try to think of your own examples which seem to fit Jameson's and Jencks' distinctions. Then ask yourself just how easy it is to distinguish between these terms in practice. How do you tell a style that is critically quoted in a building from one that is merely nostalgic? Do the distinctions really work? Are they as clear cut as Jencks and Jameson think they are?

Further Reading

Two useful books by Jencks are:

What is Post-Modernism? 1987

The Language of Post-Modern Architecture, 1991

Looking to Las Vegas

Despite all the above, Charles Jencks shows some sympathy towards the modernist theme of steel, concrete and glass cubes. His democratic 'something for all the family' approach to buildings means that modernist style still has a place. Modernists are still valid for Jencks; he simply does not want a single architectural lexicon to take over.

Another important theorist of postmodernist architecture is Robert Venturi. He tends to go further than Jencks in seeking to erase elitism from building design and urban planning (indeed, he argues that urban sites should be planned as little as possible).

Like Jencks, Venturi has no interest in creating a proper, pure style devoid of humour or playfulness. Instead, he champions the ways in which constructions are adapted to local circumstances through everyday processes of customization and personalization. He urges architects to reject the idea that ornamentation is artistically wrong, and to respect instead the variety of ways in which people gain meanings from their environment. He believes that building design should aim for communication and meaning rather than for streamlined perfection. Influenced by Pop Art (see next chapter), he finds vitality and significance not in *essential forms*, but in what modernists would see as the superfluous and trivial.

Venturi and his colleagues look at commonplace, regional building traditions for inspiration. He also looks at the streets of Las Vegas as the greatest embodiment of what he describes as a truly democratic, non-puritanical architecture. In Las Vegas Venturi discovers a dynamic interplay between diverse signs and textures. In place of one aesthetically correct blueprint imposed by a single heroic modernist expert, cities like Las Vegas revel in clutter, complexity and 'vital mess'.

Venturi favours urban sprawls, 'decorated sheds', clichés, and the proliferation of images which he drives by on the American open road, to the dry modernist monument. Rather than being static and domineering, this urban sprawl presents itself as a story – or mixture of stories – continually being re-told. Though disliked by orthodox architects and design review boards, urban sprawl can be read as a continually mutating process of creative response to current needs and to readily available materials.

Venturi praises 'the urban manifestations of ugly and ordinary architecture'. He sees billboards, flashing signs, façades, blatant commercialism, anachronistic combinations and hot-dog-shaped fast food counters as generators of meaning and experience rather than as lapses in good taste. Venturi would not, for example, be scornful of a British suburban home-owner who attached a decorative 'olde-worlde' cartwheel to the front of their house. Rather than diagnose a serious case of aesthetic misconduct, as some modernist critics would, he would see a creative bit of bricolage, a sign of individuality, a deliberate resistance to the elitist puritanism of society's would-be taste-makers, and a desire to connect with the past. In short, he would find there a 'symbolism of the ordinary'.

Two key books are:

Learning from Las Vegas, by Robert Venturi, Denise Scott Brown, and Steven Izenour (1972, revised 1977)

Complexity and Contradiction in Architecture, by Robert Venturi (1966, revised 1972)

Conclusion

Since the diversification of architecture in the 1970s, there have been many responses to the supposed demise of modernism. 'Revivalism', 'historicism', or conservative postmodernism nostalgically seeks refuge in past (pre-modernist) styles. 'Hi-tech' and 'late modernism' puts faith in modern technology but displays it for dramatic effect (rather than for functional purpose). 'Regionalism' and 'contextualism' seek out cultural identity in local and traditional forms of building. 'Pluralism' combines modern materials and methods with an eclectic mixture of features and styles. 'Deconstructivism' is an arguably more radical version of the latter. We return to it in Chapter 5.

Literature: close that gap

Modernism within the institutions of the arts often rests on ideas about its relationship with low, mass or popular culture (for the sake of convenience, I will use these three terms interchangeably). Many versions of modernism present high and low culture as two very distinct spheres: there might be degrees of influence from one to the other, but they are essentially worlds apart.

In his book *Postmodernism and Popular Culture* (1994) the Australian cultural historian John Docker uses the British literary critic F.R. Leavis (1895–1978) as a prime example of a particular kind of modernist attitude. In books like *For Continuity* (1933), Leavis sketches a view of a discriminating, minority culture which is the standard-bearer of all that is artistically and morally proper. Leavis proposes that a small handful of English, American, and European writers – including Shakespeare, Dante, Ezra Pound, T.S. Eliot, Virginia Woolf and James Joyce – represent the 'finest consciousness of the age' and he sees it as the job of critics like himself to promote their superior works. The parallel here with the arrogant self-perception of the modernist architects is hopefully quite clear: both see themselves as having superior insight into what is best for people, both think that they know what kinds of art people ought to have.

Although the writers championed by Leavis are quite diverse, he argues that what they all have in common is a rejection of over-sentimental subject-matter and over-pretty writing styles. Again there are parallels here with modernist architecture's hatred of the frivolously decorative. Leavis sees his literary hall of fame as characterized by intellectual rigour, subtlety, and wit. When he discusses writers of the modern period, Leavis makes much of the fact that they are in touch with the language of the contemporary world. However, the point of this concern with everyday life is not to celebrate or participate in it, as seems to be the case with Robert Venturi, but to subject it to criticism. In Leavis' view the role of modern literature is to oppose modern society and the cliché-ridden (and often 'Americanized') products of its mass media. Elite, minority culture must constantly be on its guard against the spread of Hollywood, advertising, 'pot-boilers' and other manifestations of facile popular culture. Film is a particularly disturbing influence because it mesmerises its audience with cheap and easy pleasures.

On this view, the mass art of the industrial age is characterized by commercialism and standardization, and these pose a serious threat to art's single-minded pursuit of timeless values. The modern world distracts people with so many forms of mindless entertainment that they are tempted away from art's traditional, more authentic standards.

By contrast, it is often argued that postmodernism tests the boundaries between what gets called high and what gets called low culture. It asks us whether such distinctions are still valid today (if they ever were), and it asks us to question the grounds on which such distinctions are made. It recognizes that contemporary society offers a vast range of different forms of entertainment, but it is less concerned with defending the 'ivory tower' against them.

Within the field of literary studies, one of the several different movements often put forward as a milestone on the road to a postmodernist attitude is Leslie Fiedler's 1969 essay *Cross that Border – Close that Gap*. Fiedler celebrates contemporary writing – such as that of Philip Roth and Kurt Vonnegut – for its ability to open the doors of the ivory tower. Where critics like Leavis had presented 'high' literature as a monolithic treasure-house surrounded by a sea of trivia, Fiedler promotes a postmodernist literature that is flexible, *pluralist* and *hospitable to the popular*. The crucial issue for Fiedler is that most assessments of literary merit are secretly rooted in social class structures. He hopes that with postmodernist writing and criticism it will become possible to judge quality in a way which does not depend on the class-based hierarchy of high vs. low.

The postmodern mood

Around the late 1960s there was much talk of 'the death of the novel' or, as the American author John Barth described it, a 'literature of exhaustion'. At this point the traditional techniques of fiction suddenly seemed obsolete or irrelevant. The complexities of the modern age were impossible to capture in a conventionally 'realist' style, but more 'experimental' or avant-garde ways of writing seemed either elitist, burned out or pointless. Writers of this period therefore faced a dilemma: on the one hand, to find a new 'voice' appropriate to the era of mass communications. On the other hand, to appeal to a popular audience, without at the same time resorting to narrative clichés (e.g. neat endings, logical sequencing of events, cause-and-effect explanations). This was difficult enough in itself. But there was also a feeling that all the good ideas had been used up. The 'great' modernists like Proust or Kafka seemed age-old, worthy but dusty exhibits in a museum.

This mood of exhaustion was a common feature of post-modernism as it was formulated into the 1970s and 1980s. In the following chapter we will encounter a similar feeling in the art world. Fredric Jameson summed it up well in 1983: 'the writers and artists of the present day will no longer be able to invent new styles and worlds . . . only a limited number of combinations are possible; the most unique ones have been thought of already'.

As in the case of architecture *pastiche* was one of the tactics for dealing with these problems. It may not be possible to make brand new, heroic statements, it was argued, but you can at least take existing forms apart and re-combine the pieces in enterprising ways. The postmodern text is openly assembled from different genres and styles. A recent review in the music magazine *Wire* puts it well: 'genius lies in the poise and skill of the blend rather than in the breathtaking innovation of the ingredients'.

A related practice is *eclecticism*. As we saw with architecture, this involves openness to a wide range of forms and devices. Postmodern artists can hop between genres at will, without appearing to privilege any. While it is impossible simply to invent a new style out of the blue, it is equally impossible to avoid having a style. Regardless of how resourceful they may be, artists are always working within pre-existing cultural languages and conventions. Eclecticism means throwing these together, re-shuffling the cards. For artists in this vein all of culture is there to be plundered, irrespective of high/low distinctions. An example is the American musician and composer John Zorn. Styles including free jazz, cartoon soundtracks, Igor Stravinsky, punk, easy listening exotica, surf guitar, Ennio Morricone and many others have entered Zorn's musical vocabulary. 'Purity' is not a virtue for postmodernists.

A brief criticism

One of the more confusing aspects of the distinction between modernist and postmodernist literature is that you can find overt references to 'low' culture in both of them. For example James Joyce's 1922 novel *Ulysses* is often seen as a classic modernist text, yet it combines self-consciously high literary styles with steamy romantic fiction and journalistic prose. Meanwhile, novelists like Umberto Eco and Kurt Vonnegut are seen as postmodernist because they *refer* to popular forms like science fiction and the detective novel.

The difference is sometimes said to be a question of motives. When modernists refer to popular culture, it is in order to mock it or improve upon it. They may even take the occasional holiday in popular fiction – they might, for example, try to liven up the 'academy' by taking prose styles from advertising or best sellers – but they still see high culture as the best place to be.

When postmodernists do the same they are said to be welcoming the plurality of contemporary cultural life with open arms. However, being seen to welcome or quote popular culture is not quite the same as being seen *as* popular culture. For instance, Vonnegut is said to refer to popular science fiction. Could he not just as easily be seen as a popular science fiction writer?

In some commentaries on postmodernism, testing the high/low border is still presented as a top-down issue – a specific problem for art more than for our thinking about the wider culture. The question often remains 'what is our art going to do about popular culture?' The hierarchy therefore stays pretty much in place.

Metafiction

A novel can be described as 'metafictional' when it wears its artificiality on its sleeve. As defined by Patricia Waugh, a work of this kind knowingly lays bare the conventions of fiction, and draws attention to the language(s) and literary style(s) it uses. In short, it is fiction about fiction. Examples mentioned by Waugh include the books of John Fowles (*The French Lieutenant's Woman* 1969), Kurt Vonnegut (*Slaughterhouse Five* 1969) and John Irving (*The World According to Garp* 1976). These writers work within the tradition of the novel as an art form, but do so with a critical, ironic awareness of that tradition. As Waugh puts it, they aim 'simultaneously to create a fiction and to make a statement about the creation of that fiction'. Devices for doing so include:

- mixing several styles or genres of writing
- commenting on (through parody, for example) other fictional works
- featuring an obtrusive voice that interrupts the novel's 'naturalistic' flow from outside of the fictional 'frame'
- deliberate use of anachronisms
- beginning and ending the story by discussing the conventions/ difficulties of beginning and ending stories
- characters reading about their own fictional lives
- directly addressing the reader in the act of reading.

Through the use of techniques like these the reader is poised between on the one hand imaginatively entering (believing in, caring about) the characters' world, and on the other hand an awareness of how the illusion of that world has been constructed.

As an example, Waugh quotes Italo Calvino's *If on a Winter's Night a Traveler* (1981): 'The novel begins in a railway station . . . a cloud of smoke hides the first part of the paragraph'. In this sentence we are reminded of the novel *as* a novel (as a culturally specific type of writing, and as a physical object). The 'paragraph' it refers to is both in our 'real' world (is part of the actual text we are reading) and is part of the fiction. Several levels or versions of 'reality' tumble over each other, all of which end up seeming fictional.

In these ways postmodernist metafiction questions realism from within: it does not pretend to offer transparent windows on the world, 'slices of life', or illusions of 'authenticity'. By drawing attention to its own status as an artefact, it instead admits that it can offer no objective, complete or universally valid representations.

The same could, however, be said of early twentieth century *modernist* texts such as James Joyce's *Ulysses* (1922), or Virginia Woolf's *To the Lighthouse* (1927). One response to this is that *all* novels have a metafictional tendency in that, although they may try to subdue the fact, they are to some degree self-conscious about their own status as fiction. Postmodernism simply flaunts or heightens this tendency. Nevertheless, some of the distinctions between realism, modernism and post-modernism can be summarized as follows:

Realist literature

In the realist novel (dominant in the nineteenth century) an all-knowing, dependable author tells of characters whose behaviour and motivations can be rationally explained, and of a cause-and-effect chain of events that follow one another chronologically. These conventions reflect and promote belief in a universally experienced, understandable and explicable world.

Modernist literature

In the modernist novel reality is represented through fallible, selective points of view. Events may be described from an uncertain position (or number of different positions). They may be presented discontinuously, according to a subjective experience in which reality, perception and the unconscious get caught up in each other. Historical or 'clock' time may get mixed up with the personal time of emotion and memory. Characters struggle against their own disintegration in the face of modern life. The smooth, transparent surface of naturalistic language is roughed up and made opaque as the author experiments with technique to achieve profound insight into life. Deep truths about the world and our place in it can be perceived, however fleetingly.

Modernism is concerned with consciousness and experience. It asks, how can we know reality?

Postmodernist literature

The postmodernist novel is concerned with *being* fiction, and with being *about* fiction. It asks, can reality be separated from the stories we tell about it?

It uses metafictional devices to suggest that novels are just one kind of fiction among countless others, none of which can adequately express the complexities of contemporary experience. It sees modernism as just one aisle in a supermarket of styles from which the author can choose.

Self-consciousness

Much of the above suggests that a central feature of post-modernist art forms is the interrogation of their own conditions of existence. This produces ironic effects. As well as using language, postmodern fiction discusses the processes of language. As well as being part of a genre, it talks about genre. As well as presenting us with stories, it asks us to consider what stories are made of. Linda Hutcheon calls this the 'contradictory enterprise' of postmodernism: 'its art forms . . . use and abuse, install and then destabilize convention'.

So things like irony, pastiche, plural coding and eclecticism can seem like ways of having your cake and eating it. And postmodernism can seem to mean not really meaning anything. But if postmodernism puts messages in quotation marks (the *poststructuralist* thinker Jacques Derrida would say it puts them 'under *erasure*'), that's because it is by definition self-conscious and self-critical. And that can be a serious business. For the postmodern text constantly asks: how do I produce meanings? How can I offer a 'true' representation of reality? For whom, and from what position, do I speak?

The self-awareness of postmodern art works has arguably been created by a consciousness of, among other factors:

- their history
- other cultures and traditions
- the mass media as producers of powerful representations
- their audience(s)
- the commercial market place in which they exist
- postmodern theory.

Further reading on postmodern literature

The Origins of Postmodernity, by Perry Anderson (1998)

Modernism, edited by Malcolm Bradbury and James McFarlane (1976)

A Theory of Parody: The teachings of twentieth century art forms, by Linda Hutcheon (1985)

The Postmodern Turn: Essays in postmodern theory and culture, by Ihab Hassan (1987)

Postmodernist Fiction, by Brian McHale (1987)

Metafiction: The theory and practice of self-conscious fiction, by Patricia Waugh (1984)

Postmodernism: A reader, edited by Patricia Waugh (1992). This includes an essay by Fiedler

The cultural mix

Consider:

Advertising has become a new art form. Many television and cinema commercials are now more imaginative, vibrant and exciting than much high art.

Many commercials also make reference to the world of art, but a lot of art equally makes reference to the world of advertising. What's the difference between them?

What *is* popular culture anyway? How many people a year need to visit your national museum of modern art, and buy postcards of the art from the museum shop, before it can be called popular?

Many commercials use classical music. Many film soundtracks (particularly horror films) are indistinguishable from experimental modernist music. Record shops are full of classical music, world music, pop music, rock, easy listening and so on. Many of us are comfortable in several different musical worlds. We are not usually restricted to just one taste. We often make our own compilation CDs which happily mix any number of 'levels' of music. Modernist critics might try to tell us what we ought and ought not watch, read and listen to, but most of us are much more eclectic (and much less puritanical) than that; we consume a very diverse range of goods offering many different experiences.

On radio, television, DVD and home computer the whole of world culture seems to be at your fingertips. The media, it has been argued, are placeless imaginary spaces which refuse to make clear distinctions between things. Adverts for ice cream and sun block interrupt an art history programme. Moving into different realities can be done at the push of a button. Everywhere you look, different, perhaps contradictory, messages, images and ideas jostle for attention. In this new media domain, anything can go with anything, like a game without rules. Or, at least, you can make up your own rules: culture can no longer be administered, there is no legislation about what can and cannot be consumed. Modernists would bemoan this as a slackening of aesthetic criteria. Postmodernists would agree, but would say 'good thing too'. They would ask, exactly whose criteria were they in the first place? And why should anybody have taken notice of them?

Flattening the hierarchy

> *Once upon a time there were the mass media, and they were wicked, of course, and there was a guilty party. Then there were the virtuous voices that accused the criminals. And art (ah, what luck!) offered alternatives, for those who were not the prisoners of the mass media. Well, it's all over. We have to start again from the beginning, asking one another what's going on*

(Umberto Eco *Travels in Hyperreality*, p.150)

I have on my desk as I write this a newspaper article expressing doubt about the fact that, as it argues, everything from anoraks to sofas to refrigerators to cars is now all equally treated as cultural phenomena by cultural theorists. This, it suggests, reveals a complete draining away of definition or judgement, an inability within postmodern conditions to tell the significant from the insignificant or the good from the bad. But even if this is true, *does it matter*?

Looking at the sorts of example we listed above, some recent writing on postmodernism has argued that the high/low model provided by Leavis and many others is no longer an appropriate way of looking at things. As the quote from Umberto Eco suggests, you can no longer accurately represent culture as two distinct levels. The map of cultural life has been re-drawn. In fact, postmodern culture *is* this new map. There is, for example, no self-evident reason why Bach should be seen as better than Bacharach. This is not to say that they are the same, just that they are equal. Everything swims in the same social sea of signs, images and meanings.

So critics and theorists need to stop thinking of culture as a building with two storeys. Culture is in a sense flat rather than hierarchical: it is a *horizontal field* in which different areas of interest mix, converse, cross over and sometimes fight with each other. It is not a vertical edifice in which influences and/or disagreements travel up and down between the top (art and literature) and bottom (mass or popular culture) floors. There is no mass culture, only a mass of cultures.

Further reading

For some interesting attempts by postmodernist critics to describe 'what's going on', as Eco says, see:

Uncommon Cultures: Popular culture and postmodernism, by Jim Collins (1991)

Postmodernism and Popular Culture, by John Docker (1995)

High-pop: making culture into popular entertainment, by Jim Collins (2002)

03

issues in high and low culture, part two: visual art

In this chapter you will learn:

- about the impact of post-modernism in the art world
- some debates about art's relationship to mass culture and consumerism
- some arguments about the 'political' implications of postmodernist art.

A note of caution

Any attempt to define postmodernism as simply a single style or period is unlikely to work. There is no single point at which postmodernism springs into being, and it is hard to find a contemporary approach to art that does not share ideas with much earlier twentieth-century work. Another difficulty is that modernism itself tends to resist simple summary. In the first place, it was manifested differently in different countries and movements. Add to that the fact that modernism is still in the process of being redefined in retrospect by *post*modernism, and it is clear that the proposed differences between the two are far from cut and dried. The important thing to remember is that being 'post' doesn't have to mean being 'anti-'; postmodernism is usually a critical dialogue with modernism, not a rejection of it.

With these warnings in mind we can begin by summarizing the 'official' account of the modernist legacy. I will then offer a potted history of postmodernism in art.

Make it new!

Most descriptions of modernism in art tend to date it from the mid to late nineteenth century, with the development of impressionist and post-impressionist painting in France (Monet, Degas, Gauguin). This is often described as the beginning of a great experimental period in art, a period in which art pursued new goals and broke free from all traditions of representation. In this simplified view of events, the impressionists triggered off a break from the past in which art learned to turn away from realistic styles of representation and move towards more abstract forms of expression.

In this revolution art progressed by means of 'heroic' experimentation – the shock tactics of the 'tradition of the new' – towards a position of highly self-conscious *art for art's sake*. The idea behind this was that art should become valid on its own terms, without having to have any obvious relation to the visual world. Via the innovations of cubism (starting with the work of Pablo Picasso and Georges Braque, around 1907) and abstract expressionism (most often associated with American painting of the 1940s and 1950s by Jackson Pollock, Mark Rothko and others), along with many other movements, modernism is sometimes said to culminate in certain highly reductive (minimalist) art forms of the 1960s and early 1970s.

Many of the key terms in the definition of modernism in visual art recall those in architecture. They are the ideas of:

- experimentation
- innovation
- individualism
- progress
- purity
- originality.

Modernism in art can be broadly defined as heavy investment in these ideas.

Playing among the ruins: a brief history of postmodernism in the art world

In the following short section I offer an overview, painted in very broad strokes, of what postmodernism has meant for recent art. This will provide a backdrop to the more in-depth discussion which follows it.

The term postmodernism first gained widespread use in the art world around the beginning of the 1980s. Although its accuracy as a description of the art receiving attention at that time was sometimes fiercely debated, it was generally agreed the term did at least signal that important changes were taking place in art.

Up until that point international art journals and big collections of contemporary art had been full of rather austere stuff. Although there had always been maverick presences around, the art that tended to be taken seriously by the 'official' (New York centred) art establishment was generally quite cerebral and dry. Various forms of minimalism in the 1960s and 1970s, for example, reduced sculpture and painting to the simplest forms and processes (bricks, cubes, slabs, grids, squares, flat fields of colour). Much conceptual art of the same period was similarly unseductive: monochrome photographs juxtaposed with dead pan text, holes made in gallery walls and artists performing endlessly repetitive 'actions' were the order of the day.

Things changed around 1980. Suddenly it became fashionable to do huge, splashy paintings *of* things. Representations of the human figure made a comeback, and in the context of an economic boom-time for the art world, a number of prominent new (usually male and pretty macho) artists made fortunes painting them. Although welcomed as a return to common sense by more traditional art critics, this supposed return to painting was greeted with dismay by other artists and critics who liked to think of (modernist) art as the cutting edge of all that is progressive and experimental in culture.

This early version of postmodernism was associated with a pluralist, 'anything goes' attitude and an obsession with the past. Old styles and techniques were re-hashed and artists quoted from the work of other artists. Abstract art was still pursued but this had a more ironic, tongue-in-cheek edge than was usually expected of abstraction. Art became more playful and (occasionally) entertaining.

This was all taken as a negation of the progress of art, with minimalist and conceptual art seen as a dead end. Art had reached the end of its progress. There was nothing new left to do. What act could possibly follow the recent spectacle of rows of bricks, piles of dirt and even empty art galleries being exhibited as art? For some there was a feeling that art had gone as far as it could go, leaving an endgame situation in which artists could choose only to re-tread art's earlier steps or to play with its left-overs. Others, as we will see, complained that art had been swallowed up by commercialism.

A handful of postmodernist approaches from this period:

Neo-geo. Combining a minimalist abstract aesthetic with references to popular culture and commodities. Key names: Peter Halley, Jeff Koons, Ross Bleckner. Influential on: Damien Hirst, Ian Davenport and many others.

Appropriation or **Simulation**. Informed by the theories of Baudrillard and others, this involved reproducing or copying works by other artists. Key names: Sherrie Levine, Mike Bidlo. Influential on: Turner Prize nominee Glenn Brown. Many contemporary artists now 're-stage' other artists' works (often by translating them into another medium).

Trans-avant-garde. An Italian movement that (ironically?) embraced traditional materials, fanciful subject matter and decorative elements. Key names: Francesco Clemente, Sandro Chia. Arguably art's equivalent to neo-classical 'revivalism' in architecture.

New Expressionism. Crude, quick, large figurative paintings from Germany. Full of references to German history and culture. Often deliberately 'primitive' looking. Key names: George Baselitz, Marcus Lupertz.

Eclecticism. Many artists worked with images appropriated from 'high' and 'low' culture and combined (or juxtaposed) them in a range of styles. Key names: David Salle, Sigmar Polke. Influential on: Fiona Rae, Kirstin Glass.

It was thought that instead of ceaselessly experimenting and offering uncompromising attacks on conventional ways of thinking about art and society, the new painting was a betrayal of all that modernism had stood for.

More cautious assessments suggested that ideas about progress, radicality and originality had been myths in the first place and were no longer sustainable in a complex, media-saturated society. Postmodernist painting could be seen as simply making the most out of the collapse of these myths. In a world orientated towards the media and mass communication, art had been made irrelevant – as an artist, you might as well just sit back and enjoy the show. On the other hand, the new painting could be seen as a lively challenge to dominant modernist ideas. It tested the assumptions of influential modernist critics, and it raised important questions about what it was that art was now supposed to do, and about how it was meant to do it.

More complex ideas about postmodernism quickly infiltrated the art world. Next to painting, photography and media-based work regained the limelight in the mid-1980s by seeming to provide a more obviously political postmodernism. A number of artists working in this field were hailed for making a specifically feminist intervention in postmodernism. Other artists began to gain notoriety for producing three-dimensional pieces based largely on showing shop-bought goods. The question for postmodernism now was not, as it had been at the beginning of the 1980s, whether the progress of art had shrivelled up, but how artists should respond to mass culture. From this perspective, mass media and commodities were seen as the instruments of a corrupt capitalist system. If art was to have any purpose in the contemporary world, it had to set itself up in opposition to this system. How could they subvert (or even compete with) the power of the media? How could they oppose the world of commodities without becoming luxury goods themselves?

In order to answer these questions, it became necessary to re-forge the links between contemporary art, the conceptual art of the 1970s, the pop art of the 1960s and beyond. It also became necessary to examine the work of a number of predominantly European postmodern theorists. The work of the French thinker Jean Baudrillard, in particular, was often used in the service of the more media-conscious brands of postmodern art, and became something of a cult among art students in the 1980s. We will have a lot to say about Baudrillard's influential theories in the next chapter. By now, the idea that postmodernist art was just a nostalgic/humourous/cynical art of quotation seemed too simplistic.

In today's art world, the 'anything goes' attitude is no longer controversial, and the word 'postmodernism' rarely raises eyebrows. Nevertheless, many changes and issues heralded by the concept of the postmodern remain current.

It is arguable that much recent art (e.g. Damien Hirst, Jake and Dinos Chapman) is conditioned by – and needs to be understood in relation to – postmodernist ideas and debates.

Further reading

Valuable snapshots of the views and controversies of the early days of artistic postmodernism can be found in:

Beyond Modernism; Essays on art from the '70s and '80s, by Kim Levin (1988)

Art Talk: the early Eighties edited by Jeanne Siegel (1988)

Thinking Art: Beyond traditional aesthetics, edited by A. Benjamin and P. Burger (1991)

On the Museum's Ruins, by Douglas Crimp (1993)

Art of the Postmodern Era: From the late 1960s to the early 1990s, by Irving Sandler (1996)

Modernism and autonomy

There are a number of widespread beliefs about art. One is that artists dedicate their lives to their art without any ulterior – especially commercial – motive. Another is that artists have unique insight into things. Finally, we often assume that art is somehow timeless. All of these beliefs suggest that art exists in a realm outside of ordinary life.

Modernism similarly believes that art is essentially independent and self-governing. Although this idea of the autonomy of art has been expressed in many different ways, one of the most common is to propose that works of art are intrinsically different from all other sorts of objects. They are governed, if at all, by rules and interests not found elsewhere, and they provoke special kinds of response in their audience. Art does not have to justify itself economically, politically, morally, or in terms of its use. It is free from social convention. It is just art. One of the most influential statements of this attitude – and the one against which postmodern art and theory most often pits itself – is the work of the American art critic Clement Greenberg. Greenberg is known for a number of essays and reviews published in art journals between the late 1930s and the mid-1960s. Let's look at two of his most well known pieces, published in the left-wing arts journal, *The Partisan Review* in 1939 and 1940.

Towards a Newer Laocoon

According to Greenberg, every historical age has a 'dominant art form', and between the seventeenth and mid-nineteenth centuries the dominant art form was literature. This means that literature became the prototype which all other art forms tried to imitate. For example, nineteenth-century salon paintings tried to tell sentimental, melodramatic tales: in doing so, they were aspiring to the condition of literature.

This is an artistic crime in Greenberg's view. The aspiration towards literary effects in painting and other art forms is a lamentable 'confusion of the arts'. In this confusion, there ceases to be any reliable standard by which artists and critics can make judgements about quality. The aesthetic worth of a painting is a question that can only be framed in relation to the specific properties, conventions, and history of painting itself. To look at a painting's ability to tell a story or to imitate a three-dimensional object is to fail to look at it on its own terms. A painting is only a painting. It is not a book or a sculpture. This argument rests on the belief that the various art forms possess – or else should achieve – characteristics of their own which separate them from all other art forms. Greenberg insists that modern art progresses through the struggle of artists to boil their art down to its barest essentials and thus to achieve genuine quality. He calls this progressive refinement a process of rigorous self criticism.

Painting's process of self-criticism involves a number of innovations:

- abandoning shaded modelling and perspective
- emphasizing brush strokes
- using harsh colours rather than subtle tonal changes
- stressing line (line is abstract because it doesn't occur in nature)
- using geometrical forms
- using 'all over' compositions
- simplifying forms.

In these ways, paintings stopped trying to fool people. Instead of pretending to be stories or windows onto another world, they called attention to the fact that they were just flat surfaces made of paint on canvas. Flatness was particularly interesting to Greenberg because being flat was the one thing which pictorial art did not share with any other art form.

Thanks to this new emphasis on materials – the integrity of the support, the resistance of the medium – painting triumphed over all the other arts. It most successfully defined its own unique essence. In doing so, it no longer had to justify itself. Like objects of nature, paintings were now their own justification.

Avant-garde and kitsch

Drawing in part from the British art critic Clive Bell, who wrote in 1914 that 'to appreciate a work of art we need bring with us nothing from life', Greenberg implied that in order to enter the space of art you must unburden yourself of social, political, practical and moral baggage. All of these things only hinder the perception of art as art. He notes that art is always surrounded by money, and that modernism was related to the expansion (in the middle of the nineteenth century) of an affluent middle class market for art. But for Greenberg economic and social factors like the existence of a system of patrons, galleries and collectors within a privileged class do not detract from the purity of the modernist enterprise – in fact, they simply create favourable conditions in which an autonomous art can flourish.

'True' culture is under constant threat from kitsch. There are two meanings of kitsch in Greenberg's essay. On the one hand, it is a sentimental sort of pseudo-art which rips off the products of 'quality' high culture. Perhaps we might think of certain performers of easy-listening music as fitting this description. Or in painting, we might think of certain artists who present 'painting for pleasure and profit' programmes on daytime TV. Greenberg would include bad high culture in this definition as well. The melodramatic paintings produced by many artists during the Victorian era would be singled out for particular contempt.

On the other hand, Greenberg also speaks with a mixture of disgust and amusement of 'that thing to which the Germans give the wonderful name of kitsch: popular, commercial art and literature with their chromeotypes, magazine covers, illustrations, ads, slick and pulp fiction, comics, Tin Pan Alley music, tap dancing, Hollywood movies, etc. etc.'. The only thing that these otherwise diverse art forms have in common is that they are all manifestations of mass or popular culture, and it seems that is reason enough for Greenberg to reject them. The only thing he leaves standing is something called 'art and literature of a high order' – namely that which achieves the supposedly self-validating status he had outlined in *Towards a Newer Laocoon*. 'High order' culture and kitsch are two separate worlds which cannot be reconciled. Any attempt to blur or cross the boundaries between them can only result in artistic catastrophe.

Presumably, if we do not recognize high order art when we see it then we, and not Greenberg's sweeping judgements, are at fault. In this respect his posture echoes that of the modernist architects and literary critics we encountered in the previous chapter. They all have incredible confidence in their own standing as arbiters of taste. They all seem to believe that they – unlike the rest of the 'common herd' – have their finger on the pulse of what is right and good in the field of culture. A postmodernist approach would see this stance as arrogant and deluded.

Summary

Art progresses, through the struggle of individual artists with their materials, towards a condition of self sufficiency and freedom. Art which lags behind or does not take part in this progress is of no interest.

The drive towards autonomy and purity in painting and other art forms is a kind of self-defence by authentic art against debased low culture. Visual art should not tell stories (or have 'content' in the usual sense) because that is literature's job and because kitsch art does it. Modernist painting draws attention to itself as medium or artifice. Kitsch doesn't. To achieve genuine quality the arts should each know their place.

Greenberg's modernism is formalist. What this means is that it is concerned less with whatever a work might be said to represent, and more with abstract matters like composition, material processes and visual stimulation. It rejects all interpretations not based mainly on the pure optical experience of art works.

Some postmodernist criticisms

In the last couple of decades there have been many criticisms levelled at Greenberg and at the general assumptions about art which his ideas represent:

- His art history is too selective. It picks and chooses only those few artists whose work seems to add to the neat story of progress he wishes to promote.
- This narrative serves nationalistic interests, in that it allows Greenberg to assert the status of American abstract painting and sculpture as a 'world beater'. For him art is like a race, with everyone running towards the same finishing post.
- He bases his argument on a simplistic picture of culture as a war between two worlds: avant-garde vs. kitsch. Culture is far more complex and multi-layered than this two-tier model can allow for.
- He is too prescriptive. He rejects out of hand any alternative ways of understanding works of art. All other academic approaches are seen as beside the point, and the pleasure people might get from finding associations in an abstract painting, for example, is marginalized as irrelevant and primitive. Enjoying art therefore becomes a matter of possessing certain skills. This serves only to mystify art, and to preserve its unreasonably high social status.

In fact, Greenberg's argument undermines its own case: in order to enjoy the *autonomous, purely optical experience* of an abstract painting, you need to have read plenty of modernist theory first.

Further reading

Many books are available which take issue with the formalist brand of modernism. Among them are:

Pollock and After: The critical debate, edited by Francis Frascina (1985)

Art and Discontent, by Thomas McEvilley (1991)

Andy Warhol, postmodernist

The re-evaluation of Greenberg, and of the whole aspect of modernist theory he represents, has been a central project of postmodernism in art. But these criticisms are present in art practice as well as in art theory (some commentaries suggest that in postmodern art the conventional line between theory and practice has disappeared). Many artists could have served just as well, but I have chosen to look briefly at the American pop artist Andy Warhol (1930–87). This is because his work has achieved a very high international profile outside of the confines of the art world, and not because he in any sense *invented* postmodern art.

Most people are familiar with at least some of Warhol's work. His various screen prints of Marilyn Monroe, produced during the 1960s, are very well known, often being reproduced on posters, greetings cards, calendars and so on. His Campbell's soup cans and cola bottles are nearly as famous. The trademarks of Warhol's art are fairly straightforward (and 'straightforwardness' is perhaps itself a Warhol trademark):

- mechanical reproduction of an image by means of photographic silk-screening on to canvas
- use of ready-made imagery from advertising, magazines, etc.
- repetition of a single image many times on a single canvas
- casually applied unnatural colours
- despite photographic sources, a lack of illusionism (perspective, realistic shading, etc.)
- non-correction of mistakes: many of the prints are mis-registered, too faint, too dark or simply crooked.

We should also mention Warhol's skill in becoming a media icon, his ability to generate hype, and the way that his art has crossed over into more mainstream culture (in addition to postcard and tee-shirt reproductions of his best known images, many adverts imitate Warhol's visual style). As well as being a hugely successful fine artist, Warhol worked at various points as an illustrator, film maker and producer, magazine editor, and band manager; contrary to the modernist myth of dedicated struggle with a single medium, Warhol was quite at ease in a range of different roles.

Seeing double: Warhol's postmodern 'hybridity'

In Greenberg's terms, Warhol's work represents a confusion of the arts. It uses popular images and sources within an art context, and semi-industrial techniques in a context that traditionally values original one-offs. It exists between screen-print and painting, original and copy, handmade and reproduced, abstraction and representation, and, most importantly, high and low culture.

Certain aspects of Warhol's work can be made to fit comfortably into Greenberg's prescriptions for modernist painting. It uses unrealistic colour schemes, flat areas of colour and all-over compositions. It is deliberately artificial-looking and makes no attempt to conceal the process of its making.

By producing work that was apparently hospitable to an abstract modernist interpretation, Warhol was able all the more quickly to succeed in the contemporary art market. By seeming to attain certain Greenbergian standards, he soon entered the pantheon of important, highly collectable modern artists.

But unlike the kind of modernism discussed above, Warhol's work was deliberately impure in that it combined these abstract procedures with mass culture images. It provided ordinary, non-modernist people with images they (as well as Warhol) could identify with. As with Charles Jencks' postmodern *multivalent* architecture (see Chapter 2), Warhol's art respects the validity of different taste cultures. It is open to the plurality of experiences and understandings that different groups can invest in images. This openness is in marked contrast to the modernist's elitist sense of expertise. To quote Howard Fox:

> *Far from seeking a single and complete experience, the post-modern object strives toward an encyclo-pedic condition, allowing a myriad of access points, and infinitude of interpretive responses*

> (quoted in *Postmodernist Culture*
> by Steven Connor (1989) p.90)

Whether you read a Warhol piece as a criticism of modernism or simply as a picture of a film star – or as both of these at once – depends on what knowledge and experience you bring to it. Against the modernist notion that art is capable of defining itself, Warhol's impure plural coding recognizes that the meanings of art (in fact, the *definition* of art) depend on where it is seen, who sees it, and what mental tools they use in order to read it.

Postmodern art like Warhol's can also be seen as recognizing the fact that being an artist does not involve *only* being an artist. The art world perhaps offers artists a particular lifestyle choice, but this does not operate to the exclusion of all other options. Social life today offers a range of different roles and functions, and art is just one of these. Artists do not spend all of their time in an autonomous bubble, breathing in nothing but art. They spend as much time as anyone else going to the cinema, shopping, playing computer games, reading magazines, and watching TV. In other words, artists (and critics) are consumers too. The issue for postmodernists is to explore the points at which these various cultural activities contradict, feed into, and merge with art. Thus postmodernism, rather than abandoning art in favour of mass culture or mass culture in favour of art, suggests that artists and their audiences occupy a slippery position between different 'cultural spaces' (the art world, the shops, the home, different social classes). Postmodern plural coding can therefore be seen as testing or playing with the boundaries.

The end of the art world as they know it?

With postmodernism there are no firm rules which can define for us exactly what the limits, purpose and status of art are. Few attempt to create universal authoritative standards (or meta-narratives) through which to measure artistic quality, and art appears to have become just another consumer choice.

Some critics have therefore lamented postmodernist developments as a decline in values. The American critic Suzi Gablik has argued that contemporary art no longer has a sense of personal commitment or moral authority. According to her, modernism aimed to bring about the spiritual rejuvenation of the Western world by being uncompromisingly opposed to material values. Postmodernism, on the other hand, is fatally attracted to commerce, mass culture, and the assembly-line mentality (Warhol called his studio 'The Factory'). From this point of view, modern day mass culture is corrupt because it is an instrument of capitalism, and art's job is to oppose it. But with postmodernism, art has been pulled down from its position of spiritual purity and sucked into the orbit of media, advertising and the *fetishization of commodities*. So opposition to the system is no longer possible. Thus the difference between modernism and postmodernism is that between serious, spiritual art with a moral centre and floppy, rootless art which commercialism has drained of meaning and emotional force.

Related but somewhat more nuanced objections to post-modernist art have been raised by the American Marxist critic Fredric Jameson. He has argued that the value of modernist painting lay in its ability to express the alienation, fragmentation and isolation of life brought about by modern society. He refers to a well known painting, *The Scream* by Edvard Munch, as a classic example of how modernism uses these themes as part of an adversary stance towards the modern world. Jameson claims that modernism was always informed by the desire to bring about a better world.

As in modernist architecture's utopian schemes, 'great' modernist painting was engaged in a search for new ways of living. Postmodernism has abandoned this project. High and commercial culture have collapsed into each other to such an extent that art cannot find a clear position from which to make powerful critical statements about society: there is no longer any real difference between art and advertising.

Postmodernism: politically weak?

Jameson and others see postmodernism as politically impotent: it refuses to envision an alternative, better way of living, it accepts the way things are, it colludes in, rather than opposes, the status quo. The question of whether postmodernist art is *critical/progressive* or *collusive/regressive* has been much debated. Some critics have sought an answer by trying to separate 'good' from 'bad' postmodernisms.

Examples of the wrangling which can take place over which kind of postmodernism is good and which is bad can be found in the work of a number of critics who publish in the American art journal *October*. Putting it crudely, the *October* critics tend to split postmodernism in the following way:

Weak postmodernism

Straight, old-fashioned painting on canvas. This has often been seen as merely backwards looking. It repeats old habits of thought, it ignores the contemporary world, it criticizes neither high nor mainstream culture; and it is all too clearly aimed at wealthy collectors (painting is still the most saleable art form).

Strong postmodernism

Photography/media-based art has more critical potential because it intervenes in mass media images and styles of representation. The mass media is seen to be an image bank full of repressive stereotypes and capitalist ideology. Strong post-modernism subverts the languages of media and consumer society, and at the same time criticizes the complacency of the bourgeois art world.

So for the *October* writers, as for Jameson, the question hinges on whether postmodern art from pop onwards celebrates the capitalist state or criticizes it.

In addressing these issues, the *October* writers look for points of connection and separation between postmodernist art and older radical art traditions.

Their art belongs to Dada

Throughout the earlier part of the twentieth century, a number of alternative movements had set themselves up, like Warhol's postmodernism, in opposition to puritanical, navel-gazing art-for-art's sake. Of particular importance in this respect are a number of art movements active between roughly 1910 and 1925. Dada, especially, is often seen as the original prototype of how art should go about the business of being radical. A noisy, miscellaneous collection of artists out to annoy the middle classes of Europe and New York in the shadow of the First World War, Dada employed a number of tactics to disrupt bourgeois fantasies about art. Most prominent of these methods was the use of 'found' materials not conventionally associated with fine art. They took materials from the gutter, images from mass culture, and styles of presentation from shop window displays.

Most famous of all, Marcel Duchamp exhibited signed *Readymades* – a urinal, a bottle rack, a comb, etc. – and eventually got them called art (or *anti-art*). For the *October* group and others, such Dadaist strategies were meant as a criticism of the rarefied, stuffy world of high art. The *October* group tended to argue that Dadaist tactics:

- draw attention to the fact that modern capitalist society has turned art into just another set of consumer goods . . .
- parody modern art's uselessness. A urinal exhibited upside-down in an art gallery is fairly detached from its normal function. In the same way, modernism has removed art from everyday life. Readymades satirize the fact that art no longer *does* anything for anybody . . .
- ridicule the high value placed on paintings and sculptures . . .
- show that art is a *social* and not a *natural* category. It is the art world itself – and the social class it is a part of – which allows some things to be called art and some not . . .
- push art off its pedestal . . .

Like Greenberg's modernism, Dada is a form of art which reflects on itself, but unlike this 'pure' modernism, Dadaists insist on remaining firmly within the concrete, material context of everyday activities. Dada can be seen as the start of a long line of art that assaults art, and that attempts to reconcile art and everyday life.

Postmodernism since Pop Art echoes many aspects of Dada. Both challenge the idea that art is autonomous, and both derive images and objects from mass culture. However, the *October* writers are often taxed by the question of whether post-modernism is a continuation or a sell out of this oppositional tradition. They still are not sure whether postmodern art celebrates or criticizes mass culture. They point out that the shock tactics of Dada have been institutionalized by museums which collect Dada pieces as though they were now 'authentic' art (something which Dada never wanted to be). They also look with dismay at the willingness of artists since Pop to embrace the market. For some critics, Dada has been transformed from a vital, radical tradition into just another old style to be cannibalized by a postmodern art world stuck for ideas, and many conclude that all art can achieve today is the impotent imitation of radical gestures: the art market can absorb and defuse everything, and mass culture turns all art into either an amusing side show or a source of imagery for commercials. From this point of view, postmodernism is just a case of exhaustion, disillusionment, and the abandonment of political motivation. It offers a mere *simulation* of the avant-garde.

Further reading

Books which usefully cover aspects of these debates include:

Art in the Age of Mass Media, by John A. Walker (1983)

After the Great Divide: Modernism, mass culture and post-modernity, by Andreas Huyssen (1986)

A criticism of the criticism

One of the assumptions of Jameson and the *October* critics is that it is not possible for art to be a valuable commodity and an expression of social criticism at the same time. It has to be either one or the other. This black-and-white approach is often more reductive than the art in question. It tries to restrict particular artists to single interpretations in a way which the art itself (at least as we have been describing it in this chapter) refuses to do. The Dada artist Hans Richter noted that 'it was . . . conventional yes/no thinking that Dada was trying to blow sky high', and what we have been calling the *between-ness* and *plural coding* of postmodernist art similarly refuses to let itself be pinned to a single interpretation. It is sometimes pointed out that postmodernism replaces *either/or* thinking with *both/and* thinking.

Postmodern art like Warhol's, instead of opting for one level of cultural activity and against another, adopts a complex position of between-ness, *border tension* or *fringe interference*:

> *postmodernism's distinctive character lies in this . . . wholesale 'nudging' commitment to doubleness, or duplicity*
>
> *The Politics of Postmodernism* by Linda Hutcheon,
> (1989) p.1

In other words, postmodernist artists can be both critical *and* celebratory of the mass culture which many (modernist) critics want art to simply condemn. They can similarly criticize the art institution at the same time as they exploit it.

Summary

Postmodernist art forms:

- aim to appeal to a wider audience.
- re-think the relationship between art and popular culture, and reconsider the supposed differences between works of art and other consumer goods.

- are against modernism's idea that art defines itself, and see the 'artness' of objects and images as defined by social acts of interpretation.
- propose that all cultural production is involved in complex social relations. Artists are very much *inside* society. Whereas the critical vs. conservative debate assumes that artists have to be in a position *outside* of popular culture and commodification in order to offer a substantial critique of them, postmodernism suggests that such a position might be neither possible nor desirable.
- criticize aspects of culture 'from within'. For example, rather than reject the languages of the mass media for something 'better', a postmodern artist would present the work that uses those languages ironically, or 'under *erasure*'.
- do not define themselves by rejecting either modernism or popular culture, but exist as an unsteady territory between the two.
- represent, or refer to, the world but in a way that questions the activity of representation and draws attention to the codes and *discourses* through which they do so. (See Chapters 3 and 4 for theories that explain why they do this.)

A final thought

A modernist view: an artist, starving in his garret, gets inspiration from popular culture for his latest masterpiece, which then goes on to outrage the academy.

A postmodernist view: contemporary British art star Damien Hirst makes a jaunty promotional video for the group *Blur*, complete with starlets from the British soft pornography industry, and doesn't outrage anybody.

04 the loss of the real

In this chapter you will learn:

- about postmodernism's inter-rogation of how (or whether) representations refer to 'reality'
- about notions of media 'spectacle' and the idea that experience is 'mediated'
- about the idea that there has been a blurring of the distinction between 'the real' and 'the artificial'
- some of Jean Baudrillard's ideas about 'simulation' and 'hyperreality'.

It is sometimes said that theories of postmodernism proclaim 'the end of the real'. While this may be something of an exaggeration, it is true to say that many of these theories do set out to raise doubts about the relationship between reality and representation. The claim here is not quite that nothing is real, but that there is no simple, direct relationship between reality and its supposed expression in words and pictures.

Within theories of postmodernism, these questions are sometimes addressed to relatively recent developments in mass communications and the electronic reproduction of sound, image and text. Television has often been central in this area. This is not to say that television is to blame for producing postmodern conditions, or that it has single-handedly given us a problem with reality. It is rather that television has often served as an emblem of the issues which theorists of postmodernism try to describe.

In this chapter we will look at a few of the ways television has been used in postmodernist theory and consider arguments that some postmodern theory puts forward about the problematic relationship between reality and image in contemporary culture. In doing this we will focus on the French theorist Jean Baudrillard.

On television

Television was an object of academic enquiry and controversy long before the concerns of postmodernism gained currency. There have been many approaches to the scholarly analysis of TV. One trend was concerned with the effects that TV might have on the cultural 'health' of the population. In the 1950s and 1960s, especially, many critics were worried that TV (and other popular forms from paperback novels to rock 'n' roll) posed a threat to both the folk heritage of 'the people', and the high arts. More recent enquiries into the uses and pleasures of popular media have attacked the arguably elitist and patronizing tone of earlier work in this area.

Echoing the concerns of postmodern and poststructuralist (see Chapter 5) theory, cultural studies has tended to emphasize *polysemy* and *pluralism*: meanings are not received uniformly by a 'mass' audience, they are negotiated by many different groups.

In another tradition, innumerable psychologists and sociologists have tried to assess the impact of TV on the psychology and behaviour of its viewers, particularly children and adolescents. On-going research into these supposed effects has proved highly ambivalent at best, with wildly inconsistent results being reported by different projects.

Neither of these more orthodox attempts to offer a definitive description of the social and aesthetic implications of TV have so far succeeded in providing a complete picture of the area. It has proved hard for theorists to account for TV in its entirety, or at least to provide a single, fully satisfactory analytical model. Even within the world of postmodern theory, there is still little consensus about how best to describe its meanings and functions. This is partly due to the sheer variety of its output, which makes it hard to find any single factor which is common to all products of TV. Another problem is that no researcher can know of all the different audiences for any one programme, or of how they might (or might not) respond to it. In its resistance to simplification or generalization, TV is sometimes seen as one of the clearest embodiments of postmodernism.

It can also be argued that the medium of TV is postmodern because it seems radically different from some of the main principles behind modernist art. From this perspective, attention might focus on the formal qualities of TV, and on aspects of TV's general dynamics. These might include the way it uses sounds and images, the experience of TV as a constant turnover of images, and the ability of viewers to zap from one channel to another.

Another important factor for theorists of postmodernism is TV's part in the expansion of *consumer culture*. TV can be examined in terms of its relation to the industrial, economic and technological developments of 'advanced' society. As well as looking at the economic and industrial role of TV in the growth of a new global mass culture, some approaches focus on the content of specific programmes by looking at how particular stories reflect postmodern social conditions.

Finally, TV is of great importance to researchers who consider themselves to be offering postmodernist accounts of popular culture. Both aesthetic and social/political aspects of TV may be considered, but the interest lies more in how to look at popular culture in a way which departs from earlier critical perspectives. It is claimed that these earlier, modernist approaches (as we saw in Chapter 2) maintained a clear-cut and elitist distinction between high and mass culture. A new, horizontal model of culture is therefore required.

Of course, the angles on TV I have identified above overlap in all sorts of ways. For instance, its visual styles may be linked in complex ways to its industrial and economic attachments. And this in turn is one of the issues addressed by theorists and researchers who wish to question the established modernist approach to cultural criticism.

TV as postmodern art form?

For the sake of clarity, some of the differences between artistic modernism and postmodern TV have been divided below into the categories of *production*, *exhibition*, and *reception*.

Style of production

To put it crudely, modernist, romantic ideas about art stressed the creativity of the individual genius, who was valued for struggling to express his or her unique emotions and insights in his or her chosen medium. With the emphasis very much on the individual at the sharp end of artistic progress it follows that modernism also valued the physical qualities of the work of art itself, and associated these qualities – present in brush-strokes, chisel marks, idiosyncratic stylistic quirks, and so on – with notions like 'integrity', 'authenticity' and 'originality'. These values were often thought to signal a stand against capitalism and consumer culture. Putting aside the question of whether these are really adequate ways of looking at art, it should become clear that they do not necessarily apply very comfortably to TV.

Unlike most works of art, a TV programme has no individual creator. Despite the possible talents of particular celebrities, script-writers, and so forth, that go into the making of a programme, and although certain directors do have recognizable styles, the final product is nearly always such a team effort that no single person can be said to have created it. Before our TV receivers pick the transmission up, the programme has been touched by a whole network of personnel, who, even if they have not directly influenced the content of the broadcast, have had some responsibility in making it happen. Hence the way TV is made does not conform to conventional notions of handicraft, or to the familiar picture of the genius pouring his or her innermost thoughts into his or her own work of art. Add to this the proliferation of repeats on satellite and cable channels, and TV appears to be witness to this 'death of the author' (see Chapter 7). This doesn't stop it promoting romantic myths about its own 'geniuses', of course. And innovative programmes still need the input of individual groundbreakers. Yet those individuals can not transcend the medium's collective nature, and all 'geniuses' are ultimately vulnerable to ratings wars and other forms of commercial pressure.

Style of exhibition

We tend to think of paintings and sculptures as being viewed in relatively exclusive spaces like galleries and museums. Some writers (notably the sociologist Pierre Bourdieu) have examined how these spaces are often organized in a way that encourages specific, modernist notions of what art is and how to look at it. In the first place, it is argued, the selection and showing of certain objects by galleries and museums instantly loads these objects with cultural baggage: it confers the status of art upon them. But, beyond that, the way art is generally exhibited (and discussed) promotes the modernist idea that works of art naturally exist in a realm of experience independent of the rest of life. Works of art are traditionally meant to be experienced at first hand by a specific, restricted audience in a specially designed high culture environment. TV is, by virtue of its style of exhibition, in stark contrast to this.

We have suggested that TV programmes are created by a long chain of personnel, rather than by a single creative being. Similarly, although each programme is made only once, it can always make a potentially infinite number of appearances on a potentially infinite number of screens. While paintings and sculptures are traditionally intended to exist as one-offs, each broadcast TV programme can therefore be said to have *multiplicity* built into it. On the one hand it may be endlessly copied, saved, exchanged, and re-shown any number of times on video tapes and DVDs around the world. To this extent TV broadcasts are a kind of art which can theoretically be owned by everyone. On the other hand, each programme is transmitted to millions of 'sites' at once and (much like information on the Internet) is in a sense free of fixed location.

Styles of reception

In the case of traditional fine art, both the architecture of the exhibition space itself and the codes of behaviour supposedly proper to the art world seem designed to encourage a private, one-to-one relationship between the viewer and the work of art. The presentation of the art work in a pristine, often white room contributes to the feeling that each piece should be attended to on its own terms, uncontaminated by either neighbouring works of art or the outside world. Reception of the art work, then, often takes place in a hushed, reverential atmosphere in which each piece apparently demands of the visitor a special aesthetic (formalist) kind of contemplation. In these ways it is possible to see the viewing of art as a somewhat *regulated* activity.

If art is conventionally confined to very particular sites and therefore to fairly specific audiences, TV seems to be the opposite: it is a mass medium watched in familiar spaces (the home, the pub, the Chinese take-away, the classroom) by a potentially unlimited audience. There are almost as many different places in which TV can be shown as there are TV sets in the world. And there are almost as many ways of using it. There are, theoretically at least, no restrictions on where it can be shown, who can watch it, or how it should be watched. Unlike the consumption of art there is – again in theory – no established social code or etiquette regarding appropriate viewing behaviour.

Where the field of modernist painting and sculpture thrives on the idea that its objects require a protracted, intent, somehow pure aesthetic gaze, TV programmes can either be gazed at in fascination, glanced at distractedly while you are doing something else, left switched on while you are in another room, sworn at or argued with, turned up to drown out another noise, or watched for entertainment or education. You can also throw things at them, and zap between them. So although schedulers and advertisers might like to imagine you in thrall to the box, it is far more likely that you use it in a variety of ways for various purposes, and that you fairly often ignore it. The consumption of TV is, then, comparatively unregulated and unpredictable.

As has already been suggested, one of the ways in which TV is used is as a source for the creation of private video archives. In this way, we can 'possess' particular programmes, and in doing so make permanent the otherwise transient moment in what is sometimes called TV's flow of sounds and images. Unless the consumer decides to store certain broadcasts on tape or disc –

perhaps frequently re-viewing them, perhaps pausing on favourite instants, and in the process making them into very different kinds of texts – the TV programme has a fleeting existence which distinguishes it from what we might think of as the traditional relationship between art and 'timelessness'.

Ways of watching TV: an open and closed case

Modernist theories of art fostered the impression that a work of art can and should be experienced in its own right, on its own terms, and for its own sake, without reference to other objects in the world. They are regularly presented as though they are permanent, timeless artefacts, requiring no external justification, and free of any 'outside' influence. The art works are somehow meant to emit a sense of their own presence. But on TV, individual programmes and images are not isolated against, or surrounded by, some polite, neutral ground. Instead they seem to fight for our attention in a crowded – some would say feverish or superficial, others would say exhilarating – environment in which representations proliferate and bounce off each other. They cannot, then, be easily characterized in terms of aesthetic purity or self-sufficiency.

An interesting case is that of the soap opera. Unlike most novels, which tend to be structured around the build-up to how they are going to end, soaps tend to present on-going stories that have no end in sight. They can go on for years, sometimes seeming to be made up as they go along, the interrelationships in their story lines constantly gathering ever greater degrees of intricacy. Single plot developments naturally reach conclusions of sorts, but in the world of the soap, the case is never really closed. New details about its fictional past are forever coming to light, cats get let out of bags, long-forgotten characters keep returning to disrupt the present, and old plot-lines are continually re-visited, revised and milked for new twists. In this world, each episode is affected by the episodes that have gone before it, and contains the seeds of numerous new developments to come. A single event in one programme can have repercussions that affect years of unfolding narrative, yet the lead-up to that single event can be traced back through an endless chain of preceding, often seemingly insignificant incidents. In a sense the separate episodes bleed into each other so that the open-ended series is a continuum in which, unlike many conventional works of art, no individual instalment wants to be seen as a complete, self-enclosed entity.

So although in one way many soaps often seem to be trapped in their own insular universe, we can see them as an example of the inherently 'open' programme. We can look in similar terms at TV commercials, which are often open in the way that they refer to other media products. Many adverts assume that viewers possess a wide knowledge of popular culture, and play on this knowledge by producing a whole range of quotes, in-jokes, *parodies*, *pastiches* and imitations of Hollywood movies, TV programmes and other adverts. In addition, they frequently appropriate their soundtracks from any point in the history of popular and classical music, or from world music. Commercials and adverts do not attempt to work independently or be seen as self enclosed wholes, but are explicitly imprinted with – and overtly made out of – their cultural surroundings.

It is possible, then, to draw a picture of TV, and the media in general, in which individual items are in various ways open to each other. But this does not mean that they are correspondingly open to the world. Rather, for some chroniclers of the postmodern, it means that the contemporary mediascape is more like a closed circuit than an open forum. So caught up are the products of the media in chatting among themselves that they have effectively shut the world out.

This is the situation described by Umberto Eco in his 1984 essay *A Guide to the Neo-Television of the 1980s*. In that short piece, Eco argues that TV is so absorbed in itself that it has now virtually turned its back on the external world. Examples of being so self-absorbed include:

- chat shows
- award ceremonies
- TV news items about TV celebrities
- TV documentaries about the making of TV
- TV quiz shows in which contestants (sometimes TV personalities) are quizzed about TV shows
- TV shows in which the public complain about/praise TV shows
- out-takes shows
- ads which recycle/spoof old ads
- game shows in which D-list celebrities are the contestants
- airing of newly discovered lost episodes of old sit-coms.

In this world of what Eco calls *neo-TV*, something being on TV is remarkable or newsworthy in itself. In nature programming, for instance, it is not the mating-procedures of certain animals which are astounding, so much as the fact that they have been captured for the first time on camera. The same goes for candid interviews with members of royalty. The very fact that the royal personage has opened her/his heart on TV can send shock waves around the globe, even when the revelations are utterly banal and predictable (especially when leaked to the press days in advance). And who would be interested in probes which did *not* send back remarkable pictures (digitally enhanced and coloured before being shown on news broadcasts the world over) of unexplored planetary surfaces? It is well known that what counts as newsworthy is often determined by what is filmed. Being caught on camera is often news in itself.

In all of these cases Eco would argue that fascination lies not in what the appearance *refers* to – the heavenly body, the royal personage, the amorous creature – but in the *fact of televisual appearance itself*. And this fascination is not only felt by the audience. As Eco would argue, TV itself is fascinated with, and is forever congratulating itself on, its own productions, its own operation, and its own ability to make history.

A note of caution

All of this begins to give the impression that TV is in a world of its own. Although, as I have suggested, no single item in the media can be seen as an isolated, self-enclosed entity, Eco's image of neo-TV talking to itself does involve taking a detached overview of TV in general and seeing it as in a sense abstract and liberated from outside influence. In this way, some postmodern accounts of TV represent it as more whole or unified than is probably the case.

Welcome to Planet Baudrillard

Umberto Eco saw the world of neo-TV as so turned in upon itself that there was little space left for the real world. Jean Baudrillard (1929–) has similarly described media culture as consumed by what he calls 'an effect of frantic self-referentiality', but he has gone much further than Eco in exploring the implications of this effect. As well as the media now operating without having to make any necessary reference to reality, we now face a situation in which, to Baudrillard's mind, the image 'bears no relation to any reality whatever: it is its own pure simulacrum.' (*Selected Writings*, 1988 p.170).

Baudrillard has been one of the key figures in the postmodernism debate. Most surveys of the subject take his work to be of central importance, and a number of theorists have taken up and adapted his ideas. Although he has actually used the term postmodern only sparingly, his work is often seen to provide especially pungent, if mind-bending, descriptions of the brave new world of postmodern society. Responses to many of his books and essays, particularly since the late 1970s, have ranged from outrage and bewilderment to uncritical enthusiasm. He has been seen as a weaver of fascinating, elusive texts which play with the (non) meanings of a world engulfed by media. And he has been seen as an infuriating apologist for just about everything that some see as bad about the media and the society that spawned them. In the following reading of Baudrillard we will touch on just part of the work he has done since his first published book, *The System of Objects* (1968).

It is often said that wherever you look, there are pictures. Tee-shirts, billboards, posters, packaging, newspapers, magazines, TV, cinema, computers and video games can all be listed as sources of imagery. Many of us also own cameras, webcams and camcorders, and most of us are regularly recorded, however unknowingly, by closed circuit surveillance cameras in shops and high streets. Some proud parents now video their children being born, and many foetuses now put in an early screen preview. For Baudrillard, this apparent obsession with images has fundamentally altered our world.

On its simplest level, Baudrillard's work suggests that all this representation has saturated reality to such an extent that experience can only take place at a remove. We can experience the world only through a kind of filter of preconceptions and expectations fabricated in advance by a culture swamped by images. How, Baudrillard might ask, can you visit, or even live in, New York City without that experience being informed by all the New York Cities you know from movies, TV shows and news reports? Or how can you even express your love for someone without that expression recalling in some way the innumerable soaps and films in which the vicissitudes of love are played out daily? Indeed, would those 'three little words' be so emotionally weighted – would you even feel the same desire to utter them upon occasion – had you *not* seen and heard them uttered a million times before?

But Baudrillard's writings offer much more than the simple study of media effects. He has looked at a wide range of cultural phenomena from all aspects of contemporary existence and much of his work, rather than occupying any one discipline or school of thought, is best seen as a sort of meeting place for linguistics, sociology, philosophy, political theory and science fiction. The analysis of TV and film, although playing an important part in Baudrillard's work, is therefore just one aspect of his theorization of the postmodern situation.

This situation appears in Baudrillard's work in several guises, and he likes to give it funky yet apocalyptic sounding names like 'hyperreality', 'implosion', 'cyberblitz' and 'the code'. All of these have fairly different connotations, and their meanings do shift and change throughout Baudrillard's work, but they are all closely related to what Baudrillard calls *simulation*. Features of contemporary life as apparently diverse as fashion, environmental design, opinion polls, theme parks, telecommunications and cybernetics have all been rolled together in Baudrillard's hands as manifestations of the single, shiny new regime of simulation. Baudrillard uses this term in a bewildering variety of ways, but often seems to mean by it little more than a generalized realm of reproductions, images, representations and models. For example, in his 1981 book *Simulations*, Disneyland, psychosomatic illness, the Watergate scandal and hijacks are all given the same Baudrillard treatment.

Dictionaries link simulation to the fake, the counterfeit, and the inauthentic. Baudrillard retains these meanings to a certain extent, but pushes them considerably further, so that simulation can no longer be seen clearly as the opposite of truth. We might naturally assume that simulation either duplicates or is emitted by a pre-given real. In this sense we might think that simulation and reality have a necessary attachment to each other. But for Baudrillard, this connection has long since snapped, so that simulation can no longer be taken as either an imitation or distortion of reality, or as a copy of an original. In Baudrillard's dizzying cosmos there is no firm, pure reality left against which we can measure the truth or falsity of a representation, and electronic reproduction has gone so far that the notion of originality is (or ought to be) irrelevant.

Computer-generated images and spaces are the most obvious example of this. They have their own sense of reality (what is sometimes called 'telepresence') which does not depend on the existence of anything outside of their virtual world. One critic, Michael Heim, has noted that 'virtual entities are not representations. They do not re-present. They do not present again something that is already present somewhere else' (*Cyberspace/Cyberbodies/Cyberpunk*, edited by Featherstone and Burrows, 1995). Although Heim makes no reference to him, this description is close to Baudrillard's definition of simulation as 'the generation of models of a real without origin or reality'. But you do not have to sit at a computer all day, or even watch a multi-million dollar special effects extravaganza at your local multiplex in order to find simulation operating. Simulation is for Baudrillard a widespread cultural condition and not an 'event' restricted to a particular technology. We have entered a state of affairs in which, as Baudrillard says, 'it is now a principle of simulation, and not of reality, that regulates all of social life' (*Selected Writings* 1988, p.120).

Images in the floating world

In a lecture called *The Evil Demon of Images*, presented at the University of Sydney in 1987, and published as a booklet in 1988, Baudrillard declared that:

> It is the reference principle of images which must be doubted, this strategy by means of which they always appear to refer to a real world, to real objects, and to reproduce something which is logically, and chrono-logically, anterior to themselves. None of this is true . . . images precede the real to the extent that they invert the causal and logical order of the real and its reproduction.

(page 13)

As you can tell, the position that Baudrillard takes can seem baffling and rather extreme. We can begin to make sense of it by breaking down the above statement into its two main propositions, and spending some time considering each in detail.

Baudrillard's first proposition: the reference principle of images must be doubted

This carries on from what we have suggested about neo-TV. For Baudrillard, the media not only talk among themselves (as they did for Eco) but are a kind of virtual collage of free-floating images which have cut themselves loose from the burden of having to represent anything other than themselves. In Baudrillard's scheme of things, representation is now on automatic pilot. In its own orbit, representation can now operate without ever having to land on the apparently solid ground of facts, reality or history. Consider three examples which might be said to bring the reference principle into doubt:

You are watching on a videotape of a contemporary film an image of a woman smoking a cigarette. She looks cool, seductive, and fairly dangerous. Her smoking gives her this sort of aura. There is something about the way she lights her cigarette . . . you find this an attractive image. Perhaps you would quite like to look like that yourself. Has any of this to do with the actuality of smouldering tobacco? Or is it intimately connected to all the other cinematic femmes fatales you have seen light up before? Is it in fact the smoking itself, or the very 'film-ness' of the image which entices you?

You wear expensive brand-name trainers and tracksuits for their fashionability, but you have no interest in sports. What 'underlying reality' do your clothes and footwear refer to? Is there any sense in trying to rationalize or explain fashion, or search for a hidden cause of which this particular fashion is the effect? Is the pricetag on your trainers determined by anything more concrete than the image of the brand name? What reality does the brand name represent other than its own? Do adverts for your trainers say anything much about their 'practical' function, or could it be that the possession of a brand image (i.e. difference from other brands) *is* their function?

What Baudrillard would see in all of these cases is a situation in which representations, broadly defined, are no longer determined by an essential connection to the things which they are supposed to represent: they are free-floating signs.

Other commentators have agreed with Baudrillard in this respect. In his 1992 book, *Postmodernism, or the Cultural Logic of Late Capitalism* (expanded from some essays first published in the 1980s), the American critic Fredric Jameson makes a similar point regarding what he sees as the 'depthlessness' of contemporary cultural production. Jameson identifies postmodern 'formal features' in art, architecture, film, video and TV, and finds in them only a superficial cutting and pasting of ready made images and styles. These are seen by Jameson as signs abstracted from their true origins and re-used in meaningless new combinations in the trivial, commercialized space created by mass culture. Unlike Baudrillard, Jameson makes little attempt to hide his disgust at the shallowness of postmodern artefacts. To illustrate his point he contrasts two famous pictures of footwear. First, he looks at a painting by Vincent Van Gogh called *Peasant Shoes*. This painting is seen by Jameson as a deep, modernist one. The very substance of the lumps and furrows of encrusted oil paint somehow offer themselves up as recordings of an authentic world of rural poverty and agricultural misery. The painting is, for Jameson, firmly embedded in a specific social, geographical, historical and personal situation, and as such deserves its status as one of the great 'canonical works of high modernism.'

On the other hand, he looks at *Diamond Dust Shoes* by Andy Warhol. Unlike the Van Gogh painting, claims Jameson, it is impossible to read anything of significance into Warhol's work. Whereas the truth of *Peasant Shoes* lies in the way Jameson can read into it the whole brutal world of peasant toil, the Warhol piece merely presents itself as a blank surface. This is partly because, as a photographically derived screen print, it is literally flat and more or less mechanical. Thus it is difficult for Jameson to read it in terms of personal expression. Another problem is that it presents the images of shoes as 'shorn of their earlier life-world'. That is to say, they simply float decoratively, placed in no particular setting. They are, in fact, pure images, in the sense that they are derived not from reality, as was the case with Van Gogh (or so Jameson supposes), but from other images. Warhol has not observed an actual pair of shoes and attempted to express through them the real way of life of which they are a part. Instead he has merely duplicated what Jameson calls the debased, depthless appearance of the glossy advertising image.

This is just one of the examples Jameson gives as symptomatic of our current social condition in which 'depth is replaced by surface'. Another writer who has expressed similar concerns is Dick Hebdige, particularly in his book *Hiding in the Light* (1988). Rather as Jameson set up two paintings in opposition to each other – one to represent the authentic old world, the other to symbolize the superficial new world – Hebdige takes two contemporary magazines, and proposes that a huge chasm separates their respective attitudes. On one side of this chasm he places a periodical called *Ten.8*, a 'serious' photography magazine with an emphasis on theory and politics, read mainly by the academic market. On the other side, he places *The Face*, perhaps the definitive, and certainly the most influential, British style magazine of the 1980s.

Hebdige sees *Ten.8* as representative of an older, graver attitude to images. In its pages writers on photography analyze images in terms of their theoretical frameworks, political implications and historical backgrounds. In this journal, words are used to ground, situate and tame images. Images are seen as in need of explanation.

Meanwhile *The Face* lets images have the upper hand. Instead of trying to pin pictures down or solve them, it sets them loose from what Hebdige calls 'the constraints imposed by the rationalist theology of representation'. In other words, *The Face* uses images for their style value rather than for some notion of their deep meaning. Unlike *Ten.8*, *The Face* and its readership do not really care where an image comes from or what it says. All that matters is the effect (Jameson calls this the *intensity* as opposed to the *meaning*) of an image *as an image*. Nowadays, of course, we are inundated with style magazines that ask nothing more of us than to be seduced by eye candy: the glossiness of the image is its own justification, regardless (arguably) of any 'deeper' meanings it may possess. Postmodernists would say in any case that 'depth' is just a surface effect, and that superficiality can be 'deep'.

As you will have gathered, the traits identified by Jameson and Hebdige are by no means restricted to a single art form. In the realm of moving images alone many critics have found similar qualities in rock videos, advertising campaigns, TV programmes and films like Quentin Tarantino's *Pulp Fiction* (1994). In this film, we get no sense that Tarantino is trying to portray a real world. We suspect that he knows little about the criminal underworld which the film seems to portray and that he is dealing almost entirely in cinematic signs, quotes, and clichés. Yet whether or not you 'get the references' is as irrelevant as which particular songs dance records get their samples from. In Tarantino's film we are not invited to be outraged by acts of violence, and critical responses to the film have tended to shy away from discussing the racist, sexist and homophobic representations in Tarantino's work. The reason for this is that the film seems to put everything in cinematic quotation marks. We hardly take it as showing anything other than a celluloid film world. It makes no attempt at revealing to us how things really are: it is purely about its own intensity, its own effect as a piece of fictional film. The title itself (as it had in the Tarantino-scripted *True Romance*) seems to signal that it is not to be taken too seriously. Like all of the examples touched on above, *Pulp*

Fiction is a case of what Baudrillard calls 'the emancipation of the sign . . . from any archaic obligation it might have to designate something' (*Selected Writings*, 1988 p.125). The use of references in the Coen Brothers' films is perhaps of this order: *The Big Lebowski* contains a sequence in the style of a 1930s musical. *The Man Who Wasn't There* is a *pastiche* of film noir. To try and figure out what they are 'really' all about is to look almost stuffy and old fashioned.

So what we are presented with in the postmodern mediascape is a matter of circulating surfaces: a zone in which signs can function without having to be plugged in to what we might think of as a fundamental, authentic realm of existence. What we have, says Jean Baudrillard, is a *centreless network of communication* that endlessly reproduces and cannibalizes its own constant production of simulations, a situation in which the image is a 'phantasm of authenticity which always ends up just short of reality' (*The Revenge of the Crystal*, 1990).

Baudrillard's second proposition: images precede the real to the extent that they invert the causal and logical order of the real and its reproduction

The big paradox in Baudrillard's work is that, while simulations are emancipated from any reference to reality, they are nevertheless firmly embedded in our lives. They may not refer to some natural, unsimulated reality, but they do have very real effects. In the course of one day we might cry along with a weepie, feel thirsty when looking at an advert for beer, have our faith in human nature shaken by the news, be scared silly by a slasher movie, get excited by seeing a celebrity in the street . . . in these ways we might say that far from being detached in their own little world, simulations are deeply connected to real life.

Baudrillard would not necessarily disagree with this point, but he might draw quite surprising conclusions from it. He would suggest something along the following lines:

• yes, life is full of simulations, but . . .
• this only shows that reality has become confused with empty, hollow signs
• yes, you could argue that because simulations have certain actual effects on people they are therefore real, but . . .
• you've got it the wrong way around: simulation is real only to the extent that reality is already simulated

- yes, this does in a sense show that simulations make reference to things, but . . .
- given that reality is always already simulated, reference can only be to simulation and not to some pure, unadulterated reality.

This is only a crude caricature of Baudrillard's subtle and evasive writing, but it does at least give an impression of the twisted logic which infests it, and which he says characterizes our current 'regime'.

In Baudrillard-land, the distinction between simulation and reality has collapsed. In *The Evil Demon of Images*, he calls this a telescoping or implosion of image into reality. We hinted at some of the ways in which this has happened when we noted how images intersect with (and, we might add, enable) certain experiences of the world. It will not surprise you to learn that Baudrillard goes a lot further than this simple observation. In fact, he turns conventional thinking about the 'logical order of the real and its reproduction' inside out, so that images do not just intersect with the real; they precede it, anticipate it, absorb it, and produce it. Even with the examples given above, Baudrillard would claim that reality was an 'effect' of representation. He makes this point rather dramatically in a passage from his travelogue, *America* (1988, first published in France 1986):

> *Everything is destined to reappear as simulation. Landscapes as photography, women as the sexual scenario, thoughts as writing, terrorism as fashion and the media. Things seem only to exist by virtue of this strange destiny. You wonder whether the world itself isn't just here to serve as advertising copy in some other world.*

(page 32)

Some examples

You turn on a fly-on-the-wall TV documentary which follows events in the day-to-day life of a typical family. It seems to bear all the marks of authenticity: there is no sense in which we think of the family as actors. These are real people, after all, and we are watching reality unfold in real time, though only as real life soap. Their lives seem full of incident, and there are some juicy, pretty heated rows. But then you wonder (as though it makes any difference): to what extent are they playing up to the recording equipment? If you were not there to watch, would there be anything worth watching? Suddenly suspicious of the whole fly-on-the-wall concept, you switch over to the news. It's a live on-the-spot report from the site of a large urban disturbance. A reporter stands before a debris-strewn street and reports, with just the slightest hint of disappointment, that all is quiet for the moment. Prompted by our henchman in the studio, she notes – a little ominously, but also perhaps a little hopefully – that there are fears that violence might flare up again later tonight. Needless to say, her prediction proves right. Had the rioters watched the news? Are they putting on a show for the cameras?

As Baudrillard asks in *The Evil Demon of Images*: 'What else does the media dream of if not raising up events by its very presence?' (page 22).

You are casting your vote in a general election. Is your vote based on some idea of real politics, or is it informed by the endless soundbites, PR exercises, photo calls, image contests and smug grins which make up the political arena today? Can you think of politics in separation from the media? Is there any distinction to be made between real (deep) and unreal (shallow) politics? In this example, we could say that image and reality are totally intertwined: notions of true versus false hardly come into the equation.

When you go food shopping you choose between designer foods, health foods, exotic foods, slim-line foods, sinful foods, luxury foods, natural foods, traditional foods, homemade foods, convenience foods, and 'TV dinners'. Some foods (especially desserts) are 'as good as granny used to make'. Others (especially junk food) are 'chip shop style' or 'American style'. Is food now ever just food, or is it always attached to a style, a lifestyle, a body image or a social type? Perhaps you base your food buying decisions on the kind of person you see yourself as. But where did you get this image from? Can you separate it from the various identities you are sold daily in advertising, fashion/lifestyle/ interior decoration magazines, sex technique videos, shop window displays, fitness programmes, pop records? Do you have any reason to suppose that the kind of person you are, or could become, is not a fulfilment of pre-existing models of thought and behaviour? Are you really anything more than a type?

All of these examples demonstrate how (as Baudrillard would see it) the line between simulation and reality has been erased. As Baudrillard would say, there is no way of identifying a real which exists outside of simulation, because we live in a society which is structured according to all sorts of beliefs, ideals, and blueprints. In short, reality is structured according to codes. Some codes are manifested in directly political ways – in the drafting of bills, the creation and enforcing of laws, and so on. Some are inscribed into concrete institutions – education, industry and prisons, for example. Others appear in less obvious ways – such as entertainment media, consumer goods, architecture and designed environments. Still more show themselves in the constant surveys, polls and questionnaires which classify the population according to their consumption patterns, income brackets, sexual orientations and so forth. None of these codes can rightfully be called natural or timeless, but all can be said to precede the real in the sense that they produce the real social order in which we all participate. And all can be said to feel real in the sense that they affect real people. To quote from Baudrillard's *America*:

> *The only physical beauty is created by plastic surgery, the only urban beauty by landscape surgery, the only opinion by opinion poll surgery . . . and now, with genetic engineering, comes plastic surgery for the whole human species.*

(page 32)

And from *Simulations*:

> *It is now impossible to isolate the processes of the real or to prove the real . . . all hold-ups, hijacks and the like are now as it were simulations . . . inscribed in advance in the decoding and orchestration rituals of the media.*

(pages 41–2)

The point about hijacks seems excessive. But Baudrillard may simply be noting terrorists' reliance on publicity. This is to say that the media are not just vehicles for reporting acts; they are part of the conditions that make those acts possible. That certain terrorists have planned their actions along the lines of action movies is also well known.

Because of the way it suggests that the real is an effect of simulation, it would be easy to discuss all of this in terms of how people are affected or manipulated by various cultural influences. We might, for instance, try to fit Baudrillard into a critical tradition which looks at how people are persuaded or encouraged to be the good consumers that the system requires in order to keep itself going. It might be tempting to try and find in Baudrillard proof of the influence of TV on the supposedly impressionable masses. And we might try to find proof of Baudrillard's theories in those people who apparently write to TV actors, believing them to be the characters they portray.

But Baudrillard is keen to distance himself from these kinds of reading of his work. The image of people being manipulated or affected is misleading because it suggests that a gap naturally exists between people and the forces which supposedly shape them. In other words, it suggests that people can exist in an independent, fundamentally unaffected state at some point prior to the system coming along and working on them. In Baudrillard's scheme of things, this is not possible. As far as he is concerned, we are always already caught up in the workings of simulation: 'the social contract has become a pact of simulation, sealed by the media and information', so we are always already part of the network. For Baudrillard, nothing is outside of the flow of signs, codes, and simulations.

How are we to react to this scenario? What impact does it have on the lives we lead and the artefacts we make and use? Baudrillard's answer is that it generates *panic*. We desperately try to get out of simulation by producing events, activities, images and objects which assure us of their (and our) reality. In an attempt to compensate for the fading of the real, we make a fetish of the supposedly authentic. We manufacture an 'escalation of the lived experience . . . a panic-stricken production of the real and the referential.' (*Simulations* pages 12–13).

Baudrillard calls this the *hyperreal* or more-real-than-real:

- jogging, weight training, aerobics, body-piercing, bungee jumping, white-water rafting, adventure holidays
- private life going public in talk shows, true-life stories, tabloid exposés, autobiographies
- interactive TV, phone-in surveys, courtroom TV, 'reality' TV, car crash/execution/surgery videos

- CDs with the built-in scratch of records, John Lennon's tinny voice on a 'new' Beatles single, groups unplugged on MTV, live recordings
- giant video screens bringing you closer to the event at stadium concerts, sports venues, party conferences
- digital special effects, surround-sound, virtual reality
- songs, ads and self-help manuals which implore you to find yourself, be yourself, do it your way, express yourself, unlock the real you, find your inner child.

You could add plenty more examples of your own to this list. They all illustrate Baudrillard's claim that 'when the real is no longer what it used to be, nostalgia assumes its full meaning. There is a proliferation of myths of origin and signs of reality; of second-hand truth, objectivity and authenticity' (*Simulations*, page 12). That is, they all attempt to deter, or provide alibis for, the disappearance of the real at the hands of simulation. The Baudrillardian irony, however, is that these attempts to increase the feel of reality are themselves simulations. Their authenticity is a special effect. They are *hyperreal* rather than *really* real.

We *manufacture the real* because of simulation. So once again we find that the real is not so much given as produced. Which basically means that we cannot win. This is why Baudrillard says that 'images precede the real', and this is why the relationship between the real and its representation is now inverted. The logical order of things might be that reality expresses itself through representations, but this has been turned upside down.

The end of theory?

For many critics, Baudrillard's work since the early 1980s has become increasingly silly. He has, it is claimed, forgotten all notions of logical argument. Relying on pure speculation, wild hyperbole and sloppy parallels between unconnected events, his whole approach is based on exaggerating for effect. Philosophy and social comment blur into science fiction. There is in his writing, as in the world it describes, a 'loss of the real.' This could, of course, be seen as its strength. An example:

In *The Transparency of Evil: Essays on extreme phenomena* (1993) Baudrillard writes a free-wheeling piece about the 'technological purification of bodies' in contemporary culture. He observes the paradox that our bodies' immune systems are weakening despite (or because of) our increasing obsession with hygiene and health. The more we protect ourselves, the more at risk we become. This generates panic, which creates further dependence on 'artificial sterilization of all environments', which further weakens our 'faltering internal immunological defences'. We have seen how hyperreality is an 'alibi' for (and proof of) the loss of the real; Baudrillard declares that Disneyland only exists to give the impression that the rest of America is real. In a similar way, he reads the postmodern body in terms of 'compensation'. Increased artificial protection compensates for the continual enfeebling of our defences. Our dependence on technology compensates for (and is proof of) the loss of the 'natural' human body. Growing knowledge of our own bodies (DNA, medical photography) compensates for (and creates) the sense that we have lost touch with them.

Warming to his theme, he then reflects on 'The 'boy in the bubble', surrounded, in his NASA-donated tent, by an atmospheric distillate of medical knowledge' and concludes that this air-tight existence is pretty close to our own. In paranoid fashion, Baudrillard speculates that we are all now 'vacuum-packed like records':

> We are already living in the bubble ourselves . . . a transparent envelope in which we take refuge and where we remain, bereft of everything yet overprotected, doomed to artificial immunity, continual transfusions and, at the slightest contact with the world outside, instant death.

Baudrillard then leads us, somehow, into an exploration of what he defines as the 'viral' nature of contemporary insecurity and panic. AIDS, terrorism and computer viruses are casually thrown together as metaphors for the system:

> they all hew to the same agenda of virulence and radiation . . . a single terrorist act obliges a reconsideration of politics as a whole in the light of terrorism's claims; an outbreak of AIDS . . . forces us to view the whole spectrum of disease in the light of the immunodeficiency thesis; and the mildest of computer viruses . . . has the potential to destabilize all data contained in information systems.

This drifts into a consideration of everything from rumours to fashions as forms of epidemic: we love, says Baudrillard to be infected by 'the ultra-rapid circulation of signs at a surface level'.

This last quote offers a clue to Baudrillard; for his critics, the problem with his work is that it, too, is in love with surface effects. He has given up trying to explain the (historical, social, or economic) causes of what he describes.

Did the Gulf War take place?

Many people lost interest in Baudrillard in 1991, when he infamously claimed that the Gulf War had been a simulation. What he seemed to have in mind was:

- the resemblance on TV screens between real war footage and video games
- the role of CNN's 24-hour reportage
- the possibility that declaration of war can be a PR exercise
- the question of what defines a 'war' at all (especially when one side suffers 20,000 losses to the other's 70)
- the fact that we cannot know, through the smokescreens of TV editorial policy and state interference, what really happened.

He didn't mean that people hadn't really been killed in conflict, but his comments were taken as, at best, insensitive to real suffering. In his book *Uncritical Theory: Postmodernism, Intellectuals and the Gulf War* (1992), Christopher Norris used Baudrillard's piece to discredit, not only Baudrillard, but postmodernism's abandonment of truth and evaluation. (We return to this last point in Chapters 5 and 8). While Baudrillard's claim that 'the Gulf War did not take place' seems problematic, it would be interesting to have a similar debate about 'the war on terrorism' that followed the terrorist attacks on America in 2001.

In summary

Baudrillard thinks we need to reconsider *what* we mean reality to be, and *where* we consider it to be in relation to its supposed reproduction.

In our 'normal' way of thinking, images and other forms of representation have a lazy relationship to the real: they are subservient to reality. Reality comes first, it is in the driver's seat. Something about reality determines or produces its 'simulation'.

In Baudrillard's way of thinking, reality has a lazy relationship to images and other forms of representation. It is subservient to representation. Reality comes second, it takes the back seat. Something about simulation determines or produces reality.

Other books by Baudrillard include:

For a Critique of the Political Economy of the Sign (1981)

America (1989)

The Illusion of the End (1995)

The Vital Illusion (2000)

The Imposible Exchange (2001)

Screened Out (2002)

The Spirit of Terrorism and Requiem for the Twin Towers (2002)

For an account of his recent work see:

Mike Gane *Jean Baudrillard: In radical uncertainty* (2000)

Influences, comparisons and dialogues

Although Baudrillard's writings do have a recognizably Baudrillardian tone, they actually feed off and develop the ideas of a number of other thinkers. As you will see, his speculations on how simulations have altered the relationship between reality and representation have a lot in common with some of the other postmodern theorists discussed later in this book. His works also show the influence of several thinkers who have developed theories about media culture from within a loosely Marxist framework. As well as being important to Baudrillard, some of them have been influential to the formation of postmodern theory in general. Most provide important touchstones for a lot of the ideas discussed in the rest of this book.

Karl Marx (1818–1883)

The political philosopher Karl Marx provided perhaps the most influential account of modernity. His arguments about the impact of industrialization and capitalist expansion have helped to shape the work of countless social analysts throughout the twentieth century, and many theories of postmodernism address themselves in one way or another to his ideas. We cannot attempt to do justice to the full scope of Marx's ideas here. But we can note some of the ideas which have informed Baudrillard's outlook on postmodern culture.

At the time when Marx was writing, modern industry was in a constant search for new sources of labour, new raw materials, new technologies, and new ways of spreading into social life. Marx looked critically at this, but recognized in it a potential for improving the material comforts of people's lives. Modernity was far from all bad: it had a great capacity for improving people's standards of living. Yet Marx also recognized that the innovations of modernity were propelled by the capitalist economic system, and he was deeply critical of this.

Marx was a historical materialist. In other words, he believed that all societies in history could only be understood by looking at the way they organized people's labour (Marx defined labour as the natural interaction of human beings with their environment). In all societies, people's lives are defined by labour, but Marx believed that labouring under capitalism defined lives in a particularly immoral way. The basis of his critique was that, under capitalism, all aspects of culture were determined by economic forces and that the overall effect of this was dehumanization and the impoverishment of creativity. Marx believed that:

In order to buy what they need to live, people have to sell their labour power (their capacity to work) for wages. Their labour is bought and sold as a commodity: a price tag is attached to everybody. Everyone is just a means of making profit.

The exchange of labour for money is not a fair swap. Employees want to do just the amount of work required to pay for their wages. But employers need workers to create wealth far in excess of this basic requirement. So only a fraction of the working week is spent replacing the value of wages. The rest is a surplus amount of work which generates wealth for the capitalist. This is exploitation.

The goods that people produce have their natural 'use value' taken away from them and replaced with false 'exchange value'. Under the dominance of the market, what counts is not what things mean or what real purpose they serve, but how much they are worth. Everything becomes equivalent to money. Money, and not face-to-face communication, now acts as the crucial social bond.

Labour becomes for most unfulfilling and uncreative. Workers are alienated from the objects they produce and from the possibility of a truly communal life. They are prevented from fulfilling their true potential. The clash between the needs of the workers and the capitalist system results in a constant class struggle, which will eventually lead to revolution.

Society has two levels:

- the *economic base*. This is the level of the production and distribution of goods. It supports and sometimes interrupts . . .
- the *cultural superstructure*. This is the level of arts, religion, shopping, entertainment, language and party politics.

Many products of the superstructure create an insatiable consumer desire, or 'commodity fetishism'. In acting as good consumers we effectively sign ourselves in to, and help to maintain, the very system which enslaves us. The superstructure tries to blind us to the true, underlying nature of capitalism. It does not let us see the economic base which creates it. Marxism, by contrast, is like a science that enables us to see through ideology.

Post Marx

Baudrillard's ideas about the society of simulation are formed in part out of a dialogue with Marxism. He retained many of the touchstones of Marx's critique of modernity, but also tried to go beyond many of them. Influenced by numerous other intellectuals on the political left – and inspired by the fact that the citizens of the west seemed reluctant to unite and overthrow the system – Baudrillard believed it necessary to bring Marx up to date. Marxism had now to account for contemporary developments in information technology, consumerism, the growth of the leisure industry and multinational corporations. We are now in a period of *supermodernity, hypermodernity, late modernity, postmodernity*. Marx needs to be souped up accordingly.

In his early work, Baudrillard was in broad agreement with Marx that the expansion of capitalism had brought about fundamental social changes. He agreed that an abstract system of values had come to replace the 'real' values that (he supposed) characterized pre-modern communities, and believed that this system had penetrated much further into all aspects of existence than Marx had envisaged. Like Marx, Baudrillard claims (sometimes rather romantically) that societies before the advent of modernity possessed more 'natural' values. He believed that they enjoyed an unmediated, collective existence, uncorrupted by outside systems of value like capitalist economics. These societies were based not on productivity or the commodification of labour, but on unprofitable, supposedly spontaneous communicative activities like gift-giving, religious rituals, festivities and so on. Marx would have described such things in terms of their use value, but Baudrillard thought that in describing them that way, Marx was unwittingly projecting capitalist ideas of utility on to 'primitive' ways of life. Baudrillard preferred the phrase *symbolic exchange* to describe such pre-capitalist activities and he believed them (it is not something he could prove) to be free of the modern-day demand that everything be put to a specific purpose and given a specific value. He also differs from Marx in claiming that:

- There has been a transition from a society of production to one of reproduction. Images and information are now more important than solid commodities.
- The cultural superstructure has power of its own. It is not just a passive reflection of whatever happens in the economic base.
- Consumerism might be more important than Marx's modes and relations of production.

As a result of these factors political oppression is not located in any one specific group, place, or action. It does not come up from some underlying economic root. Nor is it forced down on people from above by an identifiable group of fat cat capitalists. Power is an ambience. It soaks into everything. No wonder we cannot rely on the workers to spontaneously unite in revolt.

Walter Benjamin (1892–1940)

Benjamin is relevant here because of a well-known essay he published in 1936 called *The Work of Art in the Age of Mechanical Reproduction*. In that piece, Benjamin was interested in the contribution that new technologies of mass reproduction could make to the formation of politically progressive art forms. His main contention was that with the help of these new technologies art could be removed from its high-class preserve and become available to everyone.

He noted that 'original' works of art, such as paintings, gained much of their prestige from the fact that they were usually produced in editions of one. This gave them an air of uniqueness and authority which elevated the significance of the artist's 'touch'. The work of art in all its individual glory was therefore fetishized, creating an unnecessary 'aura' around it and pushing its monetary worth to ridiculous heights.

This aura could be stripped from works of art through their multiple reproduction in colour plates, postcards, posters and so on. The new art form of cinema was also important to Benjamin for similar reasons. Baudrillard's notion of simulations as copies without originals can be traced back, at least partly, to Benjamin's argument that mass reproduction has reduced the significance of authenticity and originality.

But Baudrillard might also argue against Benjamin that, rather than destroying the aura of authenticity, the predominance of simulation replaces authenticity with *nothing but* aura. Endless reproduction of a Van Gogh painting only increases (or perhaps causes) the fame of the original and the desire to see it. If Van Gogh did not have this aura conferred upon his name by constant reproduction, who would be interested? Baudrillard would say that the endless copies only produce a nostalgic desire to confront the real thing. Yet again the real is produced by its reproduction.

Henri Lefebvre (1901–1991)

A Marxist sociologist, and at one time Baudrillard's teacher, Lefebvre is known mainly for the three volumes of his *Critique of Everyday Life* (1947–1981) in which he applied some of Marx's ideas about alienation to the conditions of day-to-day social life. Building on Marx, Lefebvre argued that capitalism had now thoroughly colonized, or 'bureaucratized' daily existence and that people were now reduced to the status of mere consumers. Consequently, he attempted to push Marxist ideas beyond their traditional emphasis on production lines, factory floors and trade unions, and looked for signs of revolution in all aspects of life in the modern world.

Baudrillard picked up on aspects of Lefebvre's critique in his early books, *The System of Objects* (1968) and *The Consumer Society* (1970). In these, he took from Lefebvre the project of applying a Marx-informed analysis to such everyday matters as leisure pursuits, fashion, home furnishings and domestic gadgets. Influenced by Guy Debord and others (see below), he went further than Lefebvre in putting consumption rather than production on the centre stage of political theory.

Guy Debord (1931–1994)

Debord was a spokesman for a radical group of artists and social critics known as the Situationist International. Centred in France, and most active in the 1960s, they saw consumer and media culture as an insidious form of oppression. Believing in the power of hedonism as a force of resistance, the Situationists created art and theory which they hoped would stimulate a carnivalesque rebellion against a suffocating and falsified modern world.

In his 1967 book *The Society of the Spectacle*, Debord predicted that the economy of the later twentieth century would be driven by images rather than by the industrial production of physical goods. He argued that, with the arrival of media and consumer society, experience itself was commodified. He pointed out, for example, that we are now invited to express ourselves not through what we create, but through what we buy. Thus, to Debord, relationships were mediated by images, and social life was totally occupied by merchandise. Defining the spectacle as the 'affirmation of appearance and affirmation of all human life . . . as mere appearance', Debord argued that people could no longer take control over or actively participate in the creation of their own pleasures, experiences, and desires. People were bystanders to their own lives.

Heavily indebted to the work of Henri Lefebvre, the aim of Debord and the Situationists was therefore to turn everyday life itself into a revolutionary project – to transform the world of banality and repetition into an immediate and impassioned form of living.

Baudrillard's work is influenced by contacts he made with Debord in the 1960s. As you can see, his descriptions of simulation and implosion have a lot in common with Debord's account of how the spectacle and the commodity dominate social life. He also shared with Debord the feeling that the consumption of images is now more economically and politically significant than the production of objects.

However, Debord's description of the spectacle implied that he could make a clear-cut distinction between true and false. He and the Situationists also suggested that it was possible to find a certain amount of space between the spectacle and its consumers. It was in this space that liberating social change could be created. Finding that such distinctions and distances have now collapsed, Baudrillard is far less optimistic about this possibility.

Marshall McLuhan (1911–80)

McLuhan was a Canadian theorist with an interest in the impact of media on society and consciousness. His most famous book was *Understanding Media; the Extensions of Man* (1964), in which he charted the transition from print technologies to the 'cool' systems of electronic media as the dominant form of communication. McLuhan argued that new technologies give birth to new human environments, and believed that over the centuries the thoughts and actions of mankind have been determined by developments in our means of communication.

For McLuhan, it was the nature of media technology (how it worked, how it had to be used, how it related to the human body), and not its content (what it showed) that was significant. He formulated this belief in the well known phrase: 'the medium is the message'.

McLuhan suggested that the media revolution of the electronic age was bringing about subtle yet momentous changes in our perceptual habits, and producing a decentralized virtual community, which he famously named the 'global village'. It was thanks to *Understanding Media* that Baudrillard adopted the term 'implosion' to describe the impact of this new environment. McLuhan wrote:

> *As electrically contracted, the globe is no more than a village. Electronic speed in bringing all social and political functions together in a sudden implosion has heightened human awareness of responsibility, to an intense degree.*

(page 20)

As far as McLuhan was concerned, this electronic village involved a new kind of social bond and a high degree of audience participation. For instance, he cited the televized funeral of J.F. Kennedy as an occasion when the power of TV united a large mass of people in a ritual activity. Another example of this might be the images of war and famine witnessed daily on the world's TV screens. It is often claimed that the media age has enriched us with an ever expanding store of images of the world to which we would otherwise never have access, and in McLuhan's benign picture of things, this can bring people together in a rather mystical sort of technological consciousness. Critics have pointed out that McLuhan's 'village', far from being global, is actually emitted from a very specific Euro-American centre. The destruction of the World Trade Center in September 2001 was certainly watched globally, but that doesn't mean all audiences 'read' the events in the same way. No 'village' is harmonious. Baudrillard, meanwhile, pictures the media as a much more malign force, preventing real communication or meaning and providing only a shallow, passive experience.

Baudrillard shares with McLuhan an interest in information overload, the ability of modes of communication to alter perception and the idea that the media form a sort of environment. He also borrows from McLuhan the cybernetic vision of people wired into an all-embracing image and information network. In his later 'picture book' *The Medium is the Massage* [sic] (1967) McLuhan observed:

> *The wheel . . . is an extension of the foot . . . the book is an extension of the eye . . . clothing, an extension of the skin . . . electronic circuitry, an extension of the central nervous system.*

(pages 31–40)

Later, in *Understanding Media*, he claimed that 'with TV the viewer is the screen.' (page 272).

Baudrillard echoed this vision some years later in an essay called *The Ecstasy of Communication* (in *Postmodern Culture* edited by Hal Foster, 1983):

> *With the television image – the television being the ultimate and perfect object for this new era – our own body and the surrounding universe become a control screen.*

(page 127)

Many of these ideas seem to have been borne out by recent developments in cybertechnology, computerization and satellization. Similar ideas have also appeared in works by various science fiction and cyberpunk writers of the last 30 or so years – J.G. Ballard, Phillip K. Dick, William Gibson, Bruce Sterling – and in many films – *Videodrome*, *Bladerunner*, *The Matrix*. In some of this work, we get a vision of technology out of control, taking over the human race, making its own dangerous decisions, and so on. Some writers have criticized Baudrillard for inheriting from McLuhan a similar tendency to speak of technology as if it has human motives. Baudrillard's media seem to forge themselves out of their own technological developments, as though they are independent of personal, historical, political and economic intervention.

These are just some of the thinkers whose ideas can be traced through Baudrillard's work. There are many more. Some of those other influences come from the schools of thought known as *structuralism* and *poststructuralism*. We will have a lot to say about them in the next chapter.

05

the deconstruction of meaning

In this chapter you will learn:

- postmodernist approaches to meaning and representation
- the relationship between structuralist and postructuralist accounts of how signs work
- some of the theories involved in deconstruction
- examples of the influence of these theories.

In the last chapter we encountered a challenge to common sense ways of thinking about the relationship between reality and its representation. Via the work of Jean Baudrillard, we concentrated on how this challenge has arisen from a society organized around electronic media and spectacle. However, this area is only a small part of postmodern theory's concern with representation. In fact, Baudrillard's ideas are informed as much by recent theories of language and meaning as they are by theories of media and society.

In order to make any sense of poststructuralism, you need to know a little about structuralism first.

Although it has had most impact in the field of literary theory and criticism, structuralism is best thought of as an approach or method rather than as a clearly defined discipline. Structuralist ideas can theoretically be used in any number of different areas – they first received widespread attention with the work of the anthropologist Claude Levi-Strauss, and also affected the thinking of the psychoanalyst Jacques Lacan – and they can be applied to many different kinds of *text*. Also, although the term structuralism indicates a fairly restricted cluster of themes, there is not a single set of rules to which all thinkers who have been labelled structuralist will rigidly stick.

Structuralism is less concerned with what texts are about, and more with how they work. In order to see these mechanisms more clearly, structuralism deliberately plays down any notion of the content of a text (e.g. the moral of a story, the message of a folk tale). As the philosopher Jacques Derrida has noted, commenting on structuralism, 'the relief and design of structures appears more clearly when content, which is the living energy of meaning, is neutralized.' In other words, structuralism is about the formalities of *how* texts mean, rather than about *what* they mean.

At the most general level, structuralism brings to the fore a number of questions about meaning, representation and authorship and explores the relationships between language and knowledge. In this respect, it can be seen as part of a widespread pre-occupation with language that has affected a great deal of thought (including what we now call postmodernism) throughout the twentieth century. Anglo-American philosophy, in particular, has been dominated by a fascination with language, on some occasions believing that philosophy was ultimately *about* language, and that it therefore had a special ability to sort out any linguistic confusions suffered by other disciplines such as the sciences or political theory. Meanwhile, the philosopher Ludwig

Wittgenstein (1889–1951) was concerned with the fact that his thought was necessarily restricted by the limits of the language in which he was bound to express them. And Martin Heidegger (1889–1976) famously claimed that 'language speaks us'.

Three main structuralist themes have influenced the development of postmodernist thought:

We use language to organize – and even construct – reality. Language enables us to give meaning to the world

Reality cannot be readily separated from the way we represent it, or the stories we tell about it. Language therefore plays an active role in forming our perceptions of reality. This insight has been central to postmodern theory. Traces of it are clearly visible in Baudrillard's reflections on the power of simulation, for example (see previous chapter).

Meanings happen only in relation to structures

No single thing 'gives off' a meaning of its own accord: it does so only through its relationship to other things.

Verbal and written language provides the clearest demonstration of these structural or relational properties of meaning

Studying how language works can provide an understanding of how all cultural products create meaning.

Saussure

In the postmodern context, these ideas grew largely out of the work of Ferdinand de Saussure (1857–1913), credited as the founder of both modern linguistics and structuralism. In his *Course in General Linguistics* (first published posthumously in 1915) Saussure sought to examine the process by which language makes sense to us. He argued that in order to understand the workings of language, it was fairly pointless to look for the historical and/or 'natural' roots of particular words. Instead, words should be looked at as inter-related elements within language as a whole.

Saussure departed from previous approaches to the study of language in that he paid attention not to how it evolved over time, but to how it works as a self-governing system in the present. By denying the significance of the history of words (their etymology) and by refusing to look for their bases in nature, he anticipated the postmodern preference for surface over 'depth'.

Words and things

Common sense tells us that the world is made up of independently existing things which naturally fit the names we have given them. This implies, for example, that there is something about a rose which means that 'rose' is inevitably the right word for it. But Saussure implies that there is no direct or causal relation between a rose and the letters R-O-S-E. Any other collection of letters could conceivably have done the job just as well. It is purely a matter of social convention that roses are called roses. Thus Saussure argued against the assumption that language is made up of individual units which have natural attachments to objects and ideas.

Because there is no natural or inevitable bond between words and things, Saussure saw language as an arbitrary system. From this starting point, structuralist – and eventually postmodernist – theory abandons any question of 'truth' language: it argues that language can never be a transparent or innocent reflection of reality.

A world of signs

Saussure believed that all of culture is made up of *signs*. That is to say, social life is characterized by the circulation and exchange of forms to which convention has given meaning. A sign for Saussure is simply any device through which human beings communicate to each other. To the extent that anything can have meaning attached to it, this could be taken to suggest that just about anything can be called a sign.

One implication of this is that structuralism is not, in principle, in the business of evaluating the artistic qualities of its objects of enquiry. Thus there have been structuralist studies of cuisine, fashion, advertising, photography, music, movies and folk tales, among many other things. Everything is equally grist to the struturalist mill, and this generally means that it has little use for conventional discriminations between high and low culture.

A science of signs

Saussure argued that verbal and written language offered the best model of how signs made meaning through a system of arbitrary social conventions. Linguistics could therefore provide a strong basis for a scientific study of the life of signs in society.

This proposed science of signs would be called *semiology* (or *semiotics*: the two are more or less interchangeable). Although structuralism and semiology are not identical in meaning, they are very closely related. It can be argued that semiology is really a branch of structuralism. It can also be claimed that semiology deals with the social and political dimension of signs, while structuralism – as its name suggests – has a more abstract concern with overall systems and underlying structures. In practice, however, there is no hard and fast distinction between the two areas.

The rules of the game

Structuralism says that language has a system of rules of combination. These rules permit a large number of different words to be created, but only within the limits of the 26 letters of alphabet. Each specific language will have its own laws regarding how letters can be strung together to make meaningful (or even pronounceable) words. We cannot do what we like with letters (or invent new ones) and expect them to make sense to anybody.

An example

Rules of *combination* (known as the 'syntagmatic' axis) in English mean that 'rose' can be rearranged to 'sore' or 'eros' and still make some sort of sense. However, English does not yet permit the letters to be recombined in any meaningful way into 'rseo'. There are also rules of *selection* (known as the paradigmatic axis). These mean that the 'o' in the same word can be substituted for a 'u' to make 'ruse', or an 'i' to make 'rise', but not for much else.

Such simple rules of course extend to how words can be put into order to create phrases, sentences, novels, poems, notes to the milkman and so on.

They also extend to all other languages. In the language of clothes, the rules of selection mean that I can feasibly swap wellington boots for snow shoes, but the rules of combination decree that either kind of footwear would look rather too daring if worn in conjunction with a cocktail dress (or on the wrong part of my body).

Structuralism finds that such norms and conventions apply to all aspects of culture. Language in the sense of speech and writing simply provides the clearest embodiment of the principles which govern all sign systems.

Put at its most basic, the sign is defined by Saussure as an object, word, image, or whatever, together with its meaning. Put more technically, it is the unit of meaning produced by the relation of a *signifier* to a *signified*:

- *signifier*: the material object, the sounds that words make, the letters on a page, etc. For example 'a bunch of red roses'
- *signified*: the concept or mental image to which the signifier gives rise. For example the 'romance or passion' signified by the bunch of red roses.

The signified is what is meant by the sign. The signifier is what means it.

As we saw in the case of the relationship between words and objects, the relationship between the signified and its signifier is arbitrary. For example, there is no 'natural' reason why a bunch of red roses should signify passion – it is solely a matter of convention. Culture has coded roses in this way, and we have come to take this coding for granted.

Now, the arbitrary relationship between the sign and its meaning does not suggest that you can make signs mean anything that you want them to. Individuals can neither invent signs of their own out of nothing, nor read signs in any way they please. You are never at liberty to create purely personal interpretations of things. Understanding is always in some sense constrained by rules and conventions. It is not down to personal decision that if I send red roses to someone they will most likely interpret my gesture as a romantic (or corny) one. I have not personally endowed roses with romantic connotations; they have been coded well in advance of my own amorous wishes.

So structuralism and semiology argue that the meanings of signs go far beyond individual intention. This insight is significant for the fields of art and literature, since it calls into question the modernist, romantic view of unique, original works of art being created by individual acts of genius. We will look at this question of authorship in more detail later.

Signs of difference

The established difference between 'rose' and 'nose' is what allows a different meaning to be given to each of those otherwise similar words. In the English language the sound 'r' and the sound 'n' are registered as distinct enough to be granted significance. It is conceivable that another language would not recognize the distinction between the two sounds (or would not make it significant). Neither 'r' nor 'n' have much to say by themselves. They get meaning only by virtue of what other letters they are combined with.

Roses signify passion and romance partly because they are not poppies or chrysanthemums.

It is also important that roses are on the correct side of the arbitrary distinction we make between flowers and weeds. Few people would receive a bunch of weeds as a sign of affection.

These are all illustrations of the structuralist principle that signs mean what they do because of what the structure of language allows. In this view, signs have significance (that is, they are indeed signs) only in relation to language as a whole. Thus Saussure places little weight on isolated signs. His only concern is for relationships between signs within a self-sufficient system of differences. The meaning of a sign is never its own private property but is the product of its difference from other signs.

Structuralists at work

The suggestions touched on above have been picked up in many different ways. Here are a few examples.

The System of Objects (1968) Jean Baudrillard

Interior decoration and domestic furniture can be analyzed as sign systems structured like language. Modernity brings about a new commodification and regulation of everyday life, in which it becomes important to keep up with fashion, and to assemble goods (e.g. clothes, household furnishings) in such a way that they:

- go together and
- differentiate you (your taste, social class, etc.) from others.

Under capitalism all rooms in the middle-class home are structured around systems of goods (e.g. the 'country kitchen' look). The domestic environment is a system of objects and styles, designed to function under the logic of modernity: life gets taken over by a consumer ambience in which all commodities get their meaning from their position in networks of commodity-signs.

A particular style of armchair signifies not by itself, but in relation; to understand it, you should look at its relation to the suite of which it is a part, the suite's relation to the decor of the room, its relation to other available designs, the relationship between the theme of the lounge and the theme of other rooms in the house, and the way your possessions are encoded with mass-produced signs of 'individuality'.

Signs and Meaning in the Cinema (1972) Peter Wollen

The structuralist film critic should be on the look-out for a system of differences and oppositions. In looking at the films of a single director, the structuralist film critic is not concerned with the obvious repetition of storylines and styles through a number of films produced over that director's career. Rather, he or she is looking for an underlying esoteric structure of binary oppositions that reveals a whole complex of meaning beneath the entire spectrum of the film maker's work. Studying the Westerns of John Ford would reveal changing expressions of the binary oppositions 'garden vs. desert', 'civilization vs. savagery' and 'heroes vs. villains'. These oppositions are social constructs with political implications. Moveover, they are not produced solely out of the head of the individual director: individuals are seen by structuralism as mere channels or transmitters of social meanings. In self-expression we repeat ideals unconsciously, without being aware of their wider resonances.

Decoding Advertisements (1978) Judith Williamson

Advertising as a subtle form of propaganda designed only to buy us into capitalism. Structuralism and semiotics are the tools which enable us to take advertising apart and reveal its true mechanisms. Adverts produce meanings which have no direct connection to reality. They are all about trying to establish differences between items that (Williamson argues) are essentially the same. Aftershave commercials create very particular images for specific products so that they appear radically different from other bottles of (very similar) fragrant liquid. Two brands of instant coffee do not really differ from one another, but advertising campaigns work to differentiate them in order to stimulate false desires, and they do this through their own internal organization of words and images. They are specific structures of signs which work by making connections between things. An obvious example is that of a cigarette advert: the coming together of the brand name and the image of a cowboy on horseback creates a chain of association between smoking, masculinity, health, activity and the great outdoors.

On one level, the advert itself is the signifier (the material sign), while the product is the signified (the concept referred to). On another level, the product becomes a signifier, while its signifieds are the connotations given by the structure of the advert as a whole. This structure allows the meaning of one sign (e.g. the cowboy) to be transferred to another (e.g. the brand name).

A postmodern criticism of Williamson

In his book *Postmodernism; The Twilight of the Real* (1990) Neville Wakefield criticized Williamson's structuralist approach. He saw it as relying on outmoded modernist principles of depth analysis. Williamson sees ads only in terms of their deep meaning – to persuade us to buy the product. A postmodern view would emphasize the pleasures we might gain from the advert itself without taking much of an interest in the commodity it refers to. Postmodern ways of 'reading' media involve zapping between channels, flicking through magazines, surfing the Internet, cruising the multiplex and so on.

None of these are particularly suggestive of deep meanings or persuasion by secret forces. The postmodern consumer is a nomadic sort of window-shopper, capable of sampling a multitude of experiences thrown up by culture, but without having to have any special personal attachment to them.

The rationalist notion of deep meaning implied by structuralism and other modern forms of analysis is therefore made inappropriate by postmodernism. Dick Hebdige made a similar point (though he was rather less enthusiastic about it) in his 1988 book, *Hiding in the Light*:

> *Cruising was originally introduced as a post-structuralist strategy for going beyond the puritanical confinement of critical activity to the pursuit and taming . . . of the ideological signified. By cruising the 'reader' can take pleasure in a text without being obliged at the same time to take marriage vows and a mortgage on a house.*

(page 162)

Poststructuralism

We have seen that structuralism asks where meaning comes from. Does it come from the text itself? Does it come from the context in which the text is consumed? Is the reader free to create his or her own meaning? To what degree can the author of a text control how it is interpreted? Does the production of meaning arise from the interaction of these factors? If so, exactly how do they interact?

Poststructuralism continues to ask these questions, but refuses to find a single answer.

Structuralism and poststructuralism form much of the philosophical background of postmodern theory. Indeed, nowadays poststructuralism is often seen as postmodern philosophy. One of the dangers of this is that it can give the impression that poststructuralism is a single school of thought or academic discipline. In fact, the term is regularly used to unite the work of a fairly diverse group of thinkers, few of whom ever described themselves as poststructuralists. Also, although the word 'poststructuralism' implies that it simply took over from structuralism at some point in history, it is truer to say that, especially in the 1960s and 1970s, the two ran alongside each other and often crossed tracks.

Nevertheless it is safe to note certain major currents in poststructuralist thought. What the various poststructuralists have in common are:

• the questions listed above
• the fact that their work mixes together political theory, literary criticism, philosophy, psychoanalytical theory, semiotics, structuralism and (in some cases) feminism
• the great density of many of their writings.

They inherit from structuralism the following three broad (and overlapping) ideas:

• language cannot point outside of itself
• languages produce (rather than reflect) meaning
• language does not express individuality.

So there are certain similarities between poststructuralism and its supposed predecessor. But it has the prefix 'post-' partly because it takes the implications of structuralism further than the likes of Saussure and Levi-Strauss probably intended. There is also the important fact that it parts company with structuralism on a number of (again overlapping) points. For convenience, we can divide these into three as well:

Poststructuralism is more anti-foundational
Structuralism removed texts from the foundations of reality and individual authorship. In this way we may call it an anti-

foundational tendency. But it also suggested that although texts can be seen as flat surfaces, they are supported by deep, hidden, fundamental structures. However, poststructuralism can be seen as rejecting any such notion of ultimate, underlying grounds beneath meaning.

Poststructuralism is less all-embracing

Poststructuralists accuse structuralism of too often setting itself up arrogantly as a superior, objective viewpoint from which to observe eternal 'global facts' behind all texts. Poststructuralists see this as a totalitarian or imperialist attitude which suppresses the significance of specific minds working in particular social and historical contexts. Poststructuralists do not believe that it is possible or desirable to step outside of your objects of study and unveil a final, all-embracing explanation of everything.

Poststructuralism makes more of difference

Structuralism claimed that in language no sign had a positive meaning on its own terms. Meaning was always a product of difference. Despite this, language was seen as a relatively fixed and stable, even tyrannical, structure.

Poststructuralism brings difference into the foreground, in order to disrupt any notion of stability or unity of meaning.

In structuralism, a text is seen as complete. In poststructuralism, it is always unfinished, full of holes, and contradictory.

Poststructuralists at work

Pierre Macherey

Macherey was a Marxist critic working within the structuralist/poststructuralist arena. As a Marxist, he was concerned with how texts act to reproduce the values of capitalism. He followed the tradition within Marxist-orientated literary theory of believing that the way we habitually consume texts (and other commodities) is more or less passive and unquestioning.

So as to survive, the status quo has to give the impression of being in good working order. It also has to persuade people that the current state of affairs is simply the way things are. In other words, it has to distract people from the idea that their conditions of existence are the direct result of a historically specific social and economic structure. For Macherey, most texts and their consumers participate in creating and maintaining the taken-for-granted illusion that the status quo is inevitable, coherent and unchangeable. In short, texts (and the way we have learned to consume them) aim to reconcile us to our conditions.

They do this by creating a certain sense of smoothness, or unity. For example, when we watch most films, we tend to be interested only in the events they describe. The questions we ask concern only what is going to happen next and whether a particular character is going to win the day. Thus, whenever we admire or identify with a film star, or simply follow the actions of a character on screen, we very rarely think about acting as a form of work, or film as a form of industrial production. We give little thought to studio trade union disputes going on behind the scenes, or to the unequal pay structures between technical staff and actors. We are effectively blind to these aspects of film production, and Macherey would argue that we create this blindness for ourselves by letting ourselves be sucked into the film's unfolding yarn.

We ignore the complex pattern of edits, flashbacks, jump-cuts and all the other devices that go into the fabrication of a movie. In fact, most films are really very fragmented, highly complicated pieces of material, but in the process of viewing this fact gets lost. By getting involved (or trying to get involved) in the stories they tell, we unconsciously stitch a multitude of filmic elements (for example, frames, scenes, shots and sequences) together into an intelligible sequence. In this way attention is drawn away from the social, economic and political context in which the film is made.

For Macherey, all texts only just succeed in achieving such a sense of smoothness. Chaos is always bubbling away just under the surface. The text could easily fall into turmoil, if only we would let it. For texts are really constructed out of ill matching bits and pieces, holes, contradictions, and dislocations.

Summary

In contrast to the structuralist project of looking for the fundamental order behind texts, Macherey searches for chaos beneath the illusion of coherence: 'the concealed order of the work is . . . less significant than its real *determinate* disorder (its disarray)'. Always on the look-out for the barely hidden moments of repression and division in texts which attempt to present a coherent world view, Macherey argues that all texts are really assembled from a diverse rag-bag of different ideas. These ideas may be in conflict with each other, and may be found to disrupt or challenge a given text's intended overt message.

Texts not only try to cover over their own internal gaps and conflicts, but are created out of the meanings they omit or repress: what a text puts 'outside' of itself determines what it says.

This is an example of how, whereas structuralism saw language as a closed system, and tried to fix individual texts to rigid linguistic frameworks, poststructuralism tries to open texts up and cut meanings loose. Poststructuralists do not necessarily believe that everything is meaningless, just that meaning is never *final*.

Key work: *Theory of Literary Production* (1966) (first English translation 1978)

Julia Kristeva

Although very difficult to summarize adequately, Julia Kristeva's large and complex body of work can be seen partly as a feminist expression of poststructuralist theory. That is to say, she brings gender politics into the poststructuralist frame. Having said that, it is worth remembering that she is not particularly interested in such feminist projects as rediscovering great works of literature written by women, or in looking at the stereotypes by which women are misrepresented. Drawing on psychoanalytical theory as well as structuralism and semiotics, she is concerned with more abstract connections between language or literature and gender.

Kristeva believes that it is possible to create a 'feminine' voice in literature. But she also denies the idea that there is some essential, timeless category of womanliness from which this voice can come. For Kristeva, no text can express a universal, authentic feminine experience which is then re-experienced by the reader.

Women may not be *born* with an ability to speak in a 'feminine' tongue. But they are pushed to the edges – or put outside of – 'mainstream' systems of representation. As an example of this, note that I (being male) have just referred to women as 'they', and that it is still common for writers to use 'he' and 'mankind' to refer to people in general. In this way women can be said to be linguistically silenced. Kristeva goes on to argue that they can use this marginal position as a space from which to create subversion.

Thus it is possible to produce writing (and also ways of reading) which goes beyond what Kristeva sees as conventionally masculine values like rigour, intelligibility, stability, and structure. She argues that texts (and literary critics) should produce playful, diverse, slippery and unstable meanings; these can effect a pleasurable and progressive undermining of masculine language.

The self on trial

Kristeva argues that male-dominated society discourages multiple forms of selfhood (see Chapters 6 and 7 for a detailed consideration of this). Partly because our language only allows for she/he, her/him and so on, our identities are largely confined to rigid gender definitions. However, certain experimental ways of using language can, for Kristeva, anarchically shake up the traditional definitions of self.

In her book *Revolution in Poetic Language*, Kristeva claimed that the language of avant-garde poetry and literature could help to loosen identity and free it from socially imposed limitations. 'Marginal texts' could be produced which disturbed the imaginary positions of identification that readers normally take on in the act of reading. 'Difficult' or 'transgressive' texts (for example Joyce's *Finnegans Wake*, the plays of Antonin Artaud) prevent the illusion of being passively swept along with unfolding fictional events. For Kristeva, as for some of her poststructuralist colleagues, such acts of identification are the products of habit and serve only to confirm the way you already see yourself. Marginal works, on the other hand, contribute to what Kristeva sees as a revolutionary, liberating undoing of the imagined unity of the self.

Progressive works of art for Kristeva are fragmentary, incomplete, non-systematic, and ultimately inexplicable. They subvert normal, mainstream language, and in doing so put gendered identities on trial. In other words experimental uses of language can free people from the limits of gender.

A note of caution

One criticism of this is that Kristeva's ideas, like those of Macherey, seem mainly to be defences of non-mainstream literature. They have little respect for popular or mass culture. It could be argued that their theories are in this way elitist. To put it bluntly, can the kind of literature promoted by Kristeva really be as 'progressive' as she thinks it can if hardly anybody bothers to read it? Is hers a theory of what she thinks everybody else should be reading? And if so, what gives her the right to do this?

Key works: *Revolution in Poetic Language* (1974) (English translation 1984)

Desire in Language: A semiotic approach to literature and art (1980)

Jacques Derrida

We often wonder what people are really getting at by certain comments they make. We wonder what celebrities are really like. When we read a novel or poem, we wonder what its message is. When a shocking crime takes place, we wonder whether its true cause lies in the inherent evil of the criminal, something awful in his or her upbringing, or the fact that he or she was an avid viewer of violent films. In these and a thousand other ways we are used to talking about things as though they have an essential meaning or root cause.

As you know, postmodern thought tends to reject the idea of things having a single, basic meaning. Instead, it embraces fragmentation, conflict and discontinuity in matters of history, identity and culture. It is suspicious of any attempt to provide all-embracing, total theories. And it rejects the view that any cultural phenomenon can be explained as the effect of one objectively existing, fundamental cause.

One of the most influential figures in this postmodern turn of thought against originals, centres and foundations is Jacques Derrida (born 1930). In a long series of extremely demanding books published since the mid 1960s, Derrida has developed his own particular poststructuralist blend of philosophy, linguistics, and literary analysis. It goes by the name of *deconstruction*.

Derrida's deconstructive work is very much a part of the project, discussed throughout this chapter, of questioning what we might call the meaning of meaning. It continues the structuralist task of looking for the conditions which allow texts to be meaningful, and it shares their interest in the relationships between language and thought. However, in common with the poststructuralist topics we have discussed so far, Derrida is much more interested in how the meanings of texts can be plural and unstable than in fixing them to a rigid structure.

Conditions of knowledge

If your doctor started to rhapsodize over the aesthetic properties of a rash on your neck instead of offering a proper diagnosis of it, you would probably feel that they were finding the wrong kind of 'meaning' there. But this is not to say that their 'reading' of your rash is simply false, or that it is a misinterpretation of the facts. Rather than being inaccurate, it is simply out of place. Criteria from the field of art are being transported into the field of medicine. In other words, your doctor is going too far outside the confines of medical discourse. Meanings always have a place.

This is an example of how, as Derrida argues, fields of knowledge always put a necessary limit on what can and cannot be validly said. Any discourse – medical, artistic, legal, or whatever – is defined by the methods and understandings it makes available to its practitioners, and as such prevents meanings from ever spinning off in inappropriate directions.

According to Derrida, particular disciplines present meanings and truths as obvious. In fact, though, what counts as meaning or truth is determined by the limitations of the discipline which supposedly 'discovers' and describes them. One of Derrida's projects is to show that all meanings and truths are never absolute or timeless, but are always framed by socially and historically specific conditions of knowledge. So when your doctor finally gets round to offering a diagnosis of your rash, they are actually bringing into play a great deal of particular ideas about what counts as an illness, how symptoms relate to diseases, what doctors are for, and what constitutes medicine.

None of these things are outside of history and culture. Likewise, what they prescribe as a cure will depend on current conditions of knowledge, and these may well be subject to change (a cure today can turn out to be a poison tomorrow).

Of course, none of these issues enters into your conversation with your doctor. You will just want to get your prescription and go home. Consulting your GP for medical advice simply seems like a perfectly normal thing to do, and neither you nor your doctor is therefore likely to discuss the field of medicine as a social construct. The field of medicine, we might say, involves certain historically particular notions of illness, symptom, and cure. It also depends on certain Western ideas about scientific rationality and objectivity. For example, modern Western medicine presents itself as a science and thus as fundamentally opposed to magic. All fields of knowledge structure themselves around touchstones of their own making in this way, yet fail to draw attention to their process of construction.

To take a slightly different example, literary theorists and critics tend to present their activity of interpreting texts as though it were an obvious or natural thing to do. They do not tell us why literary criticism might be a worthwhile way of making a living, or on what grounds some texts but not others are said to count as literature. Both literature and criticism are therefore taken for granted, as if they were self-evident facts of life. Thus it is possible for a critic to make use of an inherited set of critical criteria without ever having to reveal or question it. Most film reviewers are a case in point: they never question the validity of seeing directors as the main authors who give meanings to films. Meaning is regarded as a 'presence' in the text, and the critic believes he or she somehow has a special power to drag it into the light.

Deconstruction discovers hidden assumptions. There is no 'pure' knowledge outside of society, culture, or language.

This means that all belief systems, however 'rational' they may appear (Derrida has nothing less than 'Western metaphysics' in his sights) are available for critique. The more a point of view presents itself as 'natural' or 'normal' the more Derrida wants to deconstruct it.

Against presence

Thinking of things in terms of what they 'really mean' is a habit of thought which seems perfectly natural to us, and it is hard to imagine an alternative to it. For example, I am writing here about a group of texts as if they form a single body of work which belongs to a single author (Derrida) and in which we find certain basic themes. I have also mentioned postmodern thought as if it represented a single slab of knowledge. If there *is* a single main aim in Derrida's work, it is nothing less ambitious than to dismantle this habit of thought, which he sees as an illusory belief in certainty and *presence*.

By presence, Derrida means that Western forms of knowledge – in science, philosophy, 'common sense', and so on – build themselves up on certain 'centres' and 'origins'. One of the main concerns of deconstruction is to show that those centres and origins have no basis in reality. They are myths. (This should alert you to the fact that it is dangerous to speak of Derrida having a single project, or of deconstruction having a main concern.)

Derrida's criticism of presence both develops and argues with Saussure's structuralism. He takes from Saussure the idea that language cannot point outside of itself. In other words, language is a self-referring, self-regulating system. For structuralism, you do not need to look outside of a sign-system in order to find meaning: meaning is produced by the internal relationships between parts. Thus structuralism refused to find the source of meaning in nature or in the author.

Derrida and poststructuralism agree with structuralism on this point. They both reject the significance of personal intentions or individual experience in the creation of meaning. What counts for both is not intentional self-expression but the operation of the languages we inherit: the means of representation both exceed and precede decisions made by individual human beings.

But Derrida argues that structuralism chickens out of expanding on this theme. He claims that although structuralism rejects individuality and nature as pure grounds of meaning, it still holds on to a *depth model* of meaning. In other words, it assumes that you can use structuralist ideas to cut through the surface of a text and get at its true linguistic machinery. It can 'solve' texts.

So structuralism changed where meanings were thought to come from, but it still gave meaning a foundation in deep structures. For example, Claude Levi-Strauss thought he had found a single universal structure beneath all (only superficially diverse) cultures.

Derrida calls this the 'metaphysics of presence', and it involves the myth that things are meaningful before we give words to them.

For example, because we have the single word 'postmodernism', we assume that there is also a single thing in existence to which the word corresponds. The *name* 'postmodernism' has thus in effect given rise to the *thing* so that we can now find ourselves asking 'what is postmodernism?' rather than the more appropriate question 'what does the word postmodernism do?' Derrida would say that we have succumbed once again to the metaphysics of presence: postmodernism has become an object (a presence) in such a way that we can speak of some things as being more postmodern than others.

It is by reference to such presences that interpretations and theories can claim to represent valid pieces of information. But Derrida's deconstruction seeks to expose how the language used in particular fields both creates the essential presence through which knowledge can claim to be true, and conceals the means by which it creates this presence.

Logocentrism

An important example of the metaphysics of presence is the assumption that words transmit meanings from the consciousness of their speaker to the mind of their listener. It supposes that speech is a transparent vehicle for the expression of the speaker's thoughts, and that writing tries fruitlessly to emulate this relationship. Derrida refers to this myth as 'logocentrism', and believes it characterizes all Western thinking. He deconstructs it by arguing that both speech and thought are *texts*, and that they are therefore characterized by 'différance' (see below).

Différance

In the French language the word *différer* means both to 'differ' and to 'defer'. In his book *Margins of Philosophy* Jacques Derrida has endless fun punning around this (it's not that much fun to read, though). It is not an easy word to define: Derrida says 'différance is not, does not exist', and that it 'is neither a word nor a concept'. But what he has in mind is the *semiotic* notion of language as a system of differences. This suggests to Derrida that signs always contain traces of each other, and therefore that they have no 'essential' meaning of their own. Looking a word up in a dictionary often leads to other words that you need to look up; we are always presented with further signs. So meaning is indefinitely deferred (Derrida writes of 'a detour, a delay, a relay'). At the same time any sign is meaningful only through differentiation (red means 'stop' because green means 'go'). Différance is, therefore, both the passive state of being different and the act of differing ('producing differences'). It is intended to evoke the restlessness of language and the slipperiness of meaning.

Deconstructing opposites

As we hinted in the case of our doctor's hidden assumptions about the clear distinction between science and magic, the sense of presence constructed by fields of knowledge relies heavily on systems of opposition. In this medical example, 'science' is the preferred or dominant term (the presence), while 'magic' is the inferior term against which the scientific can be defined. By putting itself on the 'correct' side of the opposition, science constructs itself as the site of objectivity and truth.

Derrida argues that all thought performs such arbitrary acts of splitting. Thus we habitually think with such oppositions private/public, nature/culture, body/soul, objective/subjective. One half of the distinction is always seen as inferior to, derivative of, less than, disruptive of or expressive of the other half, which in this process gets privileged as the pure, primary presence. There is always a bias towards one term over the other, and this becomes the assumed grounds for argument, inter-pretation and proof.

Arguments about the nature of postmodernism often act in a similar way. Whether for or against postmodernism, they often set it up (as the word itself suggests) in terms of its relation (of opposition/continuity, etc.) to a notion of modernism. In this way, modernism becomes a single thing, created in retrospect by its supposed 'post'. In this process both modernism and postmodernism come to define each other. Arguments about what postmodernism is, or what its effects are, can then proceed on the basis that it differs in some way from something that it has itself helped to make.

One major point of deconstruction, then, is to analyze the workings of binary oppositions. In doing so it aims to highlight, and criticize, the wider power structures in which they are embedded. For example:

Many modernists assume a binary opposition of high/mass culture. In this opposition, 'mass' culture is high culture's monstrous 'other'. Hence the 'high' rejects the 'mass' as 'alien' to itself, but needs it for its own sense of identity (it defines itself through a construction of difference). Moreover, any list of the 'essential' characteristics of one side of the divide (e.g. high culture as active, mass culture as passive) will include features you are just as likely to find in the other. So 'high' is defined by its not being 'mass', and 'mass' is defined by its inferiority to 'high'; since both *are* what they are *not*, neither has an essence. There is only *différance*. And if 'high culture' has no essence it has no grounds to lord it over 'mass'. A thorough deconstruction has taken place.

Try applying a similar approach to such other binaries as West/East; good/evil; light/dark; civilized/primitive; us/them, and the 'political' possibilities of deconstruction become clear. For this reason Derrida has proved useful to *post-colonial* theory and to some feminist thinkers.

Inside out/outside in

In order to make this book make as much sense as possible, I have had to hold back a great many difficulties and contradictions. I have had to make all sorts of decisions about what to include and what to exclude. I have had to draw relatively firm lines around different points in history, and between different theoretical points of view. On the other hand, I have had to suggest continuities, influences and ongoing trends, where you could just as easily find fracture, conflict and diversity. Finally, I have constantly had to decide how far back to go in tracing the history of an idea, and how far away from the supposed crux of the issue I should go in explaining various strands and influences.

So this book gets its identity from the mass of things I have decided *not* to write about. If I put some of these rejected aspects back into the text (if I made different choices about what is and what is not crucial) you would have a different book in your hands.

All of these are part of how you try to build a reasonably coherent text, especially one with the aim of being 'introductory'. But *all* texts, and not just introductory ones, work in the same way to create an illusion of coherence. The task of deconstruction is to show that this is a very precarious illusion. It would show that what this book allows you to see as central is created by what I have decided is *marginal*. This book *is* therefore partly what it *is not*.

When Derrida deconstructs a text, he goes for details which give away this process. He brings back into the foreground the very things that the text pretends it does not need. He looks for what he calls the present absences, or productive silences. Sometimes he analyzes the footnotes of books in more detail than the main thrust of the argument. Footnotes are bits of added information, little pieces of disagreement or possible contradiction which the author leaves outside. To let them back in again would upset the main body of the text, would mess up the argument, and so this is precisely what Derrida's deconstruction does.

Summary

Although deconstruction sets itself the task of digging up the hidden suppressions and exclusions upon which texts are constructed, it is far from being an act of interpretation in the normal sense. Deconstruction does not mean trying to root out what a text is 'really saying'. On the contrary, it tries to show that the grounds from which texts and theories seem to proceed are always shifting and unstable. One way it achieves this is by recognizing the active role played by the invisible or marginalized in any text. Another is by exposing a text's system of imaginary oppositions.

Conclusion

- Western philosophies (including everyday common sense) revolve around an illusory *metaphysics of presence*. This can be found in myths about 'essence', 'meaning', 'cause', and 'self'.
- But such presence is never purely *present*. Essential meanings are not *just there*: they are *put there* by the tools, knowledges and assumptions we use to look for them.
- What counts as the deep or central meaning of a text depends on where you stand.
- The language we use to put names to things plays an important part in identifying those things for us in the first place.
- All theories, arguments, texts, etc. rest on abstract systems of relationships. So they never touch down on the sure grounds of a pre-existing and pure reality.
- Structuralism sought the 'facts' about *texts*. For post-structuralism (and so for postmodernism) there are no facts. There are only interpretations.

Writing

When trying to get to grips with poststructuralism we might well ask 'what is Derrida talking about?' In literature classes, teachers often ask their students what a particular piece of writing is 'saying'. In both of these cases, we are confusing writing with speech. But for Derrida and poststructuralism, there is no author speaking to us: there is only writing on a page.

Derrida argues (or rather, I infer from writing with the name 'Derrida' attached to it) that all sciences and philosophies deny writing any significance. Writing is presented as a merely convenient medium of communication through which ideas can be transmitted. First, there is the idea. Second, this gets written down. Third, the idea is communicated by the writing to the reader. In other words, we are under the impression that writing is transparent: we can look through it and see the thoughts on the other side.

Philosophical, scientific, and other forms of factual writing therefore traditionally prosper under the illusion that writing is neutral. In a scientific paper, or in a news item, you are not invited to pay attention to the language being used. To look at the writing itself (e.g. the words, the style) would seem beside the point: you should be looking beyond them to the argument or to the facts.

But Derrida's work, and that of the other poststructuralists, rejects the idea that writing can simply be a window to the truth. Rather, it prefers to see writing as opaque. Take a piece of writing from any newspaper, for example. It presents itself – or we are used to reading it as though it presents itself – as an innocent bit of reportage. We are of course aware that sometimes newspapers get their facts wrong, and we know that they are often selective in what they tell us, but structuralism and poststructuralism would go further than that: they would look, not at how the article told (or failed to tell) the truth, but at the way language itself was being used. The idea that language is transparent serves only to distract attention from the possibility that the story could have been told in any number of other ways. The use of different words can, for instance, create very different meanings (classic examples include the choice of 'mob' over 'crowd' and 'terrorist' over 'freedom fighter'). The idea that language is neutral denies that writing always sets up particular constructions of reality, and that these constructions are always tied in to history, society and politics.

It is on similar grounds that people often argue over political correctness in matters of language and representation. Like advertisers, governments are also aware of the power of words to affect thoughts. The British government, for example, once made its Department of Social Security call unemployed people 'Jobseekers' and changed their Income Support into 'Jobseeker's Allowance'.

So poststructuralists insist that all texts are opaque writing more than approximate versions of direct speech. We (mistakenly) tend to believe that when someone speaks, the words which come out of their mouths are like hot-lines to the thoughts in their head, and can therefore be trusted. Writing, by contrast, does not, for the poststructuralist, have this privilege (and neither does speech, really, for speech too is a form of writing). So suggesting that all texts are opaque means suggesting that no texts can be trusted. We should always beware the ruses used by texts to convince us of their innocence and honesty.

These sorts of ideas have been used by many critics to praise texts which deliberately draw attention to their style or to the way they are put together. It is claimed that in doing this, certain texts reject any pretence of being neutral.

An example of this is the film *Schindler's List*. Steven Spielberg's film about the Holocaust is in grainy black and white, with some sequences in colour. This reminds us of the constructed or artificial nature of the film, the fact that we are watching a length of celluloid rather than reality unfolding. This acknowledges that no single film can adequately express the enormity of the real historical events. It acknowledges that it is a partial version of those events, constructed by Spielberg and his team in the limited form of a three-hour mainstream movie. By highlighting its own artificiality (the clearest example being a monochrome sequence in which one girl's raincoat is coloured red), the film can be said to admit that it cannot, on its own, tell the whole story. It is, after all, only a film.

In addition to this, you might find similar distancing strategies in many other recent examples. To take just three: the 1990s saw a rise in fairly unintelligible typography on record covers, club flyers and so on. The opening titles of the 1995 film *Seven* were similarly deliberately scratchy and rough looking (the *Seven* look has often been imitated in many TV commercials). Many pop videos combine different looks and textures by mixing Hi-8 video sequences with 16mm celluloid, letterbox formats with full-screen, monochrome with colour. You can probably think of many more examples like this. All of these can perhaps be called deconstructive practices in that they, like visual speech marks, draw attention to their own physical materials.

Some of these ideas have influenced the work of a number of theorists concerned with the cultural politics of representation. For example, Trinh T. Minh-Ha has written some interesting pieces on the subjective (and never 'neutral') techniques of documentary film-making (see her book *When the Moon Waxes Red* (1991) for more on this).

New historicism: a postmodern approach to history

New historicism is an approach to the interpretation of *texts* that attempts to combine anthropological and historical methods with the insights of poststructuralism. Initially a school of literary studies in America (Stephen Greenblatt identified and named it in 1982), its influence is now felt in many areas of cultural studies. New historicists aim to 'ground' the meanings of texts (note the plural) in the particular historical conditions of their production, distribution and consumption. What's 'new' about it is that their view of history and meaning is critically informed by *deconstruction*. A quote from H. Aram Veeser's introduction to an anthology of writings on new historicism gives a taste of its scope and approach:

> *The essays in this book are less concerned to project long-range trajectories than to note bizarre over-lappings: . . . of window-smashing Suffragette street actions and the 'hobble skirt' presented by the Parisian fashions house of Worth . . .; of a 17th-century hermaphrodite's criminal trial, Shakespeare's Twelfth Night, and leather and rubber gloves . . .; of an ancient Roman tax bracket and the track-system in modern high-schools . . .; of Charles Dickens, patriarchy, and literary incest in a popular '40s novel . . .*

Under the influence of deconstruction, new historicists avoid:

- overarching hypotheses, total explanations, or sweeping historical narratives
- the notion of clearly divided historical periods
- the idea that any historical 'period' has a single 'world view'
- speaking of historical 'facts' as they were accessible independently of texts
- the idea of critical objectivity or disinterest
- distinctions between high and low culture
- distinctions between literary and non-literary works
- distinctions between the social and the cultural
- distinctions between the political/historical background (context) and cultural foreground, and the related idea that texts neutrally 'reflect' history
- the idea that artworks are complete, unified objects
- the author as unique source of meaning.

They look at:

- non-'canonical' or 'marginal' works, and apparently trivial events/anecdotes
- how texts and activities are enmeshed in a network of social practices
- exchanges of ideas between 'literary' and 'non-literary' texts
- the circulation of meanings across a range of practices and institutions
- art's active involvement in structures of power and economy
- the production of local knowledge
- disputes over meaning
- culture and history as dynamic networks of texts
- links and coincidences between apparently unconnected events
- the historian/critic's own motives and interests.

They have been criticized for:

- a badly theorized approach to history
- 'canon-bashing'
- making history up as they go along but dressing it in scholarly language
- disregarding academic standards of proof and evidence
- mixing different disciplines in a cavalier manner

(We discuss some of the issues around postmodern views of history in Chapter 8.)

Influential works

Political Shakespeare, edited by Jonathan Dollimore (1985)

Renaissance Self-fashioning, by Stephen Greenblatt (1980)

Shakespearean Negotiations, by Stephen Greenblatt (1990)

The New Historicism, edited by H. Aram Veeser (1989)

Deconstruction and architecture

Since the late 1980s some of Jacques Derrida's ideas have had an impact upon the theory and practice of postmodernist architecture. An influential exhibition of 'deconstructivist architecture' was mounted at the Museum of Modern Art, New York in 1988. Architects represented in the show included Zaha Hadid, Bernard Tschumi, Peter Eisenmen and Frank Gehry. Derrida collaborated with Bernard Tschumi on the latter's *Parc de la Villette* in Paris (begun in 1983), a project the architect has described as a 'practice of disjunctions':

*The Parc de la Villette project can . . . be seen to
encourage conflict over synthesis, fragmentation over
unity, madness and play over careful management. It
subverts a number of ideas that were sacrosanct to the
Modern Period and, in this manner, it can be applied
to a specific vision of Post-Modernity.*

For Derrida, the smooth surface of a text (such as a persuasive
argument or a philosophical treatise) is an illusion created by the
attempted suppression of internal contradictions. Deconstruction
aims to dismantle this illusion. It pushes into the centre themes,
ideas and values that the text tries to push to the margins. And it
encourages the self-destruction of texts by playing on the
inconsistencies and anxieties that lurk within them.

No theory or text is a self-contained, totally coherent system. It
always exists through an 'other', which it presents as 'exterior' to
itself. This means that the text depends for its 'identity' on its
construction of an 'outside'. The outside and the inside can't,
therefore, exist without each other, so the margins between them
are unstable. So Derrida is interested in borders; he questions
what is inside and outside of the 'proper' boundaries of the text.
Twenty pages of his *Spurs* (1978) are spent discussing a five-word
marginal note by Nietzsche: 'I have forgotten my umbrella'.

Deconstructivist (or 'deconstructionist', depending on whom
you read) architects similarly believe that a building is not a self-
contained statement: it has significance only in relation to its
surrounding cultural spaces. Because it is 'meaningful' through
its relationships to (and differences from) other buildings, it
can't be experienced in isolation from the site that 'frames' it.
Hence deconstructivist buildings examine the borders between
different architectural and social spaces: they are meant to be in
critical dialogue with their surroundings (they do not aim
passively to 'blend in'). They explore the interfaces between
interior and exterior, and the relationship between the frame
and its contents.

Specific buildings, the modernist movement, and architecture
itself can all be seen as 'deconstructible' texts. For example,
modernism distinguished between the structural frame of a
building, and the ornamentation that is applied to it. Structure is
the preferred (or privileged) side of this 'binary opposition'. But
this is linked to further oppositions. The right angles, repeated
modules and white walls of modernism were seen as a rational
rejection of 'superficial' style. Objectivity was preferred to mere

fashionability. But a deconstructivist would note that these supposedly timeless values were always expressed in similar ways. In other words, an idea of 'rationality' was constructed through fashionable forms. 'Objectivity' was fashionable; instead of rejecting style, the white wall *was* a style. These are all examples of the deconstruction of binary oppositions.

By trying to hide its interest in fashion/style behind a façade of rationality/objectivity, modern architecture also concealed important aspects of its own values – particularly regarding the race, class, and gender of its practitioners.

Because they are aware of such issues, deconstructivists aim to interrogate what Eisenman has called 'the metaphysic of architecture'. This 'metaphysic' includes: ideas about the 'essence' of good design; classical notions of proportion and harmony based on the human form; the claim to represent human experience; the 'vision' of the architect. As in Derrida's approach to literary and philosophical works, all supposedly 'complete' systems or projects are treated with suspicion. Rather than seeming a conclusive statement, a deconstructivist building might therefore look unfinished, with projecting beams, exposed construction materials, or windows at unusual angles. Diagonals might replace the 'rational' right angle of modernism. In place of modernism's total schemes, deconstructivists explore fragmentation and dislocation, in effect taking the building apart and examining its component parts. The building may be more contradictory than harmonious ('harmony' is seen as false and repressive), with different materials, styles and spaces intersecting or clashing. Deconstructing the opposition between essential structure and superficial decoration, the insides of a structure might be displayed 'ornamentally' on the outside.

The extent to which Derrida's ideas really informed architects other than Tschumi has been debatable, however. It has been objected that the architects in question didn't actually read Derrida's work, and that 'deconstruction' was merely a trendy tag used to glamourize further the business of designing buildings. This may have come about partly because deconstruction sounds like another word for 'demolition'. To confuse the issue, there is also the echo of Soviet Constructivism (an avant-garde movement of around 1915–1930, associated with Vladimir Tatlin, Alexander Rodchenko and others.) Constructivism broke volumes down into their component parts and then reconstructed them into a new order. It has been said that deconstruction simply abandons the second part of this process, like taking a car engine apart but leaving no instructions on how to put it back together again.

The intention of all this is that architecture be seen as a text to be deconstructed by both designers and users of buildings. Thus, according to Tschumi, 'it is above all the historical split between architecture and its theory that is eroded by the principles of deconstruction.'

Further reading

Postmodern Design, by Michael Collins (1994)

Architecture from the Outside: Essays on virtual and real space by Peter Eisenman and Elizabeth Grosz (2001)

What is Deconstruction? by Christopher Norris and Andrew Benjamin (1988)

Rethinking Architecture: A reader in critical theory, edited by Neil Leach (1997)

Architecture and Disjunction, by Bernard Tschumi (1996)

The Architecture of Deconstruction: Derrida's haunt, by Mark Wigley (1993)

White Walls, Designer Dresses: The fashioning of modern architecture, by Mark Wigley (1995)

Concluding thoughts

We come across many examples of the postmodern *anti-foundational* attitude in this book. In this chapter we have seen Jacques Derrida and Pierre Macherey criticize the structuralists for their faith in a basic order beneath the surface of texts. In the last chapter we looked at Jean Baudrillard's argument that, in a society of simulation, images float free of reality and find a reality of their own. And in the following two chapters, we will see the impact that similar ideas have had on our ideas about the self. In all of these ways and many more postmodernism has abandoned the idea that anything is simply founded on a single, objectively existing, stable ground.

Two very influential schools of thought in particular – Marxism and Freudian psychoanalysis – have been modified and criticized at the hands of this postmodern suspicion of foundations. The traditional Marxist claim that everything which happens in culture is, at the end of the day, a reflection of fundamental conditions within the capitalist economic base has been brought to book by some brands of postmodern theory. And as we will see in the following chapter, the Freudian belief that the mental states of adults have their universal origins in infancy and in unconscious drives has similarly been criticized for being too foundational.

Doubts

Because this gives rise to the idea that there are no firm truths, but only versions of the truth, critics of Derrida find in his work a kind of nihilism. They see it as an 'anything goes', 'nothing is real' philosophy in which everything is equally meaningless. So it is no longer possible to have an opinion on anything, political and moral values are neutralized, there is no point trying to understand anything, we might as well give up and submit to anarchy.

Defence

Derrida's ideas have a more progressive potential in the sense that:

- they ask us to look for the assumptions embedded in widespread beliefs and dogmas
- they suggest we should always question the grounds on which we feel able to make value judgements
- they make us aware that we always think and act from a particular position
- there is no objective point of view which gives access to a pure global truth
- thus we can (and must) always remain open to new possibilities.

We will have more to say about these ideas in Chapter 8.

Key works by Derrida:

Of Grammatology (1967) (English translation 1976)

Writing and Difference (1967) (English translation 1978)

Margins of Philosophy (1967) (English translation 1979)

Positions (1972) (English translation 1981)

Dissemination (1972) (English translation 1982)

06

postmodern identities, part one: transformations of the self

In this chapter you will learn:

- how ideas about personal identity have been affected by postmodernism
- how the escalation of technological and social change has seemed to challenge what we see as the nature the self
- some repercussions for issues of gender and sexuality.

There are many sides to the unfolding story of postmodern identity, but the starting point is that the self is fundamentally social. Of course postmodernism did not invent this basic observation. It has been around for a long time. Karl Marx, for one, insisted on it, and sociology is in some respects founded on the idea. Nevertheless, postmodernism does inflect the notion of the social self in its own particular ways. For Jean Baudrillard (see Chapter 4) it involves a viral invasion of simulation into private life, such that it is impossible to draw a line between natural and manufactured identities and desires. For critics like Douglas Kellner and Angela McRobbie it has meant a consideration of how senses of identity can be constructed by the consumption of mass-produced objects and images. For others, as we will see in the following chapter, the outcome has been a re-think of the idea of self-expression in various forms of cultural production.

Many different models of a 'postmodern self' have been built up on the idea of the social self. But a certain cluster of different questions keep recurring:

- What are the limits of the self?
- What is the relationship between private and public or inner and outer selves? Is it possible to differentiate them in any clear way?
- Is the self whole, unified, singular? Or is it more appropriate to speak of plural or fragmented selves?

The changing nature of the self

In his essay 'Popular Culture and the Construction of Postmodern Identities' (in *Modernity and Identity*, edited by Lash and Friedman, 1992) Douglas Kellner describes what he sees as the transition to postmodern modes of identity. His description basically maps three stages:

1 Pre-modern identity

In pre-modern communities identity is social, but it is not beset by doubt or conflict. Personal identity is stable, because it is defined and maintained by long-standing myths and pre-defined systems of roles. You are part of an age-old kinship system. Your thought and behaviour are enclosed within a limited world view, and the direction your life is going to take is more or less determined for you. Thus there is no need to question your place in the world. Identity is not an issue.

You might note that Kellner suggests this view of the pre-modern past is a piece of anthropological folklore based on wishful thinking more than on fact. You can also find traces of wishful thinking in Jean Baudrillard's notion of 'traditional' cultures based on symbolic exchange (see Chapter 4), as well as in the work of a number of other thinkers who have tried to define the specific character of contemporary identity. However, Kellner does not offer an alternative view of pre-modern societies to replace this rather mythical one.

2 Modern identity

In the modern period (starting with the *Enlightenment*), identity entered into crisis for the first time. As in pre-modern cultures, your personal identity remains based on your relations with others. It retains a degree of stability, but its orientations and influences start to multiply. Where in pre-modern communities you knew exactly what your place was in the clan, modern societies begin to offer a wider range of social roles. As Kellner puts it, 'One is a mother, a son, a Texan, a Scot, a professor, a sociologist, a Catholic, a lesbian – or rather a combination of these social roles and possibilities'.

There are therefore expanded possibilities for what you can be. It becomes possible to start choosing your identity, rather than simply being born into it. You start to worry about who you really are and what you should be doing with your life. With this new self-consciousness about who you are, could be or should be, you become more desperate to achieve a recognized, stable identity. You begin to worry that your identity may be transient, fragile or false. This is all part of the peculiarly modern form of identity.

There is still assumed to be a real, innate self underneath the public roles you play, but the struggle is in finding it and being true to it. Hand-in-hand with these widespread concerns, philosophers also begin to question the nature of the self, and as time goes on the questions become more anxious. Sigmund Freud and psychoanalysis go in search of the roots of the self and find them caught between unconscious instincts and the bourgeois family. At the same time, the discipline of sociology is developed and insists that all identities have their basis in society and that they have to be studied not as some abstract entity, but in terms of how they interact with other social beings in specific social situations. Modern sociologists argue, in general, that primary encounters such as those in the home and at school help to form a relatively permanent core identity which underlies your social activities throughout adult life.

Modernity involves the belief that rejecting the shackles of tradition will forward the progress towards human emancipation. But promoting the present and the future and negating the past as a foundation for action and selfhood forces people to question the nature of their identity.

In short, identity becomes an 'issue'.

3 Postmodern identity

Social life is faster and more complex than it was in modernity. More and more demands are placed on us, more and more possible identities are paraded before us, we have to juggle a rapidly expanding number of roles as society starts to fragment.

Some theorists (for example Jameson, Baudrillard, Debord – see Chapter 4) start to look at how the selves achieved under modernity have vanished in the wake of consumerism, mass culture, and growing bureaucratization of life. Others, (such as Lacan and Foucault – see below) propose that the stable, unified self has always been an illusion. Although identity remains an issue in day-to-day life, postmodern theorists have binned any notion of the self as substantial, essential or timeless. In place of the earnest modernist search for the deep, authentic self, we have a recognition, and sometimes a celebration, of disintegration, fragmented desires, superficiality, and identity as something you shop for. According to some sociologists identity is best understood in terms of role play or style management (see the section on Erving Goffman below). Image is now all that matters. In some earlier twentieth-century philosophy, the self loses its substance and becomes the product of your own search for authenticity (for example the work of Jean-Paul Sartre). In postmodernism the self is still without substance, but fashion statements, shopping and lifestyle choices have pushed authenticity out of the equation.

This is an admittedly simplistic history of changing ideas about personal identity, but it does serve to bring some important themes to light. We will now examine these themes in more detail by looking at some of the landmarks in the terrain of postmodern identities.

The stylization of life

Commentators like Kellner approach the postmodern self by arguing that certain social conditions have produced in people a heightened awareness of appearance and style. In following this line of enquiry they trace how the making of identity has become increasingly related to what we buy (or want to buy). We now forge our identities by using goods as signals of both individuality (difference from social groups) and solidarity (a sense of belonging to other social groups). In this process identity has been freed from its 'pre-modern' foundations. Yet, as David Harris explains in his book *A Society of Signs* (1996):

> *As the consumer market is flexible and more dynamic than the older ways of regulating identities, much more fluidity is apparent: people can change their identities more frequently, experiment with them, select more options from a cultural supermarket with far less commitment than before.*

(page 207)

This is lifestyle shopping, and it involves what some critics have termed the *aestheticisation* or *stylization* of life. In *Consumer Culture and Postmodernism* (1991) Mike Featherstone relates this stylized self to the emergence of a number of postmodern social and cultural developments that have their roots in modernity. These include:

1 The intensification of image production

The increasing invasion of signs and images (in media, display, advertising and so on) into the fabric of everyday life has created a dream world of ideal lifestyles for us to fantasize about and identify with. For example, many commercials are more concerned to attach a sense of lifestyle and experience to the product being sold than to give details about the product itself. Because of this, we get as much satisfaction from consuming the images attached to goods as we do from whatever practical function the goods might serve.

2 The multiplication of cultural mediators

These might include:

- the numerous pundits who populate the media to offer advice on everything from holidays and hair styling to interior design and wine tasting
- the ever growing ranks of popular cultural commentators whose job it is to pick up on all that's new in the worlds of arts, leisure, media and fashion
- the editors of lifestyle magazines
- the makers of television programmes about heritage, architecture, antiques, etc.
- the multiplying range of caring professions, therapists of all kinds, educationalists.

3 The influence of the Bohemian tradition

Many rock musicians, often in bands formed at art school, have tried to make life into a work of art. The earlier work of David Bowie has been one of the most influential examples of this. Many bands and their managers have drawn inspiration for their images, and for the idea of blurring the gap between art and life, from radical artistic subcultures like Dadaism of the 1920s and the Situationists of the 1960s (see Chapter 3 of this book for a brief discussion of Dada, and see Chapter 4 for an overview of what the Situationists aimed at). Punk is often cited to illustrate this influence.

Many musicians also continue the romantic tradition of the aesthetic 'dandy'. Featherstone notes that the rather aristocratic aim of dandyism is to construct an uncompromising public demeanour that is a model of the superior aesthetic lifestyle. A classic example of the art/rock cross-over is the New York band The Velvet Underground: their connections with the pop artist Andy Warhol and the underground New York art scene of the 1960s relate them to both romantic, aristocratic dandyism and trash aesthetics.

Today's pop and rock stars also offer image models, but there is now a huge spectrum of such exemplary lifestyles on offer.

We will have a lot more to say about these changes later, so for now we need only note the fact that many arguably postmodern experiences of identity can be seen as specifically urban ones. It is in the city, for example, that subcultural styles, different tastes and fashions, multiple ethnic influences, and so on, blend and clash most spectacularly.

Identity in the city

Many postmodern thoughts on identity seem to be addressed specifically to city life. As such, they are built up on ideas about the urban lifestyle which have been present since the early days of the modern metropolis. In this respect the postmodern attitude can be said to amplify rather than radically depart from experiences and conditions which have been in place for over one and a half centuries. Because of this, a lot of recent writing about the postmodern city intensifies themes originally developed by early theorists of modernity.

The beginnings of the modern forms of society noted by Dougas Kellner are usually found in the explosion of large scale urban experience that took place in the middle of the nineteenth century, when over half of the population of England began to live in cities. This soon became the normal course of events as the process of modernization spread across the world. At the same time a number of writers found that the new city experience highlighted some of the ideas and questions about the self that philosophers had long been exploring. The modern city seemed to live out in concrete terms problems about the relationship between the individual and the collective, for example. With growth of the city there was a new emphasis on the fragmentary and fluid nature of experience. And with this individuals, as we have suggested, became more self-conscious about their way of life, more concerned about their social role, and more anxious about their place in the world.

For example, the French poet Charles Baudelaire, looking at mid-nineteenth-century Paris, suggested that metropolitan consciousness was dominated by a sense of the 'transitory, the fugitive, the contingent'. This picture of the city's fractured and distracted sense of time became for Baudelaire the very essence of modernity. Meanwhile the German sociologist Georg Simmel (1895–1918) more systematically studied how the experience of modernity fragmented the contemporary city-dweller's consciousness of space and time.

This emphasis on the changing nature of how we experience space and time has influenced a number of thinkers concerned with the postmodern world. We will briefly return to this interest in Chapter 8 when we discuss *postmodern geographies*.

Simmel and Baudelaire described an interaction between the metropolis and the mind in which collective solidarity was replaced by a feeling of solitude. In this situation commerce and the industrial state began to intrude too far into human affairs. Simmel pointed out that social bonds between people were now forged by formal institutions, bureaucratic organizations, and money. Money more than anything else was now the anonymous social force which mediated and 'objectified' the relationships between people. This could create a sense of alienation and dehumanization as people lost their sense of purpose, stability and belonging.

Yet the outcome of all this was, for Simmel, far from utterly bleak. On the contrary, he found that the drastic effects of the city could, by increasing people's sense of individuality, enable greater scope for their creative freedom. Although the modern metropolis could bring about a dispiriting feeling of isolation, it could just as easily liberate people from the restrictions of tradition. Simmel argued that although occupants of the modern city become more casual in their ways of life, they are also given a more stimulating, heightened sensitivity to the conditions of their existence. This, for Simmel, was the gateway to greater personal liberty.

Virtual communities

So postmodernist culture can be interpreted as an intensified version of the conditions described by Simmel and others, rather than a radical departure from them. But in his essay *Postmodern Virtualities* (in the 1996 collection *Futurenatural*), Mark Poster argues that postmodernism involves the emergence of novel forms of individual identity. According to Poster, modernity idealized rational, centred individuals (he cites the 'reasonable man' of law and the educated citizen of democracy as examples), but postmodernity gives birth to a new *subjectivity* that leaves the 'narrow scope of the modern individual' trailing far behind.

From telephone and radio to video and 'multimedia' the technologies of communication have brought about 'new configurations of individuality': where modernists defined themselves in relation to the city, postmodernists are constructed through centreless networks of information technology. In this second media age we increasingly deal with other people through communications systems that transform 'the way identifications are structured' and demand new ways of speaking and acting. The cyberspace of the Internet is the most radical demonstration of this because it:

- undermines the borders of national identity
- encourages 'unstable, multiple and diffuse' ways of communicating with each other
- upsets the traditional logic of communication: senders of messages become receivers of them, consumers are at the same time producers
- there is no central authority for signs exchanged between members
- the simulated communities of chat rooms, newsgroups, multiuser domains and so forth erode the old distinctions between public and private self
- questions the 'original' identity of community members. Authenticity seems irrelevant here. Poster quotes Howard Rheingold: 'Are relationships and commitments as we know them even possible in a place where identities are fluid? . . . We reduce and encode our identities as words on a screen, decode and unpack the identities of others'.

Cyberpeople

Into the 1990s the human subject has become a blip: ephemeral, electrically processed, unreal.

(Scott Bukatman, in *Alien Zone,*
edited by Annette Kuhn, 1987, page 196)

Over the last decade there has been an explosion of interest in the fusion of human beings and electronic technology implied by the above quote. This interest has been expressed in both cultural studies and scientific publications as well as in movies, computer games, comic books and science fiction novels. Although there are many different variations on the idea of a technology–humanity union, and although the phenomenon is far from new, the figure of the 'cyborg' and current developments in information technology have recently received a great deal of attention.

Films like *Bladerunner* (1982, Director's Cut 1993), *The Terminator* (1984) and *The Matrix* (1999) have caught the imaginations of both cinema-goers and cultural commentators. Some have seen these as raising a specifically postmodern set of questions. Giuliana Bruno, for example, finds that '*Bladerunner* posits questions of identity, identification, and history in postmodernism' (in *Alien Zone*, page 193), while Kevin Robins notes that with representations of cyberspace 'we are provided with a virtual laboratory for analyzing the postmodern – and perhaps post-human condition' (in *Cyberspace/Cyberbodies/ Cyberpunk*, edited by Featherstone and Burrows 1995, page 140).

Boundary confusion

The term *cyborg* (from 'cybernetic organism') was first coined in the 1960s, when it was originally meant to describe the kind of body/machine combination necessary for humans to endure long periods in outer space. It more generally refers to any machine/ human *hybrid* in which the body and its functions are extended in order to allow better control of its environment, or in which bits of machinery are added to the body in order to improve its performance or extend its life-span. Several commentators have suggested that we are already well on our way to becoming cyborgs in this sense and point to everything from pacemakers, prosthetic body-parts, cosmetic surgery, silicon implants, dialysis machines, test-tube babies and genetic engineering to contact lenses, remote-control handsets and the Internet as proof (and no doubt the list could be much longer than this). However, nowadays it has become common to use the word 'cyborg' to mean just about any recent variation on the old theme of the robot, android or automaton and in the following section I will tend to use the term equally loosely.

Perhaps the most important feature of the cyborg, whether real or fictional, has been its fundamental ambiguity. Many critics have noted that the cyborg either re-draws or eliminates important conceptual boundaries, notably those between mind and body, human and non-human, natural and artificial, inner world and outer world, biological and technological. The cyborgs and replicants in films like *The Terminator* and *Bladerunner* are found to explore in a particularly dramatic and accessible way this boundary confusion. In doing so, they force us to ask questions about how we define terms like 'humanity' and 'selfhood'. In this way cyborgs appear to embody the claims of a number of postmodern theorists. For instance, Jean Baudrillard claims that new technologies have produced new anxieties about what it means to be human:

Am I a man, am I a machine? In the relationship between workers and traditional machines, there is no ambiguity whatsoever. The worker is always estranged from the machine and is therefore alienated by it. He keeps his precious quality of alienated man to himself. Whilst new technology, new machines, new images, interactive screens, do not alienate me at all. With me they form an integrated circuit.

(Quoted in *The Pleasure of the Interface* by Claudia Springer, *Screen* 32:2 1991, page 310)

In *Bladerunner*, Harrison Ford's job is to destroy or 'retire' rogue replicants. This is no easy task, however, as replicants are flawless skin jobs – machines which look, act and feel exactly like the real thing. To add to the difficulties, they have emotions and even experience pain. Thus two of the main features we ascribe to 'human-ness' are also found in simulations of human beings. This human quality enables the character Deckard (Ford) to feel attached to Rachel (Sean Young), a skin job who does not even know she is one. By the end of the film – particularly in the later Director's Cut version, where Deckard himself appears to be a replicant – we are left questioning the grounds on which we base our assumptions about what makes people human. As Forest Pyle puts it: 'When we make cyborgs – at least when we make them in movies – we make and, on occasion, unmake our conceptions of ourselves' (*Film Theory Goes to the Movies*, edited by Collins, Radner et. al. 1993 page 228).

How do you differ from a replicant? In what sense are you more than a 'skin job'? It is arguable that with the possibility of artificial intelligence apparently just around the corner such questions have become increasingly urgent.

The next sexual revolution?

In various films, comic books and cyberpunk novels, interacting with computer technology brings about a new kind of human identity. It often involves an escape from the limitations, vulnerabilities and clumsiness of the physical body (cyberpunk writers dismissively call the body 'meat') and into a purer, cybernetic kind of consciousness. A common theme – now particularly appropriate in the AIDS era – is that of imaginary sex. This rather 'pure' notion of sex, involving no physical contact, has been a recurring science fiction dream (or nightmare). We see mental sex in the old Jane Fonda film *Barbarella*, and we see Sylvester Stallone and Sandra Bullock having sex via futuristic headgear in the film *Demolition Man*.

It has been claimed that in cyberspace we can escape from our real physical selves, become whoever we wish, and experiment with sexual identities at our leisure, unconstrained by the limits of either flesh or location. In this cybersex revolution we are offered the possibility of performing different sexual identities. There is also the chance not only of swapping, but getting outside of gender. This side of cyber-technology has been attractive to a number of feminist theorists, among them Sadie Plant, Claudia Springer and Donna Haraway.

In her still influential 1985 essay *A Cyborg Manifesto*, Haraway used the figure of the cyborg as a way of imagining a world in which we could transcend the social definitions of masculinity and femininity. It is argued that male-dominated society creates and exploits 'essential' distinctions between male and female in order to keep itself running. But the cyborg, for Haraway, can be seen as a creature in a 'post gender world', which could overstep all socially imposed expectations and constraints. Cybernetic technologies suggest novel ways of getting out of social (and perhaps even biological) limitations on identity by creating new, boundary-blurring images of self. In this way new political alliances can be formed which are no longer restrained by gender, class, sexuality, ethnicity or location.

Sadie Plant has also noted that women can take computer technology from the hands of men and use it to explore alternative forms of fantasized identity which are subversive – if not completely free – of male domination:

> *Like women, software systems are used as man's tools, his media and his weapons; all are developed in the interests of man, but all are poised to betray him . . . Women's liberation is sustained and vitalized by the proliferation and globalisation of software technologies, all of which feed into self-organizing systems and enter the scene on her side.*

> (*Cyberspace/Cyberbodies/Cyberpunk*, edited by Featherstone and Burrows,1995 page 58)

A note of caution

While Plant and Haraway find in cyborg technology the potential to go beyond conventional definitions of gender, it has also been pointed out that the cyberworld does remain largely male-dominated. Although there are signs that a broad spectrum of sexualities other than conventional heterosexual male fantasy has been expressed in cyborg imagery (such as that in comic books and Japanese animated films) much of it still sticks to stereotypical depictions of male and female. It has been suggested that the exaggeration of Arnold Schwarzenegger's signs of masculinity (hard muscles, stern features, etc.) in the *Terminator* films and others are a desperate attempt to hold on to the conventional representations of sexual difference at a time when technology (e.g. genetic engineering) is threatening to make such difference obsolete. A similar point can perhaps be made about the familiar image of the shiny female robot popular in airbrushed science fantasy art, with her Playboy-type features, or the 'ideal woman' created by male teenage computer-geeks in the film *Weird Science* (1985). It begins to seem that the vision of a pluralistic post-gender cyberworld is still some way off.

Donna Haraway envisages for the cyber-era a new virtual space filled with fluid, fleeting identities. This ideal of a space in which identity is effectively released from all previous social bindings echoes a lot of the postmodern thought we will look at in the rest of this book. It particularly recalls some of the influential thinking of Gilles Deleuze and Felix Guattari, whose work we will consider in the following chapter.

The post-human body

Arthur and Marilouise Kroker have explored similar themes in their anthology *Body Invaders* (1988), a book exploring the fate of the body in the postmodern condition. Their Baudrillardian essay *'Panic Sex in America'* diagnoses widespread panic about bodily fluids in the light of AIDS, and anxiety about the breakdown of the immune system. Such fears are taken by the Krokers to be symptomatic of deep paranoia in Western (especially American) society. Visible in horror movies, body art, advertising and fashion (which they describe melodramatically as 'body aesthetics for the end of the world'), this culture of panic is a response to the 'disappearances' and 'alienations' of the natural body. Two examples:

- the disappearance of biological motherhood under the 'technification' of reproduction and the 'subordination of the ovaries to the sovereignty of private property'
- the invasion of sexuality by endless media images and *discourses.*

Their work represents the more delirious, apocalyptic end of postmodernist theorizing, and therefore has something of a cult following on the Internet. Although thought provoking, they are open to similar criticisms as their guru, Baudrillard (see Chapter 4).

You will never know the real me: Madonna

Of all the superstars who inhabit popular culture, Madonna has attracted a volume of critical interest almost equal to the volume of records, videos and other by-products she has sold. Although no longer generating the kind of fanatical reception accorded her in the 1980s, Madonna has remained an icon for postmodern theorists and popular audiences alike.

Madonna first came to the attention of the world in the early 1980s, when she put out a series of successful records aimed predominantly at a teenage audience. Nothing about Madonna's early records was particularly unusual in terms of the dance music popular at that time, and as her career developed into the 1990s, she remained firmly within the musical bounds of pop convention. In fact, it is arguable that her records were just one component of the Madonna event, and that her enormous appeal lay at least as much in her media persona as in her music. She has always had a remarkable talent for courting publicity. Many of her concert performances, videos and publications have been controversial enough to ensure wide coverage, and so she maintained a high media presence.

It has often been implied that Madonna's status resulted in large part from the way she wilfully deployed images of (her own?) sexuality. It seems that as soon as any woman does this, she finds herself in the middle of a fracas, and Madonna was certainly no exception. People have wanted to know whether she represents a forward or backward step for feminism. They have argued about whether Madonna subverts stereotypes or reinforces them.

These are just a couple of the arguments you can have about Madonna, and there are surely many more. But in a chapter of his book *Media Culture* (1995) Douglas Kellner warns against adopting any one polarized view. He argues that the many images Madonna projects of herself defy any attempt to pin her down to a single meaning. He offers an overview of the career-long spectrum of guises in which Madonna has 'imaged' herself, and finds that they only add up to contradiction, multiplicity and enigma. As Madonna herself said of her supposed documentary, *In Bed With Madonna* (a.k.a. *Truth or Dare*, 1991): 'You could watch it and say, I still don't know Madonna, and *good*. Because you will never know the real me.' Not surprisingly, it proves impossible to present the Madonna 'narrative' as a coherent sequence or story of evolution. But a swift glance through the Madonna dossier might remind us of the following milestones:

1978–1986

Madonna first attracts attention as a dancer in Lower East Side New York clubs. First single and album in 1983. First public image: rebellious, exhibitionist, overtly sexual. Clothes are mix-and-match: black lace, black boots, short skirts, chains, buckles, belts, bows, bobby socks, fake pearls, crucifixes. They are teenage, cheap and easily available to the thousands of young women who soon imitate Madonna's brand of street style.

Videos include: *Material Girl* (imitates Marilyn Monroe in *Gentlemen Prefer Blondes*); *Papa Don't Preach* (appears as a teenager with cropped blonde hair); *Open Your Heart* (appears as a stripper in a peep show).

Several changes of hair colour and length, alongside 'flash trash' clothes. Markets 'Boy-Toy' range of Madonna-wear.

Starts her acting career with *Desperately Seeking Susan*.

1986–1989

Begins to display a new, very muscular physique. In videos, mixes male and female dress codes and body language. Regularly puts on a more glamourous and expensive style, often basing her image on silver screen icons like Dietrich and Garbo. Many film roles and stage shows present different versions of Madonna.

1990–present

Justify My Love video makes reference to sadomasochism, homoerotic imagery and bisexuality. Concert performances increase sexual content, with pretend orgies and masturbation.

She often wears male clothes. Male dancers in some tours wear dresses and strap-on breasts, while female dancers sport fake penises. Spearheads the vogue for wearing underwear as outerwear. *Blonde Ambition* tour: wears a hard, hi-tech outfit designed by Gaultier, and a hard, hi-tech body. Stirs up the media by publishing a soft-core photo-book presenting herself in stylish, theatrical shots, acting out a polysexual range of fantasies and identities. Claims to be freeing desire and fantasy from guilt. More recently, becomes a torch singer with a fine line in fragile ballads, and the star of *Evita*.

For some critics the whole Madonna phenomenon represents nothing but the worst excesses of commercial exploitation. She is a typical product of cynical media manipulation and her millions of fans are the brain-dead dupes of a vast capitalist conspiracy. Such scorn is not uncommon where popular culture is concerned, and it often gets poured down on the pop music industry with particular spite. Even critics who find something interesting in the way Madonna uses multiple images of sexuality and fantasy sometimes express doubts about her motives. Kellner concedes that many of Madonna's videos are interesting, and even potentially subversive, for how they represent minority points of view. But he finds that her apparently subversive tactics are really just attempts to attract the following of as many segments of the population (e.g. ethnic minorities, gay people, working- class girls, heterosexual men) as possible, and thus to increase sales by having a little of something for everyone. Madonna exploits our culture's objectification of the female body for her own material gain. By presenting herself as a sexual spectacle, she helps to maintain the importance that our sexist culture places on the appearance of women.

Others have seen in Madonna a much more positive role, and have claimed that she offers a powerful model of female assertion and self-sufficiency. They say that rather than being a victim of the system, Madonna is in complete control of her sexuality, uses it in any way she sees fit, and empowers her fans to do the same. Madonna shows that exhibitionism – or making a spectacle of yourself for erotic attention – can be active rather than passive, a skill and not a weakness. It was on these grounds that in 1992 the post-feminist critic Camille Paglia declared Madonna a 'real feminist' for her skill in manipulating and marketing sexuality.

So Madonna has been important to postmodernism for her ability to plunder the conventions of sexual and gender representation, and thus to show them all up as artificial social constructs. In other words, she 'denaturalizes' sex and gender and encourages us to play with the constructs in any way we find pleasurable. Madonna's message is that the variety of roles provided by today's culture allows identity to be as plural and playful as you wish. In doing all of this Madonna pushes questions about the politics of identity into a broad public arena in a way that could hardly be achieved by avant-garde art or highbrow theory. Whether the Spice Girls, Britney Spears or Eminem have managed a similar feat is open to discussion.

Masks of femininity

Madonna's work can be compared to that of the American artist Cindy Sherman. Sherman first came to the attention of the art world in the late 1970s and early 1980s because of a long series of photographic self- portraits, portraying herself in a seemingly endless array of cinematic guises. Each of this sequence of black-and-white photographs, called simply *Untitled Film Stills*, presented Sherman as a filmic 'type' of femininity, and in doing so played on the viewer's skill in interpreting media images. An understanding, however unconscious, of how styles of lighting, dress, and posture create meaning within our culture enabled the viewer to instantly, if sometimes dimly, identify the images. These were at once specific and generic, in that you could rarely name the source, but could almost intuitively recognize the type: Hitchcockian heroines, muses from half-remembered French art movies, femmes fatales, nice girls, troubled teenagers, traumatized adolescents from stalk 'n' slash thrillers, and so on through dozens of starring roles in stills from imaginary movies.

As is the case with Madonna, Sherman appeared to be playing with multiple images of 'female-ness'. As you travelled from one photo to another either in a book or exhibition of her work, this produced an unsettling effect: you were aware that these were self-portraits and that they were therefore of Cindy Sherman. But the photos had an obvious staged quality (they were scenes from mock movies and not slices of life), and it was clear from the start that Sherman was working with stereotypes rather than attempting to offer a simple picture of her inner, private world. In what sense was self-portraiture a suitable description of this? What was the relationship between public, mass-produced images of femininity and Sherman's real self? Did the very multiplicity of images suggest that her self was multiple or fragmented? Or did the nature of 'her' self no longer come into the question?

Madonna hoped that we would never know the real her. Similarly the cumulative effect of all Sherman's roles on the viewer is often the sense that the more images pile up, the further you get from the real Cindy Sherman. No matter how far you try to go in search of her you will always be confronted by another mask.

Changing faces

In a review first published in the journal *Screen* in 1983, Judith Williamson found that Sherman's photographs reminded her of a certain sartorial dilemma. She likened trying to decide what clothes to wear before going out in the morning to selecting a personality. How we are understood is partly dependent on how we appear. What we put on, how we do our hair, what gestures we make, all make us appear to be certain types of person. Whatever outfit we wear lends us one particular identity, which excludes others. And yet we really do not have to be fixed to any one such public identity. We can have any number of them at our disposal, can revel in our ability to 'speak' through any number of (dis)guises. Williamson observes, for example, that if she wears a little leather skirt she will be defined in one particular way, and that if she wears a smart suit another set of connotations will come into play. Each way of appearing can define you as you occupy particular social spaces, but it will fail to hint at all of the different 'yous' you can have: the sensible two-piece you wear in your high-powered job may, for your audience, firmly locate you in the stereotype of business-like-person-who-likes-to-get-things-done, but this hardly speaks of the alley-cat you turn into on a Friday night. As Williamson puts it 'often I have wished I could . . . appear simultaneously in every outfit, just to say, how dare you think any one of these is *me*. But also, see, I can be all of them' (*Consuming Passions*,1986, page 91). In the postmodern world you do not have to be pinned down to a single image of self.

Self-defence

Williamson's description of how you can toy with multiple identities depends very much on manipulating how the public sees you: other people deduce things about you from your appearance and this tends to project stereotypical identities on to you. The art critic Craig Owens once noted that this process has a particular resonance for women, since, according to him, women live under 'the masculine desire to fix the woman in a stable and stabilizing identity'.

But Williamson notes that Sherman's self portraits demand to be seen as throwing the repertoire of feminine identities 'back where they belong, in the recognition of the beholder.' They suggest that women can avoid being objectified at the hands of masculine desire by overstating or ironically adopting the pool of masks at their disposal. This is a form of self-defence against male surveillance, and we can perhaps see it in Madonna as well.

(The idea of feminine masquerade hinted at here has recently been explored by a number of feminist theorists. These have been informed especially by the French psychoanalytic thinker Luce Irigaray. Some feminist film theorists, such as Mary Anne Doane, have often found the idea of masquerade useful.)

So Sherman and Madonna have been important to the post-modern approach to the self because they make all identities appear equally artificial, including those of gender. They do not suggest that you can easily step outside of the social definitions of identity. Instead they show that culture provides a multitude of images of self and that the ability to combine these into new configurations creates a 'play of signs' in which you can construct an empowering sense of individuality.

Although the likes of Madonna and Sherman can therefore be seen as dislocating or *deconstructing* some of the stereotypes perpetuated by mass media, they do not do this through a tactic of elitist rejection: instead of presenting themselves in a superior way as overthrowing popular culture or refusing to play its games, they deliberately work on what it makes available and, especially in Madonna's case, do so on its own terms. To this extent they are both postmodern artists in the way I described in Chapter 3.

Identity as construction

By discussing some of the work of Madonna and Sherman, we have begun to see a questioning of the relationship between public and private models of identity. This questioning suggests that the connection between your inner self and the outer appearance you show to the world is not simply a relationship of expression. In other words, your public identity does not simply express what you are really like, deep down.

By the same token, some postmodernist versions of the self suggest that there is no 'deep down' to identity: the fact that Madonna and Sherman adopt so many different images suggests that there may not be a single true self that resides beneath them all. No matter how deep you go, another surface is all you get

These reflections can be formulated as postmodernism's anti-*essentialist* or 'constructionist' views of identity.

Anti-essentialism

This is opposition to the idea that people have a timeless, universal core which ultimately explains their actions. Anti-essentialism has been a hotly debated topic within recent feminist work, where it has often seemed necessary to stress the idea of gender as a cultural and not a natural or essential category. Given that attempts are sometimes made to define women's 'proper' place in terms of what is supposedly natural it has become important to dispute the way society habitually calls upon an idea of 'nature' as the ultimate explanation of things which happen within culture. The work of Judith Butler (e.g. *Gender Trouble*) is a good, challenging example of work in this area. Similar themes of anti-essentialism have been debated in relation to gay politics and in relation to ideas of racial or ethnic identity.

Constructionism

There are really two versions of this:

- Instead of being born with a particular in-built substance, we *become* what we are through being acted on by a series of social factors. You are constructed by the social and are ultimately determined by it.
- We can more or less freely fabricate our identities for ourselves. We have a degree of choice about how to represent ourselves.

You can see that these two versions of constructionism are in considerable tension with one another. For this reason, arguments over postmodernist accounts of the self often end up repeating the old philosophical debate about free will versus determinism. We do not have to enter that debate. If you side with either one of these versions of the constructed self to the total exclusion of the other, you are likely to end up in theoretical hot water. For our purposes it is safe to say that personal identity is formed out of the tension between the two, and that this tension can manifest itself in different ways as we enter different circumstances. Postmodernists would reject any attempt at a single, unified and universal theory of selfhood and would look instead at how the determined and the free versions of self construction interact with and affect each other in variable ways according to our changing social situations.

The presentation of self

In trying to sketch new conceptions of self identity, theorists of postmodernism inevitably borrow from various sources. In some cases this involves re-examining older theorists through the lens of present concerns and claiming them to be postmodernists ahead of their time. One such theorist is the American sociologist Erving Goffman. Goffman has been seen as an important precursor of the postmodern self because he studied people not in terms of what they were 'inside', but in terms of how they performed in social situations. The important text here is his 1959 book, *The Presentation of Self in Everyday Life*. In this book Goffman studied how people react to one another in concrete social circumstances. In doing so, he was working within established sociological terms, and to this extent his work should not be seen as unique. However, his work seems to have caught the postmodern-imagination because of his insistence on the centrality of what he called 'image management' to our lives. Goffman studied the various institutions that make up social life (e.g. the workplace, high school) from what he called a 'dramaturgical' perspective; mainly concerned with how people act out social roles in particular circumstances, Goffman saw life as essentially theatrical. In his book, life is divided into 'on stage' and 'back stage' moments, and people are called 'actors'.

Goffman tended to have no time for 'modernist' questions about whether the self was authentic or not. His only interest was in whether our various performances successfully promote our social survival. Hence the self 'is not an organic thing that has a specific location, whose fundamental fate is to be born, to mature, and to die; it is a dramatic effect arising diffusely from a scene that is presented, and the characteristic issue, the crucial concern, is whether it will be credited or discredited' (page 223).

So Goffman writes of the self as a series of façades erected before different audiences. These façades only *appear* to emanate from some intrinsic self inside the social performer. In fact, the self is an effect, and not a cause, of the façade. It is also not something you individually own. It arises from interaction with other actors on the social stage. Hence you are 'a peg on which something of a collaborative manufacture will be hung for a while', as Goffman puts it.

In an essay of 1992 (in the journal *Theory, Culture and Society* Vol. 9), Efrat Tseelon claims Goffman for postmodernism. Goffman's emphasis on the 'façade self', fits in well with the view of postmodern culture as a world full of flat images and simulations (see our discussion of Jean Baudrillard's work in Chapter 4, for example). In this world it is impossible to distinguish in any simple way the real from the artificial. Nor is it possible to see selves as independent individuals with essences that they then express in whatever ways they personally prefer. In postmodernism, by Tseelon's account, the idea of a real or deep self vanishes, and is replaced with a collage of social constructs. Goffman can then be seen as offering an early picture of this postmodern transition.

Summary

Postmodernism suggests in various ways that self identity is something fabricated 'on the outside'. We saw this with Madonna, with Cindy Sherman, and with Judith Williamson's quandary about what 'identity' to wear each day. All implied that appearance and behaviour *produce* the self as well as *express* it.

Your identity is a fabrication that you can manipulate more or less at will. Even your sexuality can be something you *have* or *do* rather than something you *are*. Your identity is made on the surface through what you do and how you display yourself: as the British critic Angela McRobbie has said of Madonna, she constructs herself as 'all body'.

So the visions of the postmodern self looked at in this chapter say that you are a play of surfaces, a set of shifting signs. You have no single essential self beneath all the faces you show to the world, because you are scattered over a complex network of social forces.

These ideas can be regarded as forming a specifically postmodern picture of identity on at least two grounds:

- They pose a challenge to the modernist view of individuals as independent, individual sources for the expression of unique insights. We will discuss this in more detail in the following chapter.
- The growing complexity of life under conditions of social postmodernity brings about a greater awareness of the various social roles and identities offered to us in consumer culture. There is in this way an acceleration of the demands on the notion of the self that were made in modernity. Hence the idea of the postmodern self plays a part in, and enters us into, general discussion about new ways of living in our society.
- Where the self is concerned, no clear distinction can be made between public/private; inner/outer; authentic/inauthentic.

Further reading

Modernity and Postmodernity: Knowledge, power, and the self, by Gerard Delanty (2000)

Identity Crises: A Social Critique of modernity, by Robert G. Dunn (1998)

Power/knowledge: Selected interviews and other writings 1972–1977, by Michel Foucault (1981)

Identity in Transformation: Postmodernity, postcommunism and globalization, by M. Kempny and A. Jawlowska (2002)

'The Effects of multiform narrative on subjectivity', in *Screen* Vol. 36 no.2, by Alison McMahan (1995)

The Mode of Information: Post-structuralism and social contents, by Mark Poster (1990)

Futurenatural, edited by George Robertson et al. (1996)

Digital Diversions: Youth culture in the age of multimedia, by Julian Sefton-Green (1998)

Life on Screen : Identity in the age of the Internet, by Sherrie Turkle (1995)

Cybersexualities; A reader in feminist theory, cyborgs and cyberspace, edited by Jenny Wolmark (1999)

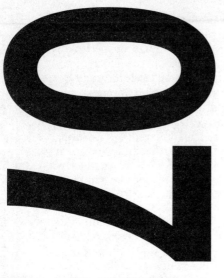

07

postmodern identities, part two: theories of subjectivity

In this chapter you will learn:

- more of the concepts that have informed and described the transformations described in the previous chapter
- theories about the construction of 'subjectivity'
- postmodernist notions of desire
- postmodernist/poststructuralist approaches to the idea of self expression.

Discussions about the self in postmodernism are often conducted with reference to the work of Michel Foucault (1926–1984). Foucault wrote elaborate histories of social institutions as diverse as the penal system, psychiatry and the social sciences. He believed that no such institutions were neutral or independent, and argued that it was an important political task to examine how they were tied to the complex operations of power in our society. This power was exercised through surveillance, monitoring and other forms of regulation of people's lives.

For Foucault, the modern-day notion of the self is bound up with, and inseparable from, the workings of social structures and institutions. This means that none of us can claim to stand apart from the exercise of power. But, as we will see, Foucault does not provide a theory of how naturally free human individuals are oppressed from above by the laws of any one dominant class or group. Instead he proposes that humanity is simply an idea and that, like any other idea, it has a history: 'the archaeology of our thinking demonstrates clearly that man is a recent invention, perhaps also approaching his end'. To approach Foucault's often demanding work there are at least two heavily used terms that you need to grasp. These are the *subject* and *discourse*.

The subject

Within much postmodern theory, and within the critical tradition from which it often draws (notably structuralism and poststructuralism: see Chapter 5), *people* do not come into the picture very often. In this body of work, the *person* is often replaced by the *subject*.

In day-to-day speech, when we talk of being 'subjective', we mean that we are basing our ideas on personal experience, that we are seeing things from our own point of view, and perhaps that our ideas reveal a certain amount of prejudiced self-interest. This is close to one definition of the subject simply as a thinking and feeling, conscious self.

As Kaja Silverman points out in her book *The Subject of Semiotics* (1983), this taken-for-granted idea of the individual can be dated back to the Renaissance, where it came to designate individual consciousness as a private, essentially free, decision-making agent and source of meaning. This modern idea of the individual 'man' assumed that 'he' was an independent, fixed entity, a 'human nature' clear of historical and cultural circumstances. This gave birth to the romantic idea that humanity can achieve a transcendent state of truth to nature through philosophy, religion and art. In his book *Collecting in a Consumer Society* (2001), Russell W. Belk similarly notes that words prefixed by 'self', such as 'self-regard' and 'self-consciousness', are relatively new to the English language. Echoing Foucault's theme of 'man' as a modern invention, he sees the self as a product of modernity, and connects its emergence to:

> *the increase in autobiographies, the proliferation of family and self-portraits, the growing popularity of mirrors, development of the concept of personality, the replacement of benches with more individuating chairs, increasingly private and specialized areas in homes, more introspective drama and literature, and the birth of psychoanalysis.*

This is, of course, the stuff of popular culture as well. Most films, for example, are about the triumph of the will, the struggle of the individual against the collective, the necessity of being true to yourself, and so forth. Whether such representations of the self can be a positive factor does not appear to have been of particular interest to Foucault, however. He would prefer to ask questions like: why have these views of the self arisen at this point in history? Where do they come from? How do they relate to the distribution of power in society?

The idea of subjectivity (i.e. being a 'subject') has been applied in many different ways by different theorists and so it cannot be said to have a single meaning. Generally speaking though, as theorists like Foucault use the term, a subject means not simply a conscious person, but a specifically social fact, a being which is at least partially *subjected* to socially produced constraints and divisions. Thus Foucault tends to deny the subject any internal substance. For him the distinction between public and private selves implied by 'human nature' is a false or at least irrelevant one. The subject cannot be reduced to individual consciousness; there are only practices or techniques of the self.

For Foucault, definitions of the self are given only in the social relations we live by. The self is political and knowledge of it is connected to power.

Discourse

Like the subject, *discourse* can have many different meanings according to who is using it. While it can sometimes designate little more than a general realm of representations, it more often refers to specific social institutions and disciplines. So we might speak of the discourse of literary criticism, for example, because literary criticism is both a particular way of putting language to use (e.g. writing criticism) and a discipline (literature) formed within a particular institution (academia). Discourse as Foucault tends to mean it involves all aspects equally – the institution, the discipline, and the language use all go together. One enables the other.

Discourses can be seen as controlled systems for the production of knowledge. Though regulated, they are not completely closed systems and have to allow for change and limited dissent. For example, literary critics will disagree over the quality of a particular poem or the meaning of a particular play, but this will not threaten the discourse of literary criticism itself. Indeed, such internal disagreements are crucial in keeping the discourse up and running. Nevertheless, discourses put a limit on what is sayable at any one time: they define what counts as 'legitimate' or 'illegitimate' statements.

Foucault sees discourses everywhere. They are the very stuff of society and they mediate all aspects of life. But discourse is not just an abstract public sphere of words and images; it exists in concrete social situations and has very real effects. One such discourse is psychology. As Henriques, Hollway et al. argue in their book *Changing the Subject* (1984), psychology has played a part in our current 'common sense' views of the self and its relation to society.

Psychology produces individuals as its objects of enquiry, and in doing so contributes to the impression that individuals need to be enquired into. The only reason for embarking on such an enquiry, in the Foucaultian view, is to keep humanity in check, to prevent 'deviants' from upsetting the social order, and to regulate people so that they can become 'useful' members of society.

In his studies of the institution of the mental hospital (e.g. *Madness and Civilization*), Foucault looks at how professional discourse employs 'scientific' knowledge to make distinctions between the sane and the insane, the normal and the abnormal. Other discourses make distinctions regarding what counts as acceptable behaviour. For example, we distinguish between legal and illegal killing, or between proper and improper sexual conduct. These judgements (Foucault calls them 'dividing practices') are always historically particular, variable from culture to culture, and subject to change.

Conclusion

Society defines itself by what it excludes. By defining and marginalizing groups of 'deviants' as criminal, mad or ill, it reassures itself of its own sanity, health and naturalness. Thus discourses are the systems of exclusion and categorization upon which society depends. We all participate in these systems.

Let's talk about sex

We are used to thinking of modern society as something which causes us to repress our instinctive sexual desires. The demands of modern life, its laws and its censorship all conspire to keep our sexual liberty under lock and key. We harbour all manner of dark desires, but the conventions of the modern world prevent us from releasing them. This repression causes misery and even illness. Discovering your true sexuality can bring fulfilment and liberty.

This is what Foucault, in his three-volume *History of Sexuality* (English Editions 1980–1986), dismissively calls 'the repressive hypothesis'. He believes that the widespread idea of repression is something of a myth. He argues that, far from being repressive of sexuality, modern Western society actually produces sexuality in the form of endless sex-talk, sex-study and sex-theory. Rather than being silenced, sex since the supposedly repressed Victorian age has grown in importance, and become a serious object of study. It has become the subject on most people's lips. The discourses of sex are constantly multiplying.

It is not hard to see Foucault's point. People often remark that our culture is obsessed with sex. Many popular films make a feature of sex, many products advertise themselves through sex appeal, Sunday newspapers are always carrying the latest 'sensational' findings of sex surveys, advice columns are pre-occupied with sex, sexual hang-ups are the stock-in-trade of the endless experts who plug their books on talk shows, sexologists make small fortunes out of discovering new ways of achieving orgasms, and so on. Add to these much more serious issues, like the promotion of safer sex in the light of AIDS, well-publicized debates about homosexuality in the armed forces, widespread media concern about the sex life of adolescents, documentaries and news items about sex crimes, their perpetrators and their victims, and it becomes clear that culture is indeed saturated by discourses of sexuality.

On one level, we could call this 'only natural' but for Foucault, the question of the 'natural' is of marginal relevance at best. He argues that the discourse of sexuality is a modern phenomenon which serves only to create the impression that there is such a thing as 'natural' sex.

You could also say that all this sex-discourse is a healthy sign on the road to sexual freedom and enlightenment. But again, says Foucault, you would be mistaken: it is just another form of social control:

> *All this garrulous attention which has us in a stew over sexuality, is it not motivated by one basic concern . . . to constitute a sexuality that is economically useful and politically conservative?*

> (*The Foucault Reader*, edited by P. Rabinow 1984, (page 317).

Discourse does not free sex: it invents it. Discussion and examination do not liberate sexuality: they make it into a problem. This is because the discourse on sexuality creates the notion that sex is an absolute, abstract category. Sex and sexuality have become the titles used to cover all bodies and their pleasures. The concept 'sex' is now the basic drive which motivates all of human life, a dark secret, a deep mystery. So it is no longer enough to simply create bodily pleasures for their own sake. All bed-time (or anywhere, anytime) activities are now sexualized, in the sense that they are seen as manifestations of a single, sexual foundation common to all of humanity. All bodily pleasures are now understood in terms of the degree to which they deviate from, conform to, improve, or avoid sex. Sex is the dominant term, the standard against which 'the body and pleasure' are measured.

And in our own society it is heterosexuality which provides this standard. Homosexuality, some 'aberrant' sexual practices, and so on, might be tolerated, but they are still identified by their difference from the heterosexist norm. The presence of this norm enables society to marginalize some sexual practices as 'against nature', and thereby to prove the naturalness of the heterosexual monogamy and family values upon which mainstream society bases itself.

Yet despite all this Foucault refuses the model of 'sexuality versus repressive society'. He notes that the discourses of sex in a sense create sexual diversity:

> The 'putting into discourse of sex', far from undergoing a process of restriction, on the contrary has been subjected to a mechanism of increasing incitement . . . the techniques of power exercised over sex have not obeyed a principle of rigorous selection, but rather one of dissemination and implantation of polymorphous sexualities.

> (*The Foucault Reader*, edited by Paul Rabinow, 1984 page 300)

In other words sex discourse 'discovers' and classifies an ever expanding encyclopaedia of preferences, gratifications and perversions. It creates a realm of perversion by discovering, commenting on and exploring it. It brings it into being as an object of study, and in doing so serves to categorize and objectify those who occupy what has been made into the secret underworld of 'deviance'. People no longer own their pleasures: they become specimens of well-documented sexual types (a 'new specification of individuals') instead. Our sexuality and our selves have been turned into a problem, and by constantly encouraging us to talk about it, the discourse on sexuality ropes us into looking for the solution: 'We must . . . ask why we burden ourselves today with so much guilt for having once made sex a sin.' (*The Foucault Reader* page 297)

Pleasures of resistance/resistance to pleasure

All of this may begin to sound a little too Big-Brotherish, but Foucault does allow for gaps in the working of discourses. He argues that wherever you find discourse you also find a conflict between those who control it (i.e. who place a limit on what can and cannot be said) and those who have been denied the right to representation through it. Wherever you find suppression, you also find subversion: no matter how frightening a particular regime may be people always find possibilities for resistance. In fact, the two go hand in hand: without subversion, society would have nothing to suppress, without suppression, there would be nothing to subvert. Certain disobedient sexual practices (for example S&M or bondage) might therefore be seen as the result, and not simply the victim, of oppression. Foucault calls this a spiralling 'double impetus' of power to pleasure, pleasure to power.

Summary

Our humanist picture of individuality is a product of modern Western systems of knowledge. These came into being with the birth of the human sciences in the age of the Enlightenment and Foucault has no interest in whether they are capable of producing a positive effect on individual lives. His concern is with how they feed into potentially oppressive ideas about the self which we still hold on to today. Modern discourses like psychiatry, criminology and sexology are 'dividing practices' which objectify and categorize us and thus fundamentally affect our experience of personal and social identity.

The deconstructed self: Jacques Lacan

Jacques Lacan (1901–81) was a psychoanalytic theorist and practitioner whose work was engaged in re-treading Sigmund Freud (the founder of psychoanalysis) in the light of contemporary theory. He believed that Freud offered fundamental insights into the life of the mind, but that the time in which he was writing prevented him from realizing the truly radical nature of his own theories and discoveries.

Freud

Freud had provided the basic texts of psychoanalysis and had furnished the field with many of its central terms. In Freud's work (for example *The Interpretation of Dreams*, 1900) the present mental state of clients was rooted in the lost events of infancy – events which psychoanalysts helped to uncover. For Freud, the family unit was the primary site of numerous dramas and conflicts which influenced the shape of the client's mental life. Despite his emphasis on the family (and thus to a certain extent the self) as a social formation, many of Freud's theories were ultimately grounded in biological models. The infant was born as an incoherent mass of naturally occurring basic instincts. Infantile dramas like breast-feeding and weaning off served to 'write over' and channel biological drives and appetites, and in doing so they transformed the child from pure biological organism to conscious social being. Put simply, Freud's work chronicles the conflicts in the psyche between instinctual and cultural forces. He finds that although we attempt to keep a lid on our unconscious natural drives, they keep 'accidentally on purpose' bubbling to the surface in day-to-day life in the form of dreams, jokes, slips of the tongue, verbal tics and other seemingly insignificant little human events.

Lacan

Lacan retains the Freudian framework but shakes it up considerably. He rejects all popular attempts to explain Freudian ideas, and takes from those ideas a model of mental life which is full of fracture and internal conflict. Where Freud (at least in the 'tamed' versions of his thinking adopted by many of his followers) suggested that the conflicts of mental life could be resolved, Lacan saw them as fundamentally irreparable: discord and fracture cannot be cleared away from the psyche because they *are* the psyche. Lacan therefore thought that the potential radicalism of Freud was hindered by the way he often resorted to permanent, universal drives as the underlying cause of mental disturbances. Lacan deflects attention away from this stress on supposedly natural causes and claims that psychoanalysis should take an interest in the cultural and the linguistic.

Language

Less emphasis should be put on the idea that self-sufficient events within the individual mind are the source of dreams, word-associations, Freudian slips and so on, as these are affected primarily by cultural rather than personal factors. Hence Freudian slips, for example, are an effect of words as much as they are the product of one person's unconscious drives. Heavily influenced by the structuralist theories of language and representation which we discussed in Chapter 5, Lacan claimed that the unconscious was structured like language.

Biology can tell us little. The unconscious is by definition unknowable, and can only be 'reconstructed' in language. The words of the client in analysis cannot act like windows into the depths of the unconscious. The analyst does not so much see through the client's words as engage in an act of reading: he or she interprets dream imagery (as described by the client in words) or a stream of word associations in much the same way as he or she would read any other kind of text. Psychoanalysis can therefore learn much from linguistics and should look harder at the linguistic processes involved in reading and speaking. For this reason Lacan's writing is, like Jacques Derrida's, dense with puns and word play. The unconscious, for Lacan, manifests itself in the way words fail to work. Thus the client in effect speaks the unconscious into being.

The mirror-stage

Lacan's vision of the self is outlined in his famous essay, *The Mirror Stage as Formative of the Function of the I*, first published in 1949 (from a lecture on *The Looking-glass Phase,* originally presented in 1936). In it he describes how, as infants, we gain a deluded sense of self-identity via identification with images and reflections.

In our first months of infancy we are in disarray. We have no co-ordination, we cannot control our bodily functions and we experience ourselves as a bunch of ill-fitting spare parts (Lacan calls this infant an 'hommelette': a scrambled little man). But in the mirror stage, which occurs at the age of six to 18 months, the infant sees its own behaviour reflected in the gestures of adults and other children and in mirrors. Fascinated by this reflection, the child (mis)recognizes itself as a whole entity for the first time. It sees an image of itself as a unified person, an image which promises for the child that it will soon achieve full co-ordination of its body. The incoherent 'hommelette' sees an image of itself as an independent being and learns to identify with this image. This is when the ego (the sense of yourself as an individual) is formed.

Thus your sense of self is fundamentally bound up with an 'exterior' image. Instead of simply coming from within, your identity is formed out of a situation in which you see yourself for the first time from the outside. For Lacan this means that alienation and division are built into your identity from the outset. The result in adult life is that you are in a constant but fruitless state of desire for some mythical inner unity and stability to match the unity and stability you thought you saw in your childhood reflection. We spend our lives trying (and failing) to make ourselves 'whole'.

So Lacan thinks that Freudian psychoanalysis has clung for too long to supposedly permanent fixtures of the self. Selfhood is really nothing but a fleeting, unstable, incomplete and open-ended mess of desires which cannot be fulfilled. Hence 'Man cannot aim at being whole. The 'total personality' is another of the deviant premises of modern psychotherapy' (*Ecrits: a Selection*, English Edition 1977, page 223).

The dispersed subject

In 1972 the Foucault-influenced philosopher Gilles Deleuze and the Lacan-influenced psychoanalyst Felix Guattari collaborated on a book called *Anti-Oedipus: Capitalism and Schizophrenia*. In that book they championed a world of fragmentation and flux in which individuals were liberated from any 'repressive' notions about the rationality, unity, or stability of the self. Because of this emphasis, the book is now often considered a major early statement of a postmodern position on identity and society.

The politics of desire

Like Michel Foucault (see above), Deleuze and Guattari were concerned with the power relationship between modern society and desire. They claimed that the institutions and discourses of modernity were a soft kind of fascism which exercised dominance by inserting repression into all aspects of everyday existence. Under modernity's capitalist system, repression and dominance were not so much forced on to people as lived by them.

In this respect, Deleuze and Guattari worked out their ideas within a very particular radical intellectual framework. As well as Foucault's work on how subjects and their pleasures are defined and controlled by the institutions of the modern state, we could also point to Guy Debord and the Situationists (see Chapter 4) as influences. Rather like Deleuze and Guattari, they believed that capitalism had infiltrated all of existence, and had taken away from people the possibility of experiencing genuine freedom, expression and satisfaction. All desires under capitalism were 'false', 'mediated' desires.

Their work is also related to that of the Frankfurt School of critical theory. Two books associated with this group of critics are:

One-dimensional Man (1964) by Herbert Marcuse

Marcuse was deeply suspicious of the way modernity had expanded communication technologies and consumerism into our lives, and saw them as central to a new, more insidious kind of totalitarianism which – through the production of 'false needs' – sought to penetrate consciousness itself, neutralize all voices of dissent, and turn us all into interchangeable components of the capitalist machine.

Dialectic of Enlightenment (1944) by Theodor Adorno and Max Horkheimer

Adorno and Horkheimer pessimistically believed that even in supposedly democratic societies (America was singled out), mass culture acted as an authoritarian force which reduced people to passive social conformity. As far as they were concerned, all of mass culture injects the capitalist status quo into people's unconscious, making its victims lose their individuality, and persuades them to willingly accept its values.

Deleuze and Guattari's work was related to the above through what they called 'territorialization'. This they defined as the process by which both society and theory (particularly Freudian and Marxist theory) attempted to tame human desire. Capitalist systems territorialize desire and creativity by channelling them into organized social areas (or codes) such as consumerism, finance, the law, psychiatry, the nuclear family unit, social class and conventional gender roles. Capitalist systems effectively control desire by attaching it to the production and consumption of goods, and by trapping social subjects in an organized network of normalizing impersonal social structures and processes. This concern with the effects of the 'rational' and anonymous systems of modern society in some respects recalls the work of earlier sociologists of modernity on the growth of the urbanized ways of life (see for example the short section on Georg Simmel in the previous chapter). But what gives Deleuze and Guattari their own particular flavour, and what have recently caught the eye of postmodernism, are their attacks on both Marxism and orthodox psychoanalysis.

Arguing with Marxism

In spite of their interest in how capitalism territorializes human life, and in trying to formulate a revolutionary theory, Deleuze and Guattari make a point of parting company with central aspects of Marxism (and Marxist-derived schools of thought like the Frankfurt School).

Where Marxism emphasized social class as the site of oppression and eventual revolution Deleuze and Guattari see the unity of the working class as a myth which suppresses diversity. For example, women, students and/or ethnic groups are often pushed by Marxists to the edges of class struggle, or are blanketed over by the single, all-embracing category of class. Rejecting this hierarchy, Deleuze and Guattari argue that social class is just one of the many lines along which both oppression and disobedience can run. Class struggle is just one strand in social life, rather than the basis of it.

Although it constantly tries to regulate all aspects of life, capitalism has the effect of undoing identity by channelling desires in many different directions at once. It continually destabilizes itself by inventing new territories for consumer desire. As commodities multiply, there are more things to desire, more images to identify with, and more lines of escape. Learning to live this proliferation of contradictory desires and identifications offers us paths for liberation and defiance. By becoming intense, 'decentred' consumers, we can pose a threat to the territorialization of private and social life.

So unlike the members of the Frankfurt school, Deleuze and Guattari did not picture the state as a single, monolithic agency. They did not see capitalism as automatically successful in its attempts to produce sameness and conformity. Indeed, against Adorno and Horkheimer's view of the capitalist system as enforced homogenization, Deleuze and Guattari believed that capitalism could generate more and more multiplicity, and that it therefore actually contains the seeds of revolution.

Arguments with Freudianism

Deleuze and Guattari also took issue with some of the founding claims of psychoanalysis. They argued that 'establishment' psychoanalysis (even Jacques Lacan: see above) reduced all of life to the single structure of the nuclear family.

Freud and his followers focused almost exclusively on conflicts in the mother-child-father relationship as the centre and base of all subsequent psychological conditions. Every mental event in adult life was connected to infantile desires formed in this triangular relationship. Deleuze and Guattari saw this as a serious reduction of the complexity of desire as it is experienced in the present. Freudianism takes the family as a pre-given, universal category. Issues of class, location or race, for example, do not come into it: all families act on the unconscious in essentially the same way, with nothing to do with social conditions or history. It does not matter to Freudianism whether the father is a miner, a banker, a trade unionist, or is unemployed. It does not matter whether the family live in a slum or a palace. Whether the parents are from different ethnic or religious backgrounds is neither here nor there. And if Freud were writing today, he would probably have little interest in what films the family members watched, what records they listened to or what magazines they read (except in so far as these could be said to express some underlying unconscious cause). None of these would fundamentally affect the essential mother-child-father triangle. In short, Freud takes politics and culture out of the family. So Deleuze and Guattari argued that the analysis of individual identity should be pushed outside of the narrow confines of 'mommy, daddy and me', and into a much wider social terrain.

> *A child never confines himself to playing house, to playing only at being daddy-and-mommy. He also plays at being a magician, a cowboy, a cop or a robber, a train, a little car. The train is not necessarily daddy, nor is the train station necessarily mommy.*

Thanks to the popularization of Freudian ideas (in Hitchcock films and dream interpretation manuals, for example), we are used to imagining an unconscious core lying deep within our minds, insulated from the world. Social roles, politics and public events are frequently understood to be things which influence us on various mental levels, but which do not penetrate deep down into this unconscious core. The unconscious has effects on us, but itself remains untouched.

By contrast, Deleuze and Guattari propose that your unconscious is constantly 'rewritten' by society and history, endlessly remade through direct contact with the outside world. It lives in the present.

One of the effects of Freudianism is the rather widely held belief that people's consumption habits can be explained by something in their unconscious. It might be claimed, for example, that if I happened to be an avid consumer of violent horror videos, the mystery of my enthusiasm could be solved by reference to a long-lost potty-training incident, repressed incestuous desires, my never having passed successfully through the oral stage of infantile development, or (most likely) castration anxiety. Thus the 'answer' would be sought in my supposedly secret past, and hopefully I could be cured.

But from Deleuze and Guattari's perspective such a view would seriously undervalue the complexity of my viewing (dis)pleasures as they are expressed in the present. For I am not simply wired into a closed-circuit relationship between myself, my video-recorder and some long forgotten 'primal scene'. You also have to take into account the relationships (and the differences) between the (dis)pleasures provided by video nasties and the (dis)pleasures I also gain from French art-house movies, Busby Berkeley spectaculars, spaghetti Westerns, kitchen sink dramas, and so on.

But you would also have to consider my entire social field: the jobs I do, the people I know, the kind of person I would like to be, the kind of person I would like not to be, the magazines and books I read, the places I shop . . .

In addition to all of these things, you would surely have to look at the social and technological conditions which enabled the video-player to come into being; the conditions of production and distribution in the low-budget exploitation film industry; the role of censorship and, in some cases, the prohibition of certain films in creating the desire for forbidden viewing, and any number of characteristics of the social and cultural traditions of Western society that my films participate in.

The point is that none of these factors are really marginal to my consumer desire. Indeed, in Deleuze and Guattari's work, there is no distinction to be made between the centre and the margin. What we have instead is a free-floating network of relationships, interweavings, cross-fertilizations and undercuttings. No unified unconscious entity occupies the centre of, or 'masters', this network. Thus, rather than express a single subjective secret meaning, my consumer desires are articulated and generated across a web of 'social flows'.

So Deleuze and Guattari argue that subjectivity should be seen as extended through or dispersed over the many complex circuits of culture and society: the unconscious 'partakes of the spread of signs from the most disparate social and material flows'. From this point of view unconscious wishes and appetites do not simply belong to you as a result of personal experience. They are public: they are constantly produced and reproduced in concrete social conditions and experience.

Desiring machines

Where Freudianism has tended to represent the unconscious as a dark and dangerous but also fixed and unchanging force, it is seen by Deleuze and Guattari as a 'desiring machine'.

'Desire' is vaguely defined by Deleuze and Guattari as a kind of creative energy, ceaselessly renewing itself and causing chaos. Imagine a reasonably benign hybrid of *The Thing* in John Carpenter's film of that name, the morphing T1000 in *Terminator 2* and the Borg in *Star Trek: the Next Generation,* and you get something close to Deleuze and Guattari's conception of desire. The dynamic force behind all social and personal actions and interactions, desire constantly flows into multiple, random connections with people and objects. It constantly spills over the territorial boundaries which modern social structures keep trying to force it into. A mercurial, ever-adaptable energy, desire is revolutionary to Deleuze and Guattari because it always seeks to transcend limits, and has no time for repressive concerns about usefulness, productivity or efficiency.

Is the postmodern condition schizophrenic?

In their search for new forms of desire and identity, Deleuze and Guattari suggest that attempts to 'cure' schizophrenia amount to a form of social control. They argue that while psychiatry and psychoanalysis reduce the 'schizo' to an 'autistic rag' cut off from the real world and removed from life, s/he in fact performs a radical unsettling of language. For them schizophrenia is best seen as the active production of a 'deterritorialized' *subjectivity:*

> *the schizophrenic passes from one code to the other . . . he deliberately scrambles all the codes, by quickly shifting from one to another . . . when he is more or less forced into it and is not in a touchy mood he may even accept the banal Oedipal code, so long as he can stuff it full of all the disjunctions that this code was designed to eliminate.*

Summary

Deleuze and Guattari:

- see the idea of stable identities as a harmful illusion and celebrate difference, chaos, and the ongoing process of change as the only liberation, and focus on the need to bring the multiplicity of our desires into being
- reject the idea that the psyche is naturally whole, unified, or coherent

- deny the possibility of providing a total or universal theory of the psyche in general
- propose an approach in which 'pure difference' reigns, and cannot be reduced to underlying foundations or essences
- see the self as a flux of desires and 'intensities' which both shoot out in many directions and absorb many influences
- argue that the production and circulation of desire in society is more important to an understanding of identity than needs or instincts.

In the postmodern view your subjectivity is seen as a kind of hybrid of different social codes and ideologies which bear on race, social class, family, age, location and gender. Who or what you are at any one point in time comes from the way these different discourses act out processes of conflict and combination within you. Although you are always socially defined, you are not necessarily stuck with just one such definition: changes in the self can come about as these different factors engage in many-levelled interactions and jostle for domination over each other.

Criticisms

James M. Glass has expressed deep reservations about what he calls the postmodern celebration of shattered selves. He argues that in picturing the self as socially defined and multiple, postmodern theory empties identity of all meaning and substance. This, he says, is an irresponsible and ill-informed thing to do. In celebrating fracture, conflict and process within the formation of identity, postmodernism makes a number of mistakes.

It fails to take seriously enough the fact that for many people the supposedly postmodern attributes of subjectivity are experienced in a painful way. What is the use of arguing, as some postmodernists do, that there is no real tension between the inner and outer self, when for many people the experience of conflict between the two is evidently a source of genuine anguish? Other critics have similarly noted with disapproval how a number of theorists (among them Fredric Jameson and Deleuze and Guattari) see postmodern culture as schizophrenic. They therefore use a traumatic mental disorder in a very casual and clumsy way as a dramatic metaphor to spice up postmodern rhetoric. Foucault is even more guilty in this respect as he has a tendency to romanticize emotionally disturbed people as subversive elements in society.

It is all very well to sing the praises of irony, playfulness and masquerade in matters of identity, suggests Glass, but what use is that to the client in therapy who does not read postmodern theory? What positive effects can come from denying that their personality has any substance? As well as going against most of our everyday experience, this implies that there is no point in therapy or analysis. Moreover, although many postmodernists do make much of disobedient so-called 'techniques of the body' and 'practices of the self', for Glass it is not easy to reconcile this aspect of their thought with the idea that people are regulated by social codes and structures. In his reading of postmodern theory, people lose most of their free will. Thus postmodernism, despite its apparent aspirations, leaves no space for people to have control over their own lives.

Other critics, more concerned than Glass with preserving a political edge in the face of what they see as postmodernism's lightweight posture of 'anything goes' (see the following chapter for more on this) have remarked on the relative triviality of the 'play, irony and surface' model of subjectivity. To see identity in these terms is a luxury which academics in free and comparatively affluent countries can perhaps afford, but it hardly speaks for the reality of the multiple forms of oppression and misery inflicted on millions of selves the world over.

See: *Shattered Selves: Multiple Personality in a Postmodern World*, by James M. Glass, 1993.

The fiction of expression

We will now discuss how some of postmodernism's questioning of the self has had repercussions for thinking about creativity and self expression. If the self is decentred, multiple or fractured, and if personal identity can be seen as fundamentally social, as postmodernists insist, what then do we mean when we speak of people expressing themselves? What are the implications for our long established notions of artistic genius and originality?

We are used to thinking about art and other forms of cultural activity in terms of these notions. For example, the belief that the value of Van Gogh's paintings resides in the way they capture his supposed insanity in oil paint is a clear case of how we habitually associate the meanings of art with the self expression of the geniuses who create it. Similar views are found in popular ideas which circulate about eccentric bohemian artists and temperamental creative types. As well as painters, poets and composers you can find this image of the artistic personality in TV documentaries about fashion designers and rock musicians. Finally the fad for releasing restored 'Director's Cut' versions of films, along with the treatment of certain directors as superstars in their own right, shows that although most films are made collectively, we tend to see directors as the ultimate originators and 'explanations' of the films which bear their names.

There has been an explosion of cultural production which seems to manage without the guiding hand of a genius. Consider the following examples:

- In music we have the common practice of sampling in rap, hip-hop and various forms of electronica. There is also scratching and mixing as a form of musical customization or *bricolage*. The availability of digital sequencers and other computerized pieces of musical equipment is making it easier and cheaper for relative beginners to make high-tech records. Many musicians now can hardly be said to be performers in the old sense of the term: making popular music no longer has to depend on virtuoso performances by 'personalities'. (A lot of dance music is now released on 'white label' records by producers and mixers with anonymous-sounding corporate names. These and other factors have to some extent displaced the traditional image of pop stars from the centre of the stage.)
- In architecture, there have been some signs of a move towards collaborative projects and away from the virtuoso performance of the master architect. A well-known example is Ralph Erskine's housing renewal project for the people of Byker in Newcastle, England. Here, locals were encouraged to take part in the design process from the beginning. Far less attention could therefore be paid (as it often had with modernist architecture) to the professional architect using buildings as a platform to show off his own great artistic vision.
- Following the tradition of Andy Warhol's pop art (see Chapter 3), many recent artists have reproduced ready-made objects, images and other works of art. To take two American examples: Sherrie Levine exhibited photographs by famous art photographers and Mike Bidlo did casual renditions of paintings (copied from art books and magazines) by Picasso and others. As with the musical practice of sampling, the use of found materials seems to shift focus away from the

importance of originals. When a painter paints a picture of a copy, he has abandoned his conventional role as an observer of forms or a narrator of anguish: there is less opportunity to contemplate his subjective experience. In addition to this there has been a move towards more 'impersonal' media such as video installation. There has also been a widespread willingness among artists to do collaborative pieces and to employ assistants to fabricate their work. So in the art world today there is far less emphasis on the artist's personal touch. Evidence of the individual artist's hand (in brush strokes, say) is much less often elevated to a position of mystical importance.

All of these practices have been called postmodern, and this is largely because they are said to subvert modernist ideas about the significance of the individual author in the making of the work. In what follows I will use the term 'author' to refer to any kind of cultural practitioner (e.g. sculptor, filmmaker, choreographer, poet). I will continue to use the term 'text' in a similarly general way, to signify any artefact produced by an 'author' and exhibited to an audience (e.g. record, painting, novel or film).

New romantics, old romantics

What is often called the modernist notion of authorship is an extension of romanticism. Romanticism was a loosely defined movement in philosophy and the arts in Europe in the eighteenth and nineteenth centuries. Drawing on the idea that the external world is in some sense a construct of (or at least cannot be separated from) the mind, romanticism exalted the individual self and celebrated the transcendent powers of the imagination. Of course this romantic attitude did not simply die out at some identifiable point in history. As well as carrying on in some modernist movements, it can still be found in popular ideas that continue to circulate about 'Bohemiam' artists and eccentric geniuses. According to the romantic view, the proper role of art is to reflect the artist's contact with both 'inner' and 'outer' reality. The artist's function is to pierce, participate in, and produce experience. John Ruskin, the nineteenth-century art critic and historian, claimed that the artist must 'go to nature in all singleness of heart, and walk with her laboriously and trustingly, having no thought but how best to penetrate her meaning and remember her instructions . . . rejoicing always in the truth' (note how artists and nature are gendered in this quote). It was seen as the artist's

Christian duty to convey to the responsive viewer how the glory of nature (and so of God) was revealed to the artistic imagination. The artist was a gifted being capable of unique insights, and the artwork was saturated with this exceptional vision.

In the case of painting, the artist's individual style was often seen as a direct materialisation of the self. As the post-impressionist painter Paul Gauguin put it: 'the work of art for him who can see is a mirror which reflects the artist's soul'. Roger Fry, in his 1909 *Essay in Aesthetics,* similarly observed that the sensations put down in paint by the creators of works of art aroused in the sensitive viewer a profoundly emotional 'special tie with the man who expressed them'. These ideas suppose that the individual artist is a vehicle for truth and authenticity, and that he or she can convey these to the gallery-goer solely through the power of sheer artistic vision. Although the sensitivity of the interpreter of the art work is considered, the meaning of art is basically seen as one-way traffic from the artist, through the artwork and to the reader.

So in the romantic (and common sense) view of authorship it is thought that the meaning found in a text can be readily traced back to its origins in the author. To quote from the French critical theorist Roland Barthes, it is as if 'it were always in the end . . . the voice of a single person, the author, 'confiding' in us'.

Postmodernist critics have attacked the way this romantic approach raises the individual author to unrealistic importance. Some feminist art historians, such as Griselda Pollock, have attacked the macho imagery and male-biased presumptions that often underlie it. You only need to look back at our quotes from Fry and Ruskin to see their point.

Roland Barthes (1925–1980) was one of the figures who helped to formulate a postmodern view of authorship. Associated mainly with structuralism, semiotics and poststructuralism (see Chapter 5), some of Barthes' work set out to question how meaning is produced in works of art. He asked: how are meanings related to their authors? And what is the role of the audience in 'finding' or 'making' these meanings?

The Death of the Author

In 1968 Barthes published a short essay called *The Death of the Author* in an obscure Parisian literary journal. In 1977, the essay resurfaced in an English translation in a collection of Barthes' essays called *Image – Music – Text* (edited and translated by Stephen Heath). Its original publication in France had caused a few ripples in the world of continental literary theory, but its reappearance a decade later brought it to a much larger audience, and triggered a tidal wave of comment.

It very quickly became something of a canonical piece, widely quoted in books and university courses on critical theory. It is still regularly cited, along with a few other Barthes essays, as an important early statement of the postmodern sensibility, even though Barthes never used the term. The notion of the death of the author also made an impact in the world of art, where it was often cited in relation to the kind of work mentioned above.

Barthes criticizes the romantic model on three main counts:

- 'the birth of the reader must be at the cost of the death of the author'
- 'the text is a tissue of quotations drawn from the innumerable centres of culture'
- 'it is language which speaks, not the author.'

Each of these phrases is taken from Barthes' essay and each can be read almost as a postmodernist slogan in its own right. So let us give detailed consideration to each in turn.

The birth of the reader must be at the cost of the death of the author

The normal idea of how meaning works assumes that three steps are taken. First, there exists in an individual author an idea, experience, sensation, or mental state. This occurs in the author independently of any verbal or visual language. It does not signify anything yet. It just is. This is close to what we mean by the moment of inspiration. Second, the author shapes inspiration into meaning by manipulating a particular medium. In other words, his or her inspiration is put into signs (words, images, etc.) Third, these signs convey the meaning given by the author and an audience is able to read them. The meaning as it occurred in the author can be read off the signs.

This model of meaning assumes that the author occupies the centre of the work and is the dominant source of meaning. The text is simply a vessel for meanings which are poured into it by the author. Language therefore simply carries meaning. The role of the reader as an interpreter of the text is essentially to receive meaning and not to create it.

But Barthes reminds us that any text can exist in any number of different times and places unforeseen when the author originally conceived it. A text moves through history, geography and culture, constantly gathering new meanings and revising old ones as it goes. There is no reason to assume that a Shakespeare play means exactly the same thing today as it did when first performed, for example. Yet when critics focus on the image of the 'genius' who produced the work, they try to restrict the changeable nature of meaning: they attempt to make the meanings of the text seem more timeless and stable than they really are.

Elsewhere in his essay Barthes notes that 'a text's unity lies not in its origin, but in its destination'. A text is only a random mass of signs until a reader comes along and binds them together in a way which lends them coherence. The most common way of binding them together, as we have seen, is in the shape of the author. But there is no reason to suppose that there even *should* be anything coherent about a text. By ignoring what Barthes calls the 'tyrannical' notion of genius, you give the signs more freedom to play, and you liberate the reader to invent new meanings. So the 'destination' of a text is its moment of being read. Of course, there can never be only one such destination, and the author has a very limited amount of control (if any) over where the text goes and what people do with it.

The text is a tissue of quotations drawn from the innumerable centres of culture

In his book *The Archaeology of Knowledge* (1969, first published in English in 1972), Michel Foucault wrote that:

> *the frontiers of a book are never clear-cut: beyond the title, the first line and the last full stop, beyond its internal configuration... it is caught up in a system of references to other books, other texts, other sentences . . . The book is not simply the object that one holds in one's hands . . . its unity is variable and relative.*

(page 23)

Borrowing the word from another of his contemporaries, Julia Kristeva (see Chapter 5), Barthes called the condition of texts described by Foucault *intertextuality*. One way of understanding this term is as a sort of environment of texts in which an author works and from which she or he draws. Whatever original idea an author might have, certain conditions must be in place in order for these ideas to 'happen'. An important aspect of these conditions is the fact that his or her text, and even the desire to produce it, exists inescapably in relation to a vast number of other texts, mostly by other authors. So no text sits in a vacuum or speaks its own tongue. Authors have to get their ideas from somewhere, and readers can only read in the light of what they have seen before.

Certain artefacts are very noticeably intertextual. That is to say, they overtly refer to other texts. Many spoof films like *Hot Shots* or *Spy Hard*, for example, are intertextual in the sense that they obviously make all sorts of references to other films (*Rambo*, *Pulp Fiction*, *Die Hard* and *Apocalypse Now*, among many others, have all been parodied in these films). Modernist novels like James Joyce's *Ulysses* (1922) also self-consciously refer to other writings. In *Ulysses* Joyce re-worked the themes of Homer's *Odyssey* and played with all sorts of styles, from Chaucer to modern day beauty-advice columns.

Intertextuality: a postmodern style?

Some critics have found the idea of intertextuality to be a good descriptions, a peculiarly contemporary aesthetic. We can all think of recent records which have mixed references to music from many different times and places, for example. Fashion design, too, is enormously wide-ranging in the way it can take ideas from any point in the entire history and geography of dress. And if you like to put your *eclectic* book, video and souvenir collections on display, then maybe even your shelves can be seen in a similar way. Since all of these might be said to 'draw from the innumerable centres of culture' they might all be seen as intertextual art forms. In this understanding of the term, intertextuality is a style intensified (and perhaps created) by the increasingly *pluralistic*, cosmopolitan nature of postmodern society and media.

Jean Baudrillard's take on such postmodern intertextuality (see Chapter 4 for more on him) is not so enthusiastic. Redefining intertextuality as a 'single dimension' of 'promiscuous' sounds and images, he notes that the whole world now appears to unfold on our televisions and radios as a haphazard mixture of contradictory information. Postmodern intertextuality for Baudrillard means being swamped by a 'pornography of information . . . a pornography of all functions and objects in their readability, their fluidity, their availability'. The problem is that in this process everything becomes equal and in doing so loses its true sense of meaning and reality.

But in fact *all* texts are intertextual. In all acts of authorship, no matter how small, we draw from a vast repertoire of codes, conventions and influences. If I were to carve a pair of initials and a love heart into the bark of a tree, for example, that act would have been informed by all the love hearts on trees I have seen represented before. And *those* representations would themselves echo countless other ways of picturing affection. And so on, down an infinite chain of influences and references.

Thus intertextuality is not so much a matter of style as a structural property which allows readers to read and texts to be produced. A text only gathers meaning because it is, as Barthes says, 'woven entirely with citations, references, echoes, cultural languages'. It is both inscribed with the traces of the texts that have gone before it, and formed in the act of reading by the encyclopaedia of references we all carry with us as participants in culture.

The reading of a text is always allowed by knowledges and expectations produced in our 'intertextual landscape'. In her *The Scorsese Connection* (1995) the film critic Lesley Stern has taken these principles on board by writing a book, apparently on the American director Martin Scorsese, that spends more time teasing out strange echoes of other films than it does on explaining Scorsese's own work. One chapter alone drifts in and out of all sorts of connections between Jerry Lewis movies, *Blue Velvet*, *The Wizard of Oz*, horror films, the New York underground cinema, the B-movie director Roger Corman, and Alfred Hitchcock. Somewhere in there are a couple of Scorsese films, but these are never presented as in any way 'central'. Rather than simply being unique pieces of art springing from the head of a one-off film artist, Scorsese's movies are treated as part of a vast intertextual field which no individual film maker can dominate. All films resonate with one another's images and meanings. As Barthes would put it, a film 'is but a space in which a variety of images, none of them original, blend and clash'. So it makes no sense to try and explain Scorsese in terms of his own talent, life story or intentions. Because you can only watch films through the rest of their cultural surroundings Sterne's book is not so much about Scorsese as *around* him.

It is language which speaks, not the author

This third phrase is perhaps the most radical claim in Barthes' essay. What Barthes is arguing against here is the taken-for-granted view that ideas spontaneously occur in the mind of the author, as if from nowhere, and are secondarily put into words or other *signs*. This conventional view suggests that there is a pure realm of ideas which exists prior to language, and that we can simply freely choose the best signs with which to express those ideas.

From Barthes' perspective, there are a couple of major theoretical problems here:

- You cannot have an idea without it *already* arriving to you in the form of signs. You cannot have a language-less thought.
- Language is therefore active: it speaks. Signs produce, rather than passively mirror, meaning.

For example: a Monet painting does not innocently capture the fleeting effects of sunlight on a boating-lake. We have simply learned to read the signs in such a way that they produce (rather than reflect) that image for us. A very different example: the clothes and behaviour of a person do not express individuality, they make it. The notion of expression suggests that meaning (in this case, individuality) is simply *there*, waiting for the appropriate signs (in this case fashion and body language) to come along and embody it. But there is not an 'individual identity' until certain clothes and behaviour have been adopted. Their expressive qualities are not invented out of the blue. They work because our culture has encoded them in certain ways. In a sense it is the whole of culture, not the 'author', which is speaking. Thus meaning does not travel *from* a vacuum *to* a sign. The sign *is* the meaning.

Summary

Authorship is (or should be) dead because:

- the author is not available for study; what we have before us is not an author, but a text
- no author can control the various interpretations that people will give to his or her work. You can't restrain the text's *polysemy*
- words generate meanings free of the author's wishes, and authors cannot 'master' language in its entirety
- the idea of genius is a mystification of art; it distracts from art's social and political meanings.

Postmodernists do not deny that there are people in the world who have intentions when they write, paint, make movies or whatever. They just ask us to reconsider the faith we place in them.

Possible criticisms

Ideas of authorship are still worth having because:

- Without the author you imply that a text is 'just' a text. In other words, you imply that it is just a free-floating combination of words and images. So despite some of the above claims, the 'death of the author' can be seen as excessively antihistorical and asocial.
- Reminding yourself of who authored a text can usefully restore it to the circumstances in which it was originally made. You cannot have a proper understanding of a text without knowing something about the 'who, where and when' of it.
- Doing away with the figure of the author erases the significance of identity politics. It negates important questions concerning what social and cultural identities are being given a voice in the text. Surely it is significant, for example, whether the author is white or black, male or female, gay or straight, but the 'death of the author' wipes these matters away.
- 'Authors' can often provide important models for people to identify with or aspire to.
- If intentions are irrelevant, if meaning is uncontrollable, we might as well give up on trying to say anything.

And a final note of caution

Barthes' essay is nearly always understood to be a general reflection on all forms of authorship and all forms of author. But an alternative reading is possible which suggests that the essay really offers a veiled form of elitism. In this interpretation, the author whom Barthes is so keen to assassinate is only the author of conventional realistic novels. Barthes can be seen as arguing for very particular sorts of 'difficult' writing, and for the writers of these works. Thus the 'birth of the reader' is not a spontaneous consumer revolution or a simple shift in what literary critics should attend to. Instead it is the outcome of experimental literature (Barthes would praise Brecht, Joyce, Mallarmé, Surrealism, etc.) which supposedly acts to make reading a more creative process than people normally undergo in their consumption of 'low culture'.

Summary

As we have seen, there are many aspects to the theorization of postmodern identity, but central is the idea of the fundamentally social self. Postmodern theory may not have the monopoly on this basic notion, but it does elaborate on it in its own particular ways. In Jean Baudrillard's terms, for example (see Chapter 4), simulation has imploded into private life to such an extent that it has become impossible to distinguish between 'natural' and 'manufactured' identities and desires. Some critics have responded by seeking a more positive view of how senses of identity can be created through the consumption of mass-produced objects and images. For Barthes and others the outcome has been a reconsideration of the idea of artistic 'self-expression'.

Key questions asked of the self by postmodernism include:

- Where are the boundaries of the self?
- Is it possible to distinguish in any clear way between private/public or inner/outer selves?
- Has the time come for the image of the whole, unified and profound self to be replaced by a multiple, fractured and superficial model?

How do we learn to handle the fact that we may already be cyborgs? What can we do with the fact that identity seems to be becoming ever more fragmentary and unstable? Of course there are no ready answers to these questions. The postmodernized self is in many ways still in the process of being defined. Theoretical accounts of it have largely remained (like the vision of the self they describe) partial and fragmentary. Foucault suggested that 'modern man' may be becoming extinct, but perhaps it is too early as yet to know how we are going to live with 'his' death.

08

postmodern
politics

In this chapter you will learn:

- postmodernism's critique of
  'totalizing' ideas
- its preference for fragmentation and difference
- ideas about cultural *relativism*
  and their consequences
- conflicts between local and
  global spaces.

Politicians often use the idea of 'we the people' in their speeches to conjure up an image of community and national identity. When they use this phrase they effectively suggest that we are all on 'the same team'. But many postmodern theorists argue to the contrary. They suggest that society is in an important sense incoherent and that no single perspective can grasp the complexity and fluidity of current conditions. They say that society has fragmented into so many conflicting knowledges, identities, needs and views that it is neither possible nor desirable to see the human race as one big family.

This situation arises partly out of the fact that our societies are becoming increasingly multi-cultural and our lifestyles are becoming more and more cosmopolitan. But it can also be taken to mean that (a) there is no agreement about what is worth believing (or even knowing) any more, (b) that social conditions are in a frightening state of disrepair, or (c) a combination of the two. Some postmodernists think that it is pointless to complain about this state of affairs. They see it as far more constructive to push the fragmentation as far as it will go and use it to your advantage.

When politicians and others use the word 'we' they are often trying to smooth out or disguise the presence of disagreement and diversity. Many postmodernists prefer to take the opposite approach. They propose that we should activate the differences between people and between the cultural spaces they inhabit; this is the only way to generate new ideas and experiences. As well as possibilities for creativity, this obviously contains the potential for violent conflict, but it seems that some postmodern thinkers would rather see violence than flabby tolerance.

We can begin to explore these points by concentrating on one of the most influential texts of postmodern theory, *The Postmodern Condition* by Jean-Francois Lyotard (1924–). Although Lyotard's focus in that work is mainly on science, we will go on to see how some of the topics he addresses have had repercussions for the study of culture at large.

Lyotard: when worlds collide

The Postmodern Condition was first published in 1979 as a report, commissioned by Quebec's Conseil des Universités, on the state of scientific knowledge and information in the late twentieth century. Lyotard's central concern is the grounds of knowledge. He is interested in how forms of knowledge come into being, who controls and has access to them, and how they become accepted as valid. His basic argument is that because of broad changes in culture and society scientific disciplines no longer assume that their theories and discoveries have universal or timeless value.

The truth is not out there

Thanks partly to commercials which use 'lab technicians' as a source of evidence about the germ-killing capacities of particular brands of bleach, or which stress the clinically proven ability of a certain sort of toothpaste to fight plaque, we are used to thinking of scientists as holders of truth. When we speak of evidence as scientific, we tend to mean that it is neutral and that it is therefore closer to reality than mere opinion. TV news and documentary programmes often make use of the fact that as soon as we are shown a man in a white coat discussing his latest discovery in a lab or book-lined study, we assume that he knows what he is talking about. We might also believe that his research is conducted in an objective spirit of scientific enquiry, that his discoveries add to our ever-growing knowledge about the universe, and that if science has a goal it is to improve the lot of humanity.

Lyotard builds his analysis of the current state of scientific knowledge around the assertion that these kinds of ideas are outmoded myths. He argues that theory is never neutral, and follows thinkers like Michel Foucault and Jacques Derrida in looking at how knowledge is always limited by the institutions in which it is created (see Chapter 5 for more on this). From this perspective, scientists can have no more direct access to 'the truth' than can philosophers or historians. For Lyotard, they are all story-tellers, and the narratives they produce (e.g. research papers, hypotheses, histories) are always governed by the protocols of the field in which they work. Each discipline is like a game: it has a special language which only makes sense within its own boundaries. Rather than being faced with infinite possibilities, a theorist or researcher can only play within the limits of a system of permissible moves.

So science is made up of *language games* which generate particular forms of narrative. Clearly this goes against the common sense view of science as a superior form of knowledge. It also contradicts modern science's view of itself. In order to maintain its high status, science has often tried to deny its own involvement in story-telling. It pretends to be beyond narrative. How does science do this? Ironically enough, it does it by appealing to what Lyotard calls grand *metanarratives*.

A metanarrative (not to be confused with 'metafiction'; see Chapter 2) is an over-arching story which can supposedly account for, explain, or comment upon the validity of all other stories, a universal or absolute set of truths which is supposed to transcend social, institutional or human limitations.

For example, a small, local narrative or language game (e.g. the result of a scientific experiment, an individual's life story) is usually granted significance only by its ability to reflect or support 'global' Enlightenment narratives like those of progress, truth and justice.

From big science to little sciences

Lyotard assumes that in earlier modern times (around the eighteenth century onwards) faith was placed in science as the source of enlightenment. For instance, instead of answering to religion as the guarantee of truth, political and economic fields developed which claimed to have the standing of science. Being 'scientific' or 'rational' was now a sign of credibility. Possessing scientific knowledge implied that you could get behind mystification and superstition, reveal the facts about the world and lead all of humanity to a brighter day.

Condensed in this view are a number of important assumptions about science:

- it is progressive, moving towards a state of 'complete knowledge'
- it is unified; there may be many different areas within science, but deep down they all share the same goal.
- it is universal – science works for the good of all of us, and aims at total truths which will benefit all of human life.

Between the Enlightenment age and the mid-twentieth century, science justified itself by claiming that it needed no justification. That is to say, it took advantage of the idea that its activities were pursued in the name of the timeless metanarratives of progress, emancipation, and knowledge. By appealing in this way to ideas whose meanings are taken to be self-evident and universally agreed, science was able to masquerade as a single project objectively carried out for the good of the 'human race'.

Lyotard claims that since around the end of the Second World War, these myths have collapsed. Some of the reasons for this collapse are outlined below:

Science's contribution to ecological disaster, and the development of nuclear and chemical weapons, have made it difficult to link scientific rationality with 'progress'. Partly as a result of this there is now widespread suspicion towards big enlightenment stories. Lyotard therefore defines postmodernism as an attitude of 'incredulity towards metanarratives'.

Explorations in the philosophy and sociology of science have recognized the influence on science of social processes, and have questioned the idea of 'objectivity' (of particular influence was Thomas Kuhn: *The Structure of Scientific Revolutions*', (1960).

Approaches like 'chaos theory', quantum mechanics, etc. have highlighted uncertainty in measurement. Because of these influences it has become harder to see science as the activity of a rational mind confronting a concrete reality.

The spirit of commercial free enterprise has entered research and has contributed to the rapid growth of computerized means of information processing. The outcome of this has been that theories and discoveries are now judged on the basis of performance and efficiency rather then truth or purpose. Scientists are now primarily interested in putting out work which will both generate further research funding and add to their own power and prestige within the academic 'market place'.

Once, ideas developed within 'natural philosophy' were bound together through theology. No hard and fast boundaries divided philosophy from science, or what we now call 'physics' from what is now known as 'chemistry'. Knowledge had not yet reached the stage where it was necessary to create these separate disciplines, and where it was a lifetime's work to master just one of them. It was possible to be a Renaissance person, capable of holding on to a thorough knowledge of many different aspects of natural philosophy. Now, rather than being a single endeavour travelling in a single direction towards a single goal, science has splintered into a mass of specialisms. In place of centralized metanarratives which bind all of these specialisms together, we now have a multitude of disciplines and sub-disciplines which all follow their own agendas and speak their own languages. According to Lyotard, sciences today are therefore more sceptical about the possibility of penetrating *the* truth or finding *the* answer.

So sciences are now carried out on a more modest, limited level. Realizing that they cannot find permanent answers to everything, they only come up with temporarily valid opinions, and seek to solve merely immediate, local problems.

So postmodern science:

- is not coherent
- can no longer be valued for the contribution it makes towards human progress
- has abandoned the idea that one day the sum of all knowledge will add up to a state of perfect information
- has become a mass of incompatible (Lyotard says *incommensurable*) little sciences with no goal other than to generate further research.

The splintering of knowledge discussed by Lyotard is paralleled by a wider sense of social and cultural disintegration. Thus his report has found many echoes in fields as diverse as political theory, cultural theory and art criticism. Indeed, later editions of the book include a postscript which concentrates on aesthetic rather than scientific issues, and the text as a whole can be read as an overview of how the 'rules of the game' have apparently changed in culture at large. It is perhaps not surprising to learn, therefore, that 'the postmodern condition' has had more of an impact on the humanities than it has had on the 'hard' sciences. In order to gauge some of this impact, we will now look at how the issues addressed by Lyotard have had repercussions for political and social thought.

The transformation of Marxism

Political thought under the influence of Marx has tended to see social class as the key site of oppression, and the resulting conflict between dominant and subordinate classes as the basis for future revolution. In this view faith is put in the proletariat as the universal class which will lead the way to socialism, and the economic structure is seen as the determining factor in social and cultural life. But much postmodern thought has challenged the idea that any one class, structure or factor can single-handedly explain history or bring about change. Following many of the themes we have touched on with Lyotard, Foucault, Baudrillard and others, this post-Marxist (post-metanarrative) tendency seeks a less reductive view of history and society, and tries to formulate a more radical version of democracy than

Marxism has often provided. It aims to address political theory to a more chaotic social landscape full of fluid identities and diverse social groups. It asks whether revolution is still possible in an age apparently without agreed values, and whether radical gestures can have any effect in a world which seems able to absorb all attempts at subversion.

There are two main aspects to this shift:

A new map of power

Since the late 1980s the collapse of communism and the apparent end of the cold war between what were once the two world superpowers have arguably re-drawn the political map of the world. This has been echoed in some countries by a gradual meeting in the middle of the main left and right political parties (e.g. the rhetoric of the Democrats and the Republicans in America, and Labour and Conservative in Britain becoming increasingly similar). This has been called 'implosion' by Jean Baudrillard and has widely been identified as the end of ideology.

Class fragmentation

Political and social identity cannot be reduced to a unified picture of an economically based class system. Gender, ethnic identity, age, sexual orientation and so on all cut across and fracture the image of class. There has also been a shift in industrial production from the standardization to the diversification of output (a move away from Henry Ford's ideas about mass production). This has resulted, among other things, in the intensification of niche marketing whereby ever more particular taste-groups are identified and 'exploited'.

Partly because of these influences reasonably affluent members of contemporary capitalist societies are more able to experiment with tastes, images and lifestyles than ever before, and as a result they are now much less likely to identify with their class origins.

The cultural politics of how minority groups are represented in the media now seems to have a louder voice than politics drawn along the traditional lines of conflict between the bourgeoisie and the proletariat. Wrangles over the right of people to express their own sexual and cultural identities have increased in prominence. Issues as diverse as the rights of the disabled, environmental protest, rural decline and animal rights have also become increasingly hot news. In India members of women's groups have threatened to set fire to themselves in protest at the

Miss World contest. In America, elections have been fought on the basis of debates about abortion. In Britain, white members of parliament have involved themselves in arguments about the lyrics of some black American rap records. These various struggles are all examples of cultural and identity politics. All of them (and of course there are many more) have seemed to push class war away from the heart of political activism. People are now more concerned with fighting over specific individual issues than they are with large-scale party politics. Public participation in elections shrinks every year, yet the number of issues available to be fought over seems to grow daily as the true diversity of human life comes increasingly into the light. The shift towards this 'grass roots level' politics is further discussed below.

In short, postmodernism erodes the three touchstones of modern politics:

- nation
- class
- belief in the wholesale transformation of the world.

Postmodern micropolitics

As Lyotard argues, there is no great blueprint which binds all 'language games' together. There is no reason to believe that different pieces of knowledge share conceptual ground or that they ultimately contribute to one vast human enterprise. Preferring the image of chaos to that of progress, Lyotard pictures a world in which all the grand ideas collapse, and no idea assumes more than a partial value. Truth is a short-term contract here. You cannot speak in the name of universal human principles and expect them to form a fixed standard by which to judge other people's perspectives. You can no longer look to ideas like morality, justice, enlightenment or human nature and expect them to form a globally agreed basis for your own point of view. It is impossible to draw up a complete map of the world in such a way that everybody would be able to recognize it as representing their own knowledge and experience. Postmodernists argue that it is no longer possible to write a 'theory of everything'; you can only take the *pragmatic* and *relativist* line that some truths are more useful than others in specific circumstances.

Micropolitics

Many theorists of postmodern society argue that power no longer works by a single monolithic state or class inflicting itself on the masses. People are not simply oppressed and exploited from above. Rather, power is exerted through the apparently mundane little networks of everyday life. Everything from advertising and other forms of representation through to interpersonal relationships and shopping can now be seen as caught up in multiple systems of power. To this extent much postmodern theory assumes that everything is in some sense political. On the one hand this means that just about anything is capable of being 'oppressive'. On the other hand it suggests that you can just as easily find acts of resistance to that oppression in the most seemingly trivial of places.

Thus postmodernism has a more modest notion of what counts as political action. Rather than aiming your beliefs at some grand Utopian scheme which will transform human destiny, postmodern politics suggests that it is more worthwhile to challenge power on a day-to-day level. Thus postmodern politics looks for ways in which we can all, as Lyotard puts it, 'gnaw away at the great institutionalized narrative apparatuses . . . by increasing the number of skirmishes that take place on the sidelines. That's what women who have had abortions, prisoners, conscripts, prostitutes, students, and peasants have been doing . . .' And, it is argued, that is what we can all do.

Rather than having to enrol in the project of total human emancipation, we are just as politically engaged every time we have a quarrel with a racist neighbour, refuse to buy a certain brand of condensed milk, or surf the net at work. Everything from defacing billboards to selling pirate copies of banned video tapes can now be seen as an attempt to gnaw from within (attack virally as Baudrillard would say) at the powers-that-be. None of these activities might strike you as particularly radical – they are perhaps not going to bring about a revolution – but from Lyotard's point of view they can be valued as disruptive skirmishes in the social system.

Lyotard's celebration of small-scale acts of dissent and his view of political commitment as a matter of personal games and tactics can be seen as part of a libertarian strand within postmodern theory: he places individual freedom at the centre of his philosophy. We already encountered something of this tendency with Foucault, Derrida and others, all of whom expressed mistrust of any kind of totalising or centralizing thought or action. Although there are differences between these thinkers, all have regarded 'universalizing' enlightenment theories (of history, progress, knowledge and so on) as more or less authoritarian ways of trying to produce conformity. Many activists have echoed this in practice. Anti-globalization and/or anti-capitalism protests have consisted of loose, temporary coalitions of multiple concerns. In Britain, marches for 'the countryside' have similarly been made up of diverse, not always compatible interest groups. In both cases, 'the enemy' is vague, and few solutions are proposed. There is no collective identity founded on a single metanarative.

Other key books by Lyotard include:

Libidinal Economy (1974, English translation 1993)

The Differend: Phrases in dispute (1983, English translation 1986).

The techniques of daily life

The postmodern view of political action as something which can take place on the most commonplace and normally overlooked of levels is influenced by a book by Michel de Certeau called *The Practice of Everyday Life* (first English translation 1989). De Certeau argues that in order to understand the present way of life you should attend less to a total picture of society as a whole and more to the seemingly insignificant details of how people go about living their lives. By doing so you will find in contemporary life not some falsely unified spirit of the age, but a complex mass of interweaving and contradictory desires, concerns and stories.

For de Certeau everyday life is creative. His approach suggests that when we go shopping we are drawing our own conceptual maps through the city streets. When we zap across the channels on our TV sets we are creating moving collages from materials provided by the mass media. When we buy fake designer labels, we are undermining the elitist fashion system. According to de Certeau everyday life is full of such acts of 'poaching, tricking, speaking, strolling, desiring'.

Hence he refuses to see us as the passive victims of consumer society. Rather than simply swallowing the goods, environments and lifestyles imposed on us by an all-powerful capitalist system, we employ *bricolage* to make our material conditions bearable and to make sense of the world we live in. Every day we engage in the creative production of our own power struggles, pleasures and acts of disobedience, and in doing so we create important cracks in the monolith of 'the dominant economic order'. We may not be able to change the world, de Certeau suggests, but at least we can migrate across the cultural environment, taking bits we need from whatever products and experiences are available. In short, day-to-day life is about making do against the system.

Summary

- Postmodernist theory is sceptical of any totalizing attempt to achieve global harmony through the wholesale application of universal ideals.
- It drops the dream of a future Utopia in favour of a politics of the here and now.
- Its view of what counts as radical instead embraces temporary acts of resistance within the limits of regional conditions and demands. (This can be compared to similar moves within postmodernist architecture – see the section on Robert Venturi in Chapter 2.)
- It celebrates a world in which principles are constantly in the process of being fought over and redefined. It sees no reason to hope that this process will some day come to an end.

Criticisms of post-Marxism

A number of thinkers who place themselves politically on the left have had their doubts about the claims outlined above. They see in the theories of Lyotard, de Certeau and the rest a sell-out of genuinely radical political ideas, and find in their place a lazy acceptance of the way things are. From this point of view postmodernism is, despite its radical sounding terminology, a deeply conservative response to the ideals promoted by modernity. Its theories are too close for comfort to the ideas they pretend to oppose:

- Its celebration of fragmentation and difference in society seems to strike at the heart of socialism's fundamental faith in community and collective action. It complies too happily with the idea of the 'free market'.
- Its rejection of the idea of progress implies that there is no point in anyone trying to make the world a better place.

- Its fascination with commodities, fashion and the media shows that it is so seduced by capitalism that it has lost its critical distance.
- Its interest in how consumers make the best of a bad situation seems far too laid back and defeatist.
- Its emphasis on the 'politics of identity' is a poor substitute for genuine 'hard' political activity.

One of the key figures in the critical response towards post-modern theory is Jurgen Habermas.

Habermas takes on postmodernism

Habermas (1929–) continues the enquiries of the Frankfurt School of critical theory, whose work we have come across elsewhere in this book (see Chapter 6 for example). He shares with them, and also with many postmodernists, a general uneasiness towards rational systems, and agrees with them that the technical rationality of science should be treated with suspicion. Like Lyotard and others, Habermas believes that the products of modernity (technology, science, capitalist economic systems, etc.) have so far failed to live up to their potential. They have tended to enslave people rather than liberate them, and instead of enriching creativity they have often impoverished it. However, Habermas sees postmodern thought as 'the end of the Enlightenment', and goes against Lyotard by believing that the project of modernity is still worth pursuing.

Although he is very wary of present political and economic systems (whether capitalist or communist) which regulate people's lives, Habermas is no anarchist. He sees postmodernism's apparent embrace of irrationality as morally bankrupt and believes, contrary to Lyotard, that some sort of universally agreed-upon framework is both possible and necessary in order to ensure that freedom and justice are achieved. We can move towards this goal by bringing the spheres of morality, science and art back together, removing them from the experts and professionals who currently monopolize them, and restoring them to ordinary people. Habermas disputes the claims of some postmodern thinkers that human identity is unstable, fragmented, or 'in process' (see Chapter 6 for more on this): for him we all, deep down, share eternal human needs and desires. The failure of the postmodernists is that they refuse to propose a route towards the fulfilment of these.

Lyotard argued that it is impossible to create any single ethical scheme which does not silence or alienate minority voices, but Habermas responds that as long as we can freely communicate with each other we will one day all agree about what the true values are and how to make them happen. Disputing the postmodernist's *relativist* claim that all moral concepts are open to different interpretations, he asks: How is it possible to follow a moral programme if you do not believe it to be universally right? Unless we believe that the great ideals of freedom, justice and democracy can be fully realized, we will never be able to progress towards the global emancipation of humanity. Through the process of open and rational conversation we need to keep searching for the common ethical ground which lies beneath our superficial differences.

So Lyotard is mistaken in his belief that the Enlightenment project is exhausted. This attitude is conservative in that, seeing principles as nothing more than language games, it opens the way to the casual acceptance of any and every aberrant point of view. For Habermas, unlike Lyotard, it is not modernity's ideas of enlightenment, reason and rationality that are wrong, so much as the misuse to which history has sometimes put them. Mistakes may often have been made in the name of modernity but we still need to hold on to at least some of its aspirations. By opening up knowledge and the means of communication to people it is possible to enhance their understanding of themselves and others, and in doing so to promote progress towards human happiness. Thus the promise of the modern 'project' needs to be completed rather than abandoned.

One of Habermas' key books is *The Philosophical Discourse of Modernity* (1995). His most well known essay is 'Modernity: An Incomplete Project'. This can be found in *Postmodernism; a Reader*, edited by Thomas Docherty (1993).

Lyotard's defence

It can seem that Lyotard's kind of postmodernism involves a complete rejection of morality. And it is true to say that the trend has been for promoting the pursuit of pleasure over moral responsibility. But Lyotard's anarchic abandonment of 'universal' ideals is motivated largely by an idealistic desire to maximize freedom and creativity. Out of this desire he has expressed concern with the control of knowledge in our society, and has argued that in order to shift power back from systems to individuals the public should be granted free access to all information. So Lyotard does have quite firm ethics. He just does not believe they can ever apply to all people for all time. The difficulty then is how to persuade people that your values are correct without at the same time appearing authoritarian or violent (by trying to silence 'marginal' voices).

Lyotard has compared speaking to fighting and claims that what we should aim for is not so much the satisfaction of winning as the pleasures of keeping up the fight. Difference is always more desirable than agreement, for it is from difference that invention arises. The lines should always be kept open: universal agreement about values should be discouraged rather than encouraged, because consensus – if such a thing is even possible – only 'does violence to the heterogeneity of language games', as Lyotard says. So the fear among postmodernists is that universal principles threaten cultural diversity by seeking to force a single way of life on people. As far as Lyotard is concerned the only way to avoid such terroristic suppression of different experiences, identities, and expressions is to forget the prospect of unity and to dismantle any institution which aims at 'governing the social bonds':

The idea that I think we need today in order to make decisions in political matters cannot be the idea of the totality, or of the unity, of the body. It can only be the idea of a mutiplicity or of a diversity.

Steven Best & Douglas Kellner, *Postmodern Theory: Critical Interrogations* (1991) page 89

Problems

Postmodern or post-Marxist politics gives critics a range of problems. It can be argued that while the postmodern approach is constructive in its search for new possibilities for political radicalism, it easily slips into a far too passive 'anything goes' attitude. So the strength of the kind of angles discussed above lies in their desire to support all forms of cultural and individual diversity. But their weakness lies in the fact that this desire can often result in an enfeebling form of relativism. For example, one result of this in the area of cultural studies is that many researchers now want to celebrate rather than criticize popular culture. To exercise your critical skills on the little politics of identity and consumption is to allow yourself the luxury of being distracted from the real problems of poverty and injustice that still beset this supposedly late capitalist society. What use, after all, is a theory of mass consumption to people forced to live on the streets? Hence the British critic Simon Frith has argued that too many analysts of culture have left political engagement behind in favour of the sound of the cash register. Another British critic, Colin MacCabe, has similarly suggested recently that postmodernism has encouraged too much cultural 'pick and mix' and not enough hard thinking. The time has come, he says, for theorists to reject all this disabling pluralism and learn how to make value judgements again.

Further reading on the political ramifications of postmodernism:

The Orgins of Postmodernity, by Perry Anderson (1998)

The Illusions of Postmodernism, by Terry Eagleton (1996)

The Politics of Postmodernity, by James Good (1998)

Religion, Modernity and Postmodernity, edited by Paul Heelas (1998)

'Feminism and Postmodernism', by Joanna Hodge in *The Problems of Modernity*, edited by Andrew Benjamin (1989)

Political Theory, Modernity and Postmodernity: Beyond enlightenment critique, by N. J. Reagger (1995)

Postmodernism, truth and history

There are many examples in this book of how postmodern theory challenges ideas about truth. One common theme is that truths exist only in relation to specific *discourses*. For example, Lyotard (drawing on thinkers like Paul Feyerabend and Thomas Kuhn) argues that scientific truth-claims can only be *legitimated* by reference to the specific scientific *language game* in which they are made. There are no absolute or universal facts, only stories that 'work' at particular times for their particular 'speakers'. *Pragmatism* in philosophy puts forward a similar argument. Structuralists, poststructuralists and *new historicists* argue that it is impossible to access reality except through *texts*. Foucault and other *discourse* theorists suggest that it is not truth that counts, but who defines it, and what uses they put it to; knowledge is used in the exercise of power. In short:

- observers are never neutral or disinterested. Truth-claims serve specific interests
- you can only look at an object of enquiry from a particular viewpoint, and through a specific set of expectations and requirements
- no account of historical reality is free of narrative – because you can't reconstruct the past as it 'really' happened, you can only tell stories about it.

This can be seen as a *relativist* outlook. It can be glibly asserted, but it has important consequences. One positive aspect is that it can lead to a critical engagement with history. It enables new histories to be written that reveal the significance of previously neglected groups, or which challenge dominant but biased accounts; feminist histories or Marxist histories would be two examples of this. The negative side is the suggestion that, since all histories are stories, historians needn't worry about evidence, accuracy or validation. It seems to be an invitation to make things up. Some critics have therefore argued that postmodern theory (however unintentionally) opens the door to irresponsible, even dangerous, revisions of history, but gives itself no grounds on which to dispute them. How, for instance, do relativists refute 'historians' who deny the existence of the Holocaust? How helpful is it to imply that there are no clear boundaries between history and fiction? In a case like this we surely need to believe that there are such things as undeniable, objective facts.

While the arguments over this issue are complex and often circular, a couple of defences can be made of the postmodernist's point of view (whether these are strong defences or not is, of course, central to the debate):

- It isn't a matter of choosing between pure facts on the one hand and fantasy on the other. You can establish that one account is truer than another without assuming that your knowledge is perfect or that new facts won't come to light.
- Postmodernist relativism makes us aware of the rules and conventions under which claims are made. In the case of the holocaust denier, then, we can show that s/he is not 'playing' by the agreed rules (not applying the standards) of the historical community. As Lyotard would say, s/he is not 'in' the history language game; s/he is not a historian at all.

Further reading

Telling the Truth about History, by Joyce Appleby et al. *(1994)*

What is History? by E. H. Carr

Postmodernism and Holocaust Denial, by Robert Eaglestone (2001)

In Defence of History, by Richard Evans (1997)

The Differend: Phrases in dispute, by Jean-François Lyotard (1988)

The Postmodern History Reader, edited by Keith Jenkins (1997)

Postmodern space

Thanks in part to this interest in miniature tactics of political resistance – what Michel Foucault (see Chapter 7) called 'the little tactics of the habitat' – recent thinking about post-modernism has taken a particular interest in space and location. Let us look at some examples.

Edward Soja

An American geographer, Soja has argued that we tend to see history (or time) as the major force behind culture and society, as though it travels under its own steam, influencing people and places as it moves along. Once again it is Marxism that Soja wants to give a facelift in this respect. He claims that traditional Marxism places too much weight on the idea of the progress of history towards a single goal. This view shunts geography too far into the background, making it the canvas on which history paints itself. In other words, space is seen as something which is merely acted on by time. Soja sees this model as too simplistic and aims to go beyond it by putting space into the foreground. Pointing out that we live in concrete environments as much as we live in abstract constructs like society and time, he argues that spaces actively affect history rather than passively receive it.

Soja asserts that it is pointless for thinkers with radical political aspirations to simply wish postmodernism away. Postmodernism is not an attitude you can choose to approve or disapprove of. It is a set of concrete conditions which now affect all aspects of contemporary life, and they will continue to do so whether you like it or not. He believes that the future of radical politics depends on its ability to come to terms with these conditions.

Over the last few decades a postmodern reorganization of space has emerged which has begun to radically alter both the way we live and the way we see the world. He looks in particular at the postmodern city (which he calls the 'post-metropolis'), and observes there a mixture of transformations in the arrangement of urban places. Cities have been undergoing many complex processes of postmodernization which have affected what Soja sees as 'urbanized' ways of living and thinking. Among the (sometimes contradictory) restructurings noted by Soja are:

Drastic changes in industry

These include the computerized design and production of goods alongside craft-based industries, the growth of industries (e.g. the stock exchange, financial advisors) based on selling information, a widening of the gap between rich and poor (often living in close proximity to each other) and a weakening of trade union power.

The growth of global cities

Soja cites the ways in which multinational corporations spread their offices, outlets, advertising campaigns, logos and factories all over the world, the Internet continues to grow, there is an increase in 'global identities' as more and more people seek work away from their home countries, and there is an international division of labour between 'First', 'Second' and 'Third' worlds.

Increasing surveillance

Soja points out that communities and individuals are becoming more and more obsessed with security, and notes that in the USA at least 30,000 communities are literally fenced off to keep intruders at bay. Crime prevention is now an industry in its own right. Ever increasing numbers of city streets are being installed with surveillance cameras. Numerous identity card schemes and neighbourhood watch schemes are introduced. The post-modernized space is a site of prohibition and supervision.

Soja's key work is *Postmodern Geographies: The reassertion of space in critical social theory*, 1989.

Fredric Jameson

We have noted elsewhere in this book that Jameson, although partly excited by the dynamic and witty quality of some postmodern culture, is worried about what he sees as its superficiality. From architecture and literature through to music videos and cinema, too much of today's culture, he suggests in his book *Postmodernism, or the Cultural Logic of Late Capitalism*, is made up of hollow signs thrown together in meaningless combinations. Jameson sees everywhere a general 'waning of affect' and defines this as a loss of historical awareness which makes everything seem equally lightweight. We now live in a dangerously short-sighted 'perpetual present' in which society has lost its ability to know its own past. Profound meanings and deep interpretations have been replaced by surfaces which play among themselves in the centreless space of global media.

For Jameson this postmodern culture of surfaces is intimately related to certain technological, economic and political changes. Borrowing themes from a number of theorists of what has been called 'post-industrial' society (especially Daniel Bell and Ernest Mandel), he proposes that postmodernism is the 'cultural logic' of our current stage of capitalist expansion and implies that everything produced within it is postmodern in character. Although the transition to this logic cannot reliably be dated to a single point in time, Jameson puts forward the following broad shifts:

Market capitalism
Associated with the eighteenth and nineteenth centuries, this phase was based on industrial growth within individual nations. It was characterized by the rise of the 'self-made man' (the factory owner, the 'fat cat' capitalist).

Monopoly capitalism
Associated with the mid-nineteenth to mid-twentieth centuries, this is the so-called imperialist phase in which capitalism profited from the creation of more and more foreign markets for the production and consumption of goods. Colonized nations (e.g. those in the 'third world') were exploited for cheap labour and raw materials.

Multinational capitalism
Also known as 'consumer', 'late' or 'post-industrial' capitalism, this is the current state of affairs in which we witness the growth of an international market in images and information. Jameson paints this phase as a world of global telecommunication networks and huge media webs spanning continents. Here representations and data become commodities circulated electronically in virtual networks. These run over national boundaries, and a vast network of multinational business corporations holds more power than individual nation states.

At the same time, capitalist expansion has created ever smaller groups of consumers – with specialized tastes and interests – for their ever-growing range of different commodities. As a result of these changes, the population might seem to have fragmented into a bewildering diversity of markets for consumer goods. As Jameson argues, individual and national identities have been shattered by a global image market which 'reflects . . . the absence of any great collective project.' However, these are ultimately ruled by one 'global totality' (late capitalism) which has relentlessly spread its tentacles across all nations and into all aspects of life. Most theorists of postmodernism are horrified by the idea of sameness, and Jameson likewise fears that late capitalism has squeezed the world into a single system which neutralizes individual and cultural differences. In such a world, local cultures struggle to have any meaning and we all lose our sense of historical and geographical place.

Jameson talks about how we are caught in a mass of 'depthless' and centreless multinational communication networks so vast and complex that it is impossible to mentally grasp them. In doing so, he represents postmodernism in terms of transformations it has made to our relationships to space.

Jameson checks into postmodern space

The way postmodernism alters our experience of space is explored by Jameson in a passage of his book which describes his visit to the Bonaventure Hotel in Los Angeles, designed by John Portman. Although he pays a lot of attention to this one building, Jameson does not see it as one of a kind. He notes that similar points could equally have been made about the Pompidou Centre in Paris or the Eaton Centre in Toronto. You may be able to find in the following summary echoes of buildings you have visited yourself.

A popular building, visited by both locals and tourists, entering it, according to Jameson, is a disorientating experience in itself. It is hard to find the entrances (the one Jameson used seems to go round the back and up a walkway), and you can readily find yourself in a part of the building you did not intend to be in. Once inside, you might struggle to find your way to the reception desk as various passages (and apparently a shortage of signs) send you drifting in the wrong direction. But rather than being a totally frustrating experience, the Bonaventure can be exhilarating. In it you find yourself in a space full of many different pleasures and levels of experience. Escalators and elevators (Jameson describes these as like air-borne gondolas) rise up and down but take you nowhere in particular. Balconies, shops, gardens, columns and gigantic hanging streamers make the interior of the hotel feel like a miniature, self-enclosed city. This is confirmed by the difficulty of finding your way in and by the fact that the building has a reflective glass skin. The effect of these glass walls for Jameson is that, like mirror shades which stop you from seeing people's eyes, they repel the surrounding city, confirming Jameson's view of the place as a little world complete in itself. Trying to make sense of this place, your senses are both stimulated and bewildered as you immerse yourself in a crowded yet superficial 'hyperspace'.

Jameson sees the Bonaventure as symbolic of postmodern times because of the way it mixes in a 'depthless' space many different, fleeting, 'overstimulating' images and experiences. Jameson finds that in this uncanny space you are literally swept along by corridors and lifts. The building seems able to take over, making you feel passive and complacent as you drift around trying to take it all in. You lose your sense of perspective and place. In the process of being sucked into the building's confusions and charms you lose, according to Jameson, all capacity for rationally distanced judgement. Everything becomes equal and weightless. In these ways the Bonaventure is taken to be symptomatic of the whole global postmodern experience.

Criticism of Jameson

Jameson defends grand, sweeping social theory against the postmodern faith in modest micropolitics and difference. But critics see the *metanarrative* he provides about the postmodern situation as far too all-embracing.

On the one hand Jameson suggests that postmodern conditions are too huge, complex and merged into everyday life for us to be able to fully comprehend them. On the other hand he reduces this complexity to a single all-powerful system which he thinks can explain everything. His own perspective is so monolithic that he ends up repeating the very flattening of cultural differences that he is out to condemn.

Out of this perspective, Jameson presents isolated objects (a hotel, an Andy Warhol painting) and assumes that you can simply read vast social systems off them. How is this possible?

What about the different meanings which those objects might have for people who have no interest in theories of post-modernism and late capitalism?

Linked to these criticisms is the idea that Jameson grants himself too much authority. He argues that under postmodern conditions 'we' have lost our sense of history, but the implication is that his own historical awareness has remained miraculously intact. Admittedly he does get lost in the Bonaventure, but he is able to give a detached (Marxist, deep down) critique of his experience. The rest of us have been mesmerized by the dazzling world of consumer capitalism but Jameson can stand above it all and see this world for what it really is. Where does he get this power from?

This arrogance comes from the belief that a single set of tools (in his case certain Marxist concepts) can be used to (a) explain everything and (b) draw up a template for collective human destiny.

Theorizing the city

The 'post-metropolis' described by Soja, Jameson and others does not come from nowhere. It is built on aspects of urban life which have been present since the early days of the modern city. To this degree the postmodern social situation amplifies rather than radically departs from conditions which have been in place for over one and a half centuries. Because of this, a lot of recent writing about the postmodern city intensifies themes originally developed by early theorists of modernity.

The beginnings of modern forms of society are usually found in the explosion of large-scale urban experience that took place in the middle of the nineteenth century, when over half of the population of England began to live in cities. This soon became the normal course of events as the process of modernization spread across the world. At the same time a number of writers found that the new city experience highlighted some of the ideas and questions about the self that philosophers had long been exploring. The modern city seemed to live out in concrete terms problems about the relationship between the individual and the collective, for example. With the growth of the city there was a new emphasis on the fragmentary and fluid nature of experience. And with the modern urban lifestyle, individuals (as we saw in Chapter 6) became more self-conscious about their way of life, more concerned about their social role, and more anxious about their place in the world.

Lyotard continues this theme. He draws inspiration for his ideas from the kinds of cosmopolitan experience offered by Jameson's world of global media, travel and corporations. In an often quoted passage, he writes with a mixture of excitement and disapproval that:

> *eclecticism is the degree zero of culture: one listens to reggae, watches a Western, eats McDonald's (sic) food for lunch and local cuisine for dinner, wears Paris perfume in Tokyo and retro clothes in Hong Kong; knowledge is a matter for TV games.*

The Postmodern Condition, page 76

It is worth remembering that Lyotard has grave doubts about this kind of mix-and-match approach to culture. As the reference to game shows indicates, he regrets that too often it can lead to complacency. Everything can become too easy, too flat, too wishy-washy. There is no room for struggle. (It is also interesting to note that part of this regret comes from his feeling that in this 'period of slackening' art no longer has a special status.)

One writer more enthusiastic about the kind of picture Lyotard paints is the British critic Iain Chambers. Unlike Fredric Jameson's image of the postmodern 'cultural dominant' as rather all-powerful and unchanging, Chambers' description of life in postmodern space emphasizes qualities like vibrancy, flux, experimentation and discontinuity. Chambers does not attempt to provide a complete map of this space and thinks that it would be impossible to do so (see the section on critical modesty below). But he explores in often exciting prose the many ways in which different pockets and levels of reality can overlap, intersect, (sometimes violently) conflict and rub shoulders with each other. In the following passage he continues the theme of cultural mixing that was touched on by Lyotard, but adds to it a concern with how different ethnic, racial and cultural groups can co-exist:

> *. . . many young black Britons of both sexes sport fashionable Italian track suits and, remixing the examples of New York B-Boys (and Girls) with Jamaican roots, reggae rhythms with rap anthems, dub with scratch, electronic grammar with British syntax, have transformed the multi-ethnic traditions of a once colonial and colonized subject into local and more immediate sense. It suggests a black integration,*

Iain Chambers *Border Dialogues; Journeys in Postmodernity(1990)* page 75

Local versus global culture

In our discussions of Soja and Jameson we noted that the new spaces of postmodernity feature a complicated interaction between universal and regional factors. On the one hand there is the continuing expansion of global markets for music, fashion and so on, coupled with the growth of boundary-crossing media and communications systems. On the other hand there is a heightened sensitivity to regional and particular issues of the kind championed by Lyotard and de Certeau. The apparent contradiction between these two aspects – which we can can perhaps translate as a dynamic tension between sameness and difference – can be seen as one of the defining features of the postmodern landscape and is explored below.

Shifting boundaries

Rather like Fredric Jameson, David Morley and Kevin Robins (in their book *Spaces of Identity*) suggest that global satellite and cable broadcasting systems have created a postmodern environment which has changed the shape of national, ethnic and cultural identities. Echoing Gilles Deleuze and Felix Guattari's idea of 'deterritorialization' (see Chapter 7), they argue that recent technologies of communication and transport have created new geographies based less on the physical boundaries of land and more on the flow of information and signs. In postmodernity, people, information, images and objects migrate around the globe. In the process they make it harder to define the limits of a community or a nation. National and even natural boundaries are still there, of course, but they do not even begin to tell the whole story. They are constantly over-ridden and undermined by 'spaces of transmission' with boundaries of their own. Thus the old categories of national, racial and cultural identity must be balanced by the greater 'symbolic boundaries of language and culture' provided by the mass media, global markets, computerization and the rest.

Morley and Robins argue that although these new geographies have brought about a crisis in the idea of the nation they have at the same time created a new awareness of regional locations and activities. For example, there has been a growth of local and specialist radio stations as the airwaves have become progressively more deregulated. On one level the entertainment industries are controlled by a shrinking number of multinational companies (film production and distribution is a good example of this monopolization). On another level, the media are expected to maximize consumer choice. Again, the spread of the Internet over an ever wider area and into ever more homes and institutions has similarly created a mind-boggling range of special-interest websites. Finally, a television channel broadcasts the same programme to millions of sets at once, but that programme will be seen in many different kinds of places by many different kinds of people and in many different kinds of ways. In all of these cases what we see is a complex combination of global 'virtual communities' and small-scale concerns.

Non-places

The French anthropologist Marc Augé has argued that we are living in a 'supermodern' society increasingly dominated by what he calls 'non-places.' For example, we spend more and more of our time in hypermarkets, out-of-town leisure complexes, motorway service stations, departure lounges . . . More and more of our everyday transactions take place over the phone, listening to a digital voice, at a computer . . . We are 'born in the clinic and die in hospital'.

Once (Augé's time scale is rather vague) there was an organic, creative link between places and their occupants. Places were formed by peoples' lives in them, and were lived according to local knowledges and customs. They were therefore rich with cultural memory. They were, as Augé puts it, 'encrusted with history.' Our experiences of places now come prepackaged and mediated by a 'proliferation of imagined and imaginary references': in France, for instance, road signs tell drivers they are 'entering the Beaujolais region' (in Britain there is 'Hardy Country' and 'Bronte Country'). Floodlit monuments and listed areas turn places into museums. Information panels guide visitors to 'places of interest' and point out designated 'city walks'. In tourists' brochures, places become scenery and history becomes image.

An old town or village may have a monument in its market square, perhaps symbolizing a community held together through the 'indigenous fantasy' of a closed world 'founded once and for all long ago.' Non-places, by contrast, are centreless and have no contours or frontiers. A place is where people belong. A non-place is something you pass: 'motorway travel . . . avoids all the principle places to which it takes us.' When you phone a call centre about train times you can be talking to an operative on another continent. High-street stores are identical from city to city. Exotic and out of season produce is available throughout the year in temperature controlled western supermarkets. The world becomes both smaller and more complex through satellite TV, the Internet and global transit. Traditionally, a town centre comes to life at intervals: markets appear on specific appointed days; shops open only at certain times. Non-places do not demarcate time in this way: they are 24/7.

'Particularities,' says Augé, are eroded by all of this: there is a loss of place, community and 'reference points for collective identification' that produces new kinds of solitude. This in turn can give rise to nostalgia, nationalism or conflict as people seek their mother country of land and roots.

Yet place can't be destroyed completely. Inspired by Michel de Certeau's idea that ordinary people 'invent the everyday' through spontaneous 'tricks in the art of doing' (see above), Augé notes that people 'deflect global/urban modernity through everyday tinkering.' They clear spaces for themselves within a homogenized culture by tracing personal routes and establishing their own décor. The customization of urban spaces by skateboarders or graffiti artists could be seen as examples of this improvized creation of a meaningful local place.

Further reading

Non-places: Introduction to an anthropology of supermodernity by Marc Augé (1995)

The Production of Space by Henri Lefebvre (1991)

Further reading on postmodern space

Space and Social Theory: Interpreting modernity and post-modernity, edited by Georges Benko (1997)

The Spaces of Postmodernity: Readings in human geography, by Michael J. Dear and Steven Flusty (2002)

City of Quartz, by Mike Davis (1998)

Magical Urbanism, by Mike Davis (2000)

Postmodern Urbanism, by Nan Ellin (1995)

Globalized identities

The American critic George Lipsitz has touched on similar themes. He has agreed that social changes of the kind outlined by Soja, Jameson, Morley and Robins have changed identities and culture. But he argues that these changes have to be measured against the many continuing forms of oppression and inequality to which many people are still subjected. The late capitalist world of mass consumption, computers and multi-national communications can hardly be said to affect everybody equally.

Lipsitz has looked at how hip-hop and rap music have taken root in many different countries across the world. Originally rising from the ghettoes of North America, they are now listened to the world over. As Lipsitz says, it as though the whole world is listening to what happens in the South Bronx. Lipsitz contends that African cultures have historically been dispersed by the movement of low-wage black labourers from country to country; it is through the production, distribution and consumption of popular music that ethnic and cultural identity can be restored and expressed. Thus a form of music with its source in a very specific region has become the basis of an imaginary global community that crosses national boundaries. Moreover, it is a form of music that plunders from and mixes together a whole range of influences. For instance, many rhythms and samples can be taken from the history of black music (e.g. jazz, soul, funk) and combined with bits and pieces borrowed from mainstream white culture (e.g. news broadcasts, film soundtracks).

For Lipsitz, such acts of *bricolage* and *appropriation* have a critical edge. 'White' appropriation from Afro-American music, meanwhile, is seen as an oppressive act, a colonization of its true meanings.

A criticism of Lipsitz

Paul Gilroy has criticized Lipsitz's optimistic view for implying that particular kinds of music intrinsically belong to particular ethnic groups. In the first place, you need to take into account the fact that hip-hop can be listened to by white middle-class schoolchildren in rural areas as well as by disadvantaged black youths in the inner cities. In other words you cannot expect any form of music to stay within the boundaries of a single identifiable audience. In the second place one of the points of sampling, scratching and re-mixing is to undermine the idea that culture is the property of a single group. Finally, Gilroy argues that seeing hip-hop and rap as authentic forms of racial expression denies the fluid and contradictory character of identity by implying that a certain kind of outlook or experience is fundamentally and essentially 'black'. The postmodern world is multi-cultural, interracial and eclectic: in such a world identities and lifestyles can, like contemporary black music itself, be collages of many different influences. They are far too fragmentary and fleeting to permit any appeal to an underlying ethnic nature.

Post-coloniality

One of the most important facts about the postmodern geography outlined by Lyotard, Soja and others is that the world is becoming 'post-colonial'. What this means is that the political map of imperialism and colonization across the world is in the process of being redrawn. While it would be a serious exaggeration to suggest that the world has now got over colonialism (Native Americans, to take just one example, would dispute the idea: post-colonialism cannot mean the same thing for everybody), it is safe to say that the world has recently witnessed the meltdown of empires. The progressive shrinking and weakening of the British Empire is a good example of this. In other cases the idea of the post-colonial situation has more to do with the fact that across the world people seem to be becoming more migrant. Thus the notion that the world is witnessing post-colonial times suggests that important changes are taking place on an international scale in political, economic and social areas. The postmodern spaces described by Soja, Jameson and Chambers are part of these changes: they are physical or imaginary sites in which different voices converge, and can be seen as post-colonial in the sense that they seem to erode the rigid boundaries of nationality and race.

The idea of the post-colonial also refers to the theory and in some cases the practice of marginal voices getting a say in representation. This version of post-colonialism is about how the arts and media can and should respond to life in an interracial, multi-ethnic world. Thinkers often classed as post-colonial in this sense include Edward Said, Homi Bhabha and Gayatri Spivak. We cannot do justice to their work in the space available, but we can note their main concerns in a general way.

Who speaks?

You may have noticed that in this book I have had a tendency to use plurals in apparently unusual places. I have written at various points of knowledges, histories, and sexualities. This may seem an annoying grammatical quirk on my part (it is a usage not recognized by the spell-check on my word processor), but it follows the practice of many theorists influenced by the terms of postmodernism. We have seen throughout this book a general sensitivity within postmodernism to the issue of difference. The desire to speak in the plural of things which once seemed perfectly happy to be singular is part of this concern to preserve diversity at all costs. To speak of sexualities, for example, is to recognize that not all sexuality expresses the same thing or arises from the same impulse. Feminist and post-feminist critics, among others, have argued that the universal desire or urge implied by generalized talk of sexuality is actually a male heterosexual idea. Or again, to speak of history is to deny that what passes as an objective or 'true' account of historical events might be open to different interpretations by groups with different interests. It implies that you have access to the only correct version. By referring to multiple histories, you suggest that no single overview can do justice to the full complexity of historical events and their effects, and you raise the question of whose history is being told. Speaking in the plural in this way acknowledges that diverse perspectives and experiences always exist to disrupt metanarratives.

This is just one of the effects that the growing awareness of diversity has had within the humanities. It can be seen as part of a general sense of caution which postmodernism has brought to the study of culture and society. One major concern has been to ask of any act of representation: Who is being allowed to speak in this representation, for whom, and to what end? Who 'hears' it and who is excluded from it?

Critics informed by the 'posts' argue that it is better not to speak on behalf of oppressed, under-privileged or marginalized people. All groups should have access to self-representation. Speaking for others is a form of 'grammatical violence', as Lyotard would say, which invests 'them' with your own values. This brings us to the next point.

Sensitivity to centrisms

Back in the early 1980s a group of musicians in the UK released a hit charity record in aid of famine relief called 'Do They Know it's Christmas?' Its lyric tugged on the nation's heartstrings by pointing out that starving children in Ethiopia would not be sampling the joys of the festive season that year. However, Great Britain could become Santa Claus by buying the records and delivering to Africa the 'greatest gift they'll get this year [which] is life'. The problem with this idea is that there was no reason why the starving in Ethiopia *should* have known that it was Christmas time at all. Christmas as we know it is hardly a universal idea; many of its traditions are European and of quite recent origin, a large proportion of the world's religions do not recognize it and even in countries that do celebrate it there is a great diversity of customs. Thus the question raised by the title of the song was entirely European in origin. In other words it was Eurocentric. Similar cases of Eurocentrism can be found in many ideas about 'primitive' as opposed to 'civilized' cultures, and in exotic portrayals of 'the orient' as a mysterious land full of eastern promise. The way the globe is often divided into first, second and third 'worlds' works in much the same way: in what sense do Ethiopians living in Ethiopia feel themselves to be living in the 'third world'?

You may remember from our discussion of Jacques Derrida in Chapter 5 that postmodern theory is always on its guard against centres. This concern is sometimes reflected by the desire to uncover various centrisms of the kind noted above. So post-colonial critics look for evidence of Eurocentrism in the media and literature. Others look for the hidden signs of 'phallocentrism' (having a 'masculine' bias), 'heterocentrism' (having a heterosexual bias) and any number of other 'centrisms' in seemingly innocent texts.

Postcolonial Studies, by Bill Ashcroft et al. (2000)

Islam, Globalization and Postmodernity, edited by Akbar S. Ahmed (1994)

Postcolonial Theory, by Leela Gandhi (1998)

Colonialism/postcolonialism, by Ania Loomba (1998)

Beginning Postcolonialism, by John McLeod (2000)

A Companion to Postcolonial Studies, by Ray Sangeeta (2002)

Critical modesty

As a result of the above influences, and many other of the postmodern issues outlined in this book, critics often now make value judgement much more tentatively. The British sociologist Zygmunt Bauman has called this a change in the role of intellectuals from 'legislators' to 'interpreters'. What he means is that academics are becoming reluctant to put forward moral or aesthetic distinctions between 'good' and 'bad'. My own use of inverted commas around these words echoes this sense of caution.

Intellectuals begin to renounce their own authority. Instead of trying to lead us to how things *should be* (as though, superior to the rest of us, they know what is good for us) they are now more inclined to spend their time modestly probing the way things *seem* to be. In postmodernism, we become so aware of the existence of other difference – and of the historically and socially limited nature of our own – that treading carefully increasingly appears to be crucial.

Through the work of Lyotard, Derrida and many others we learn to forget the idea of universal values. As old certainties start to crumble, there is a tendency to feel that all views are equally valid. With the fall of the grand metanarratives (Lyotard) more attention is paid to the 'little narratives' of regional issues and everyday life. The commonplace is converted into culture. There arrives a cloud of relativism and a flurry of deliberately 'weak thought'. This last phrase belongs to the Italian philosopher Gianni Vattimo. Partly recalling the writings of Jean Baudrillard, he argues that the age of mass communications produces such an 'apparently irresistible pluralization' that we have been released from the shackles of once authoritative principles of reality. As Baudrillard himself has argued, the media are so saturated with information, and with so many different voices demanding to be heard, that it is no longer possible to know what you either know or want any more. In postmodernism, value systems and identities become so multiple and so tenuous that a humble, more open approach to philosophy is necessary which lets go of whatever hold it once thought it had on the truth.

Does postmodernism mean not believing in anything? Some problems of cultural relativism

Because of these and other debates, postmodernism can be seen as a *relativist* trend: in other words, it emphasizes the culturally particular over the 'universal'. All values are created by, and are only relevant to, particular circumstances (e.g. your culture). This forces us to recognize that our ideas and observations are not impartial; we always speak from a particular position. There is, for example, no global agreement about what constitutes justice; there are many definitions, and each makes sense only in relation to the specific *language game* in it is embedded. A modernist might ask: 'is this good?' But a postmodernist might ask 'who/what is it good *for*?'

The implication seems to be that everyone's ideas and values are equally valid. Hence there is no reason to suppose that 'Western' or 'Enlightenment' beliefs should hold sway over any other possible world-view. 'We' have no moral high ground from which to criticize 'their' actions. Nor are 'their' views any more valid than 'ours'. We will never (and nor should we, because it could only be achieved by coercion) arrive at universally agreed norms. For Lyotard society can never be an organic whole: it is a mesh of *incommensurable* languages. So the ideal of shared standards is put aside in favour of *pluralism*. But the questions generated by this position are not easily answered:

Lyotard and others seem to celebrate difference, but what are the limits of tolerance?

How do you ensure that plurality is maintained? What do you do about regimes that don't share your relativist position?

Can you stand up for your values – can you argue against something – without believing that you are in some sense absolutely 'right'? Since I must think there are good reasons for holding the views I do, it surely isn't possible to be a pluralist all the time.

Postmodernism aims at preserving the maximum number of competing value systems: Lyotard calls this 'the possibility of continuing to play the game of the just'. So it would seem to offer a liberating, democratic vision. But is fragmentation and diversity always beneficial? Doesn't oppression thrive on the principle of 'divide and conquer'?

Some responses

Finding that postmodernism lacks positive answers to these questions, critics have argued that relativism is a dead end. For them (e.g David Harvey, Terry Eagleton, Alex Callinicos) it unhelpfully implies that tolerating oppression and exploitation is better than 'imposing' your own values. Making any concept of justice appear problematic, it can't tell us why one culture should bother to challenge the tyrannical practices of another. This argument sees postmodernism's relativization of all truth claims as inhibiting rather than liberating: it becomes impossible to make moral or aesthetic evaluations. Worse than that, it is a luxury of the privileged – while postmodernists get excited about the loss of stability and certainty, many disempowered people are desperate for those very things.

But it has often been pointed out that value judgements are unavoidable: Lyotard's declaration of 'war on totality' is a moral imperative. In her book *Contingencies of Value* (1988) the *pragmatist* thinker Barbara Herrnstein Smith argues that taking a relativist view does not remove your capacity for ethical decision-making. She lists your 'memory, imagination, early training and example, conditioned loyalties, instinctive sympathies and antipathies' as factors that enable you to take 'moral action'.

David Harvey meanwhile suggests that postmodernists embarrassedly hide the fact that even they cannot dodge the idea of universal values. The difficulty lies in how to marry such values to respect for diversity. Societies have somehow to reconcile necessary 'principles of exclusion' (not all points of view can be tolerated) with the recognition of difference and dissent. Some kind of global agreement about the principles of social justice are desirable, but these have to be arrived at in a way that avoids *Enlightenment*/modernist illusions of *essentialism*. We have to position ourselves, says Harvey, between 'absolutism' and 'anything goes'.

Kate Soper has suggested in a similar vein that rejecting the idea of grand truth does not mean abandoning the more pragmatic idea of agreed standards. She suggests that shared, inclusive systems of representation have to be created in order to realize diversity and open-ended dialogue.

Further reading

Situating the Self, by Seyla Benhabib (1992)

The Idea of Culture, by Terry Eagleton (2000)

Uncritical Theory, by Christopher Norris (1992)

Principled Positions: Postmodernism and the recovery of value, edited by Judith Squires (1993)

From the centre to the margin

Postmodern and/or post-colonial theory seeks to free up the means of representation for of those 'others' normally pushed to the edges of mainstream cultural expression. In doing so it aims to shatter all 'centric' accounts of history, culture and society and to open up an infinitely more plural, inclusive mixture of world views.

Part of this project involves studying texts which capture something of the deterritorialised nature of postmodern geography. Salman Rushdie's *The Satanic Verses* (first published in 1988) has been read in this light by Gayatri Spivak. She sees it as a telling portrait of the postmodern feeling of fractured and plural cultural identity. In its uneasy mixture of Eastern and Western traditions Rushdie's novel contains an unresolvable tension between the author's experience of a migrant, hybrid way of life and his sense of belonging to a specific nationality. The feeling of openness, liberty and boundary-blurring which can, as we have seen, be offered by the new postmodern spaces of supersonic travel, migration and media is accompanied by a contradictory sensitivity to the edges between different cultures. Again, there is the sense that in the postmodern world we live on the sometimes jarring, sometimes merging borders between the global and the local, the fluid and the fixed, the old and the new.

Spivak also noted that it was now impossible not to read *The Satanic Verses* in the light of the fatwa issued by the Ayatollah Khomeini in 1989. The novel had become entwined in the sometimes violent disputes and protests that have surrounded it. Many Muslims felt that Rushdie's supposedly postmodern mixing of fact and fiction and east and west, was part of a blasphemous conspiracy against Islam: it brought cultural plurality and mixing into what some saw as the decidedly *un*mixed historical truth and integrity of the prophet Muhammad's revelation. Rushdie's aim had been to express the doubt that characterizes life in our times as we become ever more aware of different people's histories, views and needs. The problem was that for some Muslims such a state of uncertainty did not apply to their system of beliefs. With the issue of the fatwa and the subsequent conflicts surrounding it, *The Satanic Verses* was arguably both an expression and a victim of post-colonial insecurity.

The fact that such insecurity was thought by some not to apply to their faith raises awkward questions:

- Does anybody have the right to criticize other people's beliefs?
- Do postmodernists have the right to urge other people to embrace *their* beliefs?
- Can postmodernism tell us anything useful about the experiences of people whose world view is *not* as hybrid and cosmopolitan as that of postmodern theorists?
- If postmodernism is a 'global' social condition, does it affect all people in the same way?

In short, it expresses what is perhaps the fundamental (and impossible to resolve) concern of postmodernism – the difficulty of living with difference.

Postscript

It has been suggested that the greatest virtue of the term 'postmodernism' is its lack of precision. Although it has been around for a long time, it still refuses to settle into a single meaning. As we have seen, one of postmodernism's recurring themes is this very instability of meaning: meanings, it is argued, are never unified; they are at all levels disrupted by difference. To this extent we might say that postmodernism practices what it preaches. In doing so it allows ideas to stay mobile, constantly re-inventing themselves and adjusting to changing circumstances. Because it is about finding new ways of describing the world, we can regard it (as Habermas said of modernity) as unfinished. It can be seen as an ongoing project to find new ways of looking at new times.

So it is difficult to write a conclusive conclusion for this book. Because so many of the topics we have addressed remain open-ended, there is no simple way of closing the case. Theorists like Derrida, Lyotard and the rest would at any rate suggest that this is how it should be, and would resist the idea that their work can be summarized in one easy package. Nevertheless, that is what I have tried to do.

Certain matters are, of course, no longer 'hot'. *Pluralism* in the art-world, for example, is rarely debated today. Similarly, the 'blurred' distinction between high and low culture now seems normal rather than novel. Indeed, thanks to postmodernism, terms like 'high culture' are now difficult to use without irony. So these are not signs that postmodernist conditions have disappeared. On the contrary, it may be that we are now more thoroughly 'in' postmodernism than ever. Seen in this light, the debates of the 1970s and 1980s seem like a period of transition: changes were observed and were often resisted; 'modernists' clung to ideas declared obsolete by 'postmodernists'. The dust generated by these scraps has now settled. 'Postmodernism' may no longer be the most fashionable name for our times, but nothing has yet replaced it. It may even be that the 'incredulity towards *metanarratives*' described by Lyotard is now so widespread that finding one name for 'our times' (whose times?) seems an impossible task.

Yet many of the problems and conditions postmodernism identifies are likely to persist. In some cases they will intensify. The conflict between local and global cultures and the issues of cultural difference now seem more urgent than ever. Information technology and the 'mediascape', observed by commentators like Baudrillard and Jameson, continue to expand. New ways of *commodifying* our lives are constantly being discovered in ways thinkers like Guy Debord could never have anticipated. Developments in genetic science and artificial intelligence ensure the relevance of postmodernist debates about the limits and nature of the self. You can easily add to this short list.

I therefore believe that claims to have reached the 'end' of postmodernism are not only premature, but distract attention from some of the important challenges it lays down.

I hope I have given you a taste of how the term postmodernism, however slippery and contradictory it might be, offers a way into debates about contemporary societies, cultures and lifestyles. I also hope that you now feel able to tackle them head-on by reading directly some of the theorists we have discussed.

If you have read this book, you'll know that a chronology of postmodernism should be taken with a large pinch of salt. History bears little resemblance to an orderly timetable. Past events that seem important now may have seemed insignificant in their day. Two things sharing a date aren't necessarily connected. Although I therefore present the following chronology with tongue partly in cheek, it may be still be useful to have an 'at a glance' guide to some milestones. Because it reflects the scope of this book, there are huge gaps in it; filling them for your self might create new maps of the field.

1807   The invention of the 'camera lucida', an ancestor of the camera, makes it easy to trace from real life.

1826   Niépce makes a photograph on a pewter plate.

1863   Charles Baudelaire, in 'The Painter of Modern Life', calls for an art which records the transience of modern experience.

   A fax message is sent by 'typotelegraph' between London and Liverpool.

1867   Karl Marx, *Capital* Volume 1.

1875   Edison's phonograph.

1876   Bell invents the telephone.

1880   Newspapers print photographs for the first time.

1886   In *Thus Spake Zarathustra* Friedrich Nietzsche declares that 'God is dead'.

1888   The snapshot is born when Kodak introduces the box camera.

1895	The first paying audience for the projection of a film.
1900	Sigmund Freud, *The Interpretation of Dreams.*
1901	First wireless communication between Europe and the USA.
1907	Pablo Picasso paints *Les Demoiselles d'Avignon* (cubism is said to 'begin' a year later). The experience of modernity is pictured as fragmented; rational renaissance perspective is broken down.
	The first photocopier is marketed.
1913	Igor Stravinsky, *The Rite of Spring.*
	Bakelite records replace cylinder recordings.
	Einstein, *General Theory of Relativity.*
1916	Ferdinand de Saussure's *Course in General Linguistics* founds structuralism and semiotics.
1917	Marcel Duchamp's *Fountain*, a 'readymade' urinal signed 'R. Mutt', is rejected from the first exhibition of the American Society of Independent Artists. Is the readymade a modernist, anti-modernist or proto-postmodernist gesture?
1919	The Bauhaus school is founded in Germany: Walter Gropius, Mies van der Rohe and others develop ideas about a rational new architecture which would declare its functionality and be stripped down to 'essentials'.
1922	James Joyce's *Ulysses* experiments radically with language and style.
1923	Kodak markets the first home movie equipment.
1925	*Battleship Potemkin,* directed by Sergei Eisenstein, makes leaps in the art of film montage.
1936	Walter Benjamin, 'The Work of Art in the Age of Mechanical Reproduction'.
1945	Atomic bomb dropped on Hiroshima.
1946	T. W. Adorno and M. Horkheimer, *Dialectic of Enlightenment.*
1947	The beginning of the large-scale decolonization of the British Empire.

1954 Arnold Toynbee describes a 'post-modern' civilization characterized by irrationality, contradiction and technological dominance.

1959 New York sociologist C. Wright Mills refers to a 'post-modern period' in which conformity and consumerism have begun to replace the Modern Age of liberal ideals.

Irving Howe's "Mass Society and Post-Modern Fiction" (in the journal *Partisan Review*) argues that 'mass society' has undermined the intelligence and courage of modernist literature.

1960 Daniel Bell, in *The End of Ideology*, notes that the prosperous West has moved beyond the industrial phase of capitalism, and that in the age of consumerism class conflict is effectively over. His analysis will go on to inform Jean Baudrillard and Francis Fukuyama.

1962 The first computer game: 'Space War'.

Thomas Kuhn, *The Structure of Scientific Revolutions*.

Marshall McLuhan, *The Gutenberg Galaxy*.

1965 Leslie Fiedler's essay 'The New mutants' (*Partisan Review*) celebrates a genre-hopping new 'postmodern literature' based on hallucinogenic drugs, civil rights and drop-out culture.

1966 Michel Foucault, *The Order of Things*.

Jacques Lacan, *Écrits*.

1967 Jacques Derrida, *Of Grammatology*.

1967 The May *événements* upset the Parisian bourgeoisie, as students, workers and situationists take over the streets and try to revolutionize everyday life. It all amounts to nothing, and an air of disillusionment descends on the French intellectual scene. Lyotard and Baudrillard never recover.

1968 Robert Venturi *Complexity and Contradiction in Architecture*.

1969 Man lands on the moon.

The American Advanced Research Project Agency goes online (ARPANet): the beginnings of the Internet.

1971 Ihab Hassan *The Dismemberments of Orpheus: Towards a postmodern literature.*

The first word processor is introduced.

1972 In *Anti-Oedipus,* Deleuze and Guattari observe that 'a schizophrenic out for a walk is a better model than a neurotic lying on the analyst's couch'.

'Pong' is the first home video game.

Sony markets Betamax, the first videotape system for domestic use. New ways of viewing are born.

The prize winning modernist Pruitt-Igoe housing development, in St. Louis, Missouri is demolished. According to Charles Jencks this signals the death of modern architecture.

1974 Paul Feyerabend, *Against Method.* A relativist view of science, arguing that no truth is disinterested.

Roland Barthes, *Image – Music – Text.*

1975 Charles Jencks, *The Language of Post-Modern Architecture.*

Ernest Mandel, *Late Capitalism.*

1976 Benoit Mandelbrot, *The Fractal Geometry of Nature.* Constructs a model of geometry based on fragmentation, randomness, infinite division and repetition. Lyotard will describe Mandelbrot as a postmodern scientist.

1979 Jean-Francois Lyotard, *The Postmodern Condition: A report on knowledge.*

First tests of the cellular phone.

The Sony Walkman enters the market.

Dance music based on scratching and mixing other people's records becomes popular.

1980 In Frankfurt, Jurgen Habermas delivers his lecture *Modernity – An Incomplete Project.* Condemns the 'conservatism' of postmodernists (especially Lyotard). The enlightenment project needs to be revived to heal the fragmentation of knowledge under late capitalism. Communication and agreement among language games is both possible and desirable.

CNN brings 24-hour news to the world.

1981 MTV goes out on cable television 24 hours a day.

1982 *Bladerunner*, directed by Ridley Scott. Its view of the city is to become one of the icons of postmodernism.

Boston Institute of Arts 'Endgame' exhibition popularises 'simulation' art and 'commodity art'.

Richard Rorty, *The Consequences of Pragmatism*. Philosophy might as well give up looking for universal principles of reality, goodness or truth. What's useful is more important than what's 'true.'

Jean Baudrillard, *Simulations*.

CDs go on sale.

1983 William Gibson, *Neuromancer*.

Fredric Jameson's essay 'Postmodernism, or, the Cultural Logic of Late Capitalism' is published in *New Left Review*. Eventually to be expanded into a mammoth tome.

Museum of Modern Art New York: exhibition of 'Deconstructivist Architecture'.

Umberto Eco, *The Name of the Rose*.

The CD-Rom is introduced. Ever larger amounts of information are available in ever smaller spaces. Some 'interactivity' is possible.

Musical Instrument Digital Interface (MIDI) means any sound can be captured in digital code. Sampling in music gains in sophistication.

1986 David Lynch directs *Blue Velvet*.

Digital AudioTape (DAT) is marketed.

1989 The demolition of the Berlin Wall symbolizes the collapse of communism. Millions of people rejoice (Francis Fukuyama among them). Seems to confirm Daniel Bell's idea that we have reached the 'end of ideology.'

Salman Rushdie's *The Satanic Verses* angers many Muslims. In a political move, the Ayatollah Khomeini issues a *fatwa* on Rushdie. A troubling issue for cultural relativists.

The disposable camera arrives.

1991   CNN brings the world the Gulf War as it happens.

Jean Baudrillard argues that the Gulf war did not take place ('La Guerre du Golfe n'a pas eu lieu', *Libération* 29 March 1991).

1992   Francis Fukuyama, *The End of History and the Last Man.*

Text based browser opens up the World Wide Web for general use. A democratization of information? Proliferation of virtual communities. General excitement about 'hypertext': a newly non-linear, *rhizomatic* way of reading.

1997   Following the death of Diana, Princess of Wales, Elton John's revised version of 'Candle in the Wind' sells millions. The more mourning is shown on TV, the more people go to the streets of London to mourn. Conspiracy theories fairly quickly spread on the Internet.

2000   Like the millenium bug, the new millenium doesn't really happen – as Baudrillard pointed out, we had already been living 'the end' for years.

2001   Terrorist attack on the World Trade Centre, New York. Conspiracy theories proliferate almost instantly on the Internet. Fukuyama admits that history hasn't ended after all (yet).

glossary

What follows is intended to supplement the main text; I have tried to make it more useful and interesting than a simple list. I have included a few terms that don't appear elsewhere in this book, but that you may come across if you pursue post-modernism further.

anomie Postmodernity is sometimes seen (by those opposed to it) as a time of anomie – in other words, a period of social instability in which shared values and standards have disintegrated.

appropriation Taking possession of something, or taking something over, without permission. Seen as a key strategy of postmodernist arts, sometimes as a symptom of the end of 'originality'. In the 1980s a number of influential American artists became famous for re-presenting (photographing, copying) already existing images. In popular music sampling may be seen as a form of appropriation. There is a 'politics' to this activity: subcultures appropriate images from 'mainstream' culture and in doing so are said to subvert their meanings. On the other hand, one culture can be criticized for appropriating from another (e.g. popular music borrowing 'global' sounds, fashion borrowing 'ethnic' designs). It can be difficult to distinguish appropriation from quotation, *pastiche* and other forms of *intertextuality*.

bricolage This term was used by the structural anthropologist Claude Lévi-Strauss to describe the everyday creativity of improvising with materials that are close to hand. It means making do with available resources, and in the process changing their function (e.g. using a book to steady a wobbly table). Languages develop unpredictably through the activity of bricolage: words constantly gain new meanings through being 'customized' by their users and applied in new situations.

code Loosely, the conventions which enable *signs* to be organized into meaningful systems. In order to be meaningful any *text* must have an audience familiar with its conventions. Practices like *parody, metafiction* and *eclecticism* depend on an awareness of codes. Postmodernist artworks often display self-consciousness about their own 'codedness', and poststructuralists stress the idea that codes are dynamic rather than static. Things start to get complicated when you realize that different audiences can bring different codes to the same text, yet find it equally meaningful. There has therefore been debate about whether reading a text is a process of 'decoding' (i.e. interpreting the codes to get at its meanings) or 'encoding' (i.e. reading your own cultural codes into to it). Thinking about questions like this often leads to ideas like *relativism* and *polysemy*.

commodification Many commentators, from both 'for' and 'against' positions, observe that contemporary society is increasingly surrendered to the logic of the marketplace. In late capitalism everything becomes an object (or sign) to be bought and sold: commercial/commodity value is the only value that counts. Sometimes this is seen as the basis of postmodern *anomie*. Some critical theorists argue that postmodern art forms merely accept, rather than resist, the victory of commodification.

cyborg A mixture of machine and body. Its *hybrid* nature makes the cyborg a model of postmodern identity. Though it seems merely a future possibility, it has often been argued that we already live as cyborgs. This is implied by some of Marshall McLuhan's writing of the 1960s, and is developed by more recent thinking on new technologies. The cyborg is an appealing figure for postmodernists because it questions such oppositions as human/non-human, natural/unnatural, organic/technological, self/other. While thinkers like Donna Haraway (*Symians, Cyborgs and Women*, 1991) embrace the cyborg, many science fiction films suggest that the possibility of cybernetic identity is something to be afraid of.

deconstruction Associated with the work of Jacques Derrida, deconstruction is a method of reading which effectively turns *texts* against themselves in order to reveal their repressed *polysemy*. It involves looking for moments when a text's rhetorical strategies (i.e. the language it uses, the way it's constructed) contradict what the author claims to be saying. It teases out the *multivalency* of specific words; looks for absences (what the author doesn't say); hunts down hidden hierarchies; examines what the text pushes to the margins (e.g. into footnotes); shows the text to be woven from strands which are at cross purposes with one another. Critics of deconstruction see it as little more than an academic word-game, and claim that it has nothing useful to say about the texts it looks at. However, Derrida's methods – and the philosophy behind them – have influenced *postcolonial* criticism (e.g. Gayatri Chakravorty Spivak) and some feminists (e.g. Judith Butler). It is not just another word for analysis.

deconstructivism   A movement in architecture supposed to be influenced by Jacques Derrida. Mixes hi-tech materials and methods with postmodernist *pluralism* and a collage-like sense of design.

différance   Jacques Derrida coined this term but noted that it 'is neither a word nor a concept'. Language is a system of differences in which *signs* mean only in relation to each other. Because signs therefore always contain traces of other signs, they have no 'essential' meaning of their own. Looking a word up in a dictionary leads to other words that you need to look up; we are always presented with further signs. So meaning is forever deferred. At the same time any sign is meaningful only through differentiation (red means 'stop' because green means 'go'). So différance refers both to the passive state of being different and the activity of 'producing differences'.

discourse   This term has many different meanings, but can be defined as a way of using language that, however unconsciously, embodies a particular (historically and culturally specific) set of beliefs or concerns. In semiotics and poststructuralism it refers to the way ideas and meanings circulate across many *texts*. The work of Michel Foucault examines complex relationships between discourses, institutions and social practices (e.g. discourses of criminology, penal institutions and practices of discipline). In Foucault's sense, discourse is a 'regime' or domain of language inseparable from the social 'formations' that organize and use it. Also from Foucault comes the term 'reverse discourse'. This is the practice of an oppressed group *appropriating* oppressive language for itself (the word 'queer' is a well known example). Postmodernists are particularly interested in how we 'live' the discourses that define us (e.g. discourses of class, race, nationality, gender etc.), and in how those discourses might contradict each other.

double coding   Charles Jencks' term for the stylistic *pluralism* of postmodernist architecture. Double coded buildings combine contemporary techniques with traditional building styles, and can therefore communicate both to the general public and to architectural 'experts' (which is not to say that everybody likes them). They are not simply old fashioned or 'retro'; they do not reject modernism, but put it into dialogue with other possibilities. Architectural styles are in this way *relativized* and put under *erasure*. Many other art forms use codes in a similarly *hybrid* way to address different audiences (e.g. David Lynch's 2001 film *Mullholland Drive* combines film noir and mystery codes with avant-garde techniques; the 1970s music of Miles Davis mixes together James Brown's funk, Duke Ellington's jazz and Karlheinz Stockhausen's avant-garde experimentation). Jencks sees this as an anti-elitist, inclusive approach. His description of architecture in terms of codes and communication reflects the influence of *semiotics,* and echoes postmodernism's general preoccupation with *textuality*. Sometimes the phrase 'plural coding' is preferred.

eclecticism Collecting themes, styles, ideas etc. from various sources. While it could be argued that all creative acts are eclectic, the postmodernist 'period' is generally regarded as explicitly, self-consciously, so. Technologies from print to television to the Internet have made available a vast (and ever expanding) pool of resources from which to draw. This is sometimes regarded as a rather passive practice (eclectics can appear to have no ideas of their own and seem to see everything as equally valid). On the other hand it can be seen as a deliberate affront to notions of good aesthetic sensibility, a refusal to accept hierarchies of taste and value. In the 1970s and '80s, the merits of eclecticism (e.g. in architecture) were much debated, but it is now so normal that it longer seems an issue.

enlightenment As used in postmodern theory, the Enlightenment was a project that began in eighteenth-century Europe. Sometimes used as another word for 'modernity', it was a progressive movement involving the belief that science, rational enquiry and open debate can free humanity from oppression and fear. It aims to control nature, organize society and lead to the moral improvement of 'mankind'. But it has a dark side. Postmodernists (e.g. Lyotard) see it as an oppressive *metanarrative,* because its faith in universals (humanity, truth, progress, history) denies cultural *pluralism* and difference. The Enlightenment dream of a utopia based on rationality turns into the nightmare of totalitarianism (e.g social engineering).

erasure Jacques Derrida's *deconstruction* often puts ideas 'under erasure' – in some of his texts words are even printed with lines crossing them out. Like a stronger version of using inverted commas to signal irony, it involves using a concept for strategic purposes without committing yourself to all of its meanings. As a philosopher, Derrida has to use the language of philosophy: stating that it is used 'under erasure' is his way of saying that it has to be *deconstructed.*

essentialism The belief that a thing has inherent characteristics or a fundamental nature. Postmodernism is anti-essentialist because it stresses the cultural over the natural, surface over depth, and difference over sameness (these are all binary oppositions which postmodernism deconstructs).

hybridity The condition of being composed of different elements. Postmodernity can be seen as the experience of hybridity: hybrid identities (e.g. the crossing of human/machine); hybrid cultures; hybrid art forms. Hybrids are always uncertain – they have no *essence.*

hyperreality Not to be confused with 'unreality', this is Jean Baudrillard's term for *signs* that seem more real than reality. Images in advertising are often hyperreal: they seem to magnify and improve on reality (e.g. the beads of condensation on a bottle of cola) while at the same time leaving it behind (bottles of cola never look that good). This paradoxical condition doesn't stop them having real effects (I feel thirsty). The use of computer aided design has increased this quality. An image may be hyperreal when it refers to other images that are part of our (real) experience (e.g. *Pulp Fiction* is hyperreal when its sense of reality seems to derive from the world of film). Baudrillard sometimes speaks of hyperreality as an excess of 'reality effects'. Reality game shows might be an example of this.

incommensurability The situation of having no common measure or shared ground. Borrowing from Thomas Khun (who, in *The Structure of Scientific Revolutions* discussed the 'lack of common measure' between distinct scientific 'paradigms') Lyotard suggests that postmodernity is the proliferation of incommensurable *language games.* In other words, there can be no translation between two languages, two cultures, or two systems of ideas. In Lyotard's view incommensurability is only ever overcome by force: understanding or agreement only come about when one language game becomes dominant. Hence constant dispute is preferable to consensus.

intertextuality The way *texts* refer to other texts. It is often taken to mean practices of referencing other works, as in *eclecticism, parody* etc. In this sense anything from *Gargantua and Pentagruel* to *Austin Powers* is intertextual. But for thinkers like Julia Kristeva and Roland Barthes, all texts are intertextual in that they are (knowingly or otherwise) composed of influences, paraphrases, echoes, genre conventions, discourses, etc. Intertextuality can be seen as a necessary condition of creativity and meaning. There may be different kinds of intertextuality, but no text is independent of the network of texts that surround and precede it.

language game   Society is made up of communities that make use of specific *discourses* and have their own *codes* which affect what can be said and done. These frame the possibilities of meaning and provide the grounds on which claims can be *legitimated*. Playing a language game means acting within these bounds. For example, being a historian involves playing a language game with rules (i.e. standards agreed within the discipline) about verification, documentation, how to present an argument, etc. For Lyotard, this has important consequences:

Notions like meaning and truth can only be locally defined (i.e. they are relative).

There may be no common ground between different language games.

Society is endlessly fragmented as language games compete with each other.

Lyotard suggests that consensus between language games is neither possible nor desirable, but their boundaries can be quite porous. Indeed, Lyotard's *The Postmodern Condition* quite *eclectically* ranges over scientific, philosophical and aesthetic discourses; whether these different language games merge satisfactorily or sit at odds with each other is debatable.

late capitalism   Ernest Mandel's description of our current social and economic order (*Late Capitalism*, Verso, 1975). It involves the growth of multinational corporations, the expansion of information technology, and the turning of representation into a commodity. Mandel's description greatly influenced Fredric Jameson. *Commodification* (and a subsequent acceleration of styles and fashions) penetrates everything from art to lifestyle.

legitimation   How a community, a practice or a form of knowledge gains authority. For example, capitalism legitimates itself through 'common sense' ideas about individual rights, responsibilities, and freedom of choice (these ideas must themselves be legitimated through a further set of authorities).

Lyotard argues that all *discourses* validate themselves through narrative. Hence modern science is legitimated by its narratives of objective knowledge, emancipation from superstition, and human progress. According to Lyotard postmodernity faces a 'legitimation crisis' as faith in *metanarratives* is breaking down; *language games* now find it difficult to get authority from supposedly universal principles. Forms of knowledge are increasingly legitimated by *pragmatism*, profit and productivity (e.g. academics write papers in order to get funding to write more papers, and thereby to gain status).

logocentricity/logocentrism   The myth, as Derrida would have it, that words simply communicate meanings that exist in the consciousness of their speaker, and that those meanings are received by the listener. The assumption is that words are transparent signs, that speech immediately expresses the speaker's thoughts, and that writing tries (and fails) to imitate this relationship. Derrida calls this the 'metaphysics of presence' underlying all Western thought. He *deconstructs* it by arguing that both speech and thought are *textual* (speech is another form of writing, as *polysemic* as any other) and that they are therefore characterized by *différance*. This sense of the term is often expanded to include any way of thinking that seeks single points of origin or cores of meaning.

metanarrative   *Language games* gain *legitimation* through the local stories (or 'micro-narratives') they tell. But there are certain 'grand-' or 'metanarratives' that claim to be globally valid. A metanarrative, then, is a theory that arrogantly offers total, all-embracing answers. In doing so it tries to overarch other, more modest language games, and erase the differences between them. Marxism and the Enlightenment project are often called metanarratives. Early *semiotics* could be seen as a metanarrative because it sought to apply a universal model of meaning and language across a diversity of *texts*. Lyotard sees metanarratives as dangerously authoritarian and observes that in postmodernity 'we' are sceptical towards them. Given that many groups of people think the world would be a better place if it converted to their beliefs, this widespread scepticism may be wishful thinking on Lyotard's part. Indeed, the very notion of postmodernity could be seen as a metanarrative.

multivalency   See *polysemy*.

new historicism   A trend in literary criticism that attempts to combine poststructuralist ideas with a historical approach to analysis. The key figure is Stephen Greenblatt. At the same time as examining texts in relation to their historical situations, new historicists question the notion of history, and refuse to see texts as mere reflections of context. Though critical of what they see as postmodernism's denial of history, they share many of its concerns (e.g. scepticism about the idea of 'origin', emphasis on *polysemy*) and draw on the work of Foucault and Derrida.

parody   A parody is a mocking kind of *pastiche.* To parody something (such as the work of a particular author) is to produce a version that exaggerates certain features for humorous (often satirical) effect. Popular culture is full of this. The rapid circulation of texts in the media and the knowingness of their audiences results in things being parodied almost instantly. The film *Scary Movie* was a parody of films like *Scream,* which parodied teen horror movies of the 1980s. While these 1980s 'originals' were often pastiches of each other, they also often parodied their own genre (e.g jokey references to the shower sequence in *Psycho*). Parodies are ambiguous objects because in order to work they have to be close to their original. The music of Frank Zappa could provide a case study – many of his records seem to parody musical genres (e.g jazz) while at the same time being examples, or even improvements, of them.

pastiche   Related to *eclecticism,* pastiche is the imitation of a recognizable style. According to Fredric Jameson, it is weak and complacent in comparison with *parody.* It is shallow because it randomly mimics dead styles without having anything intelligent to say about them. Jameson says that pastiche is the defining trait of postmodern art works.

pluralism   If postmodernism had a central idea, pluralism might be it. At its simplest, it means preferring the many to the one. A pluralistic society allows minority cultures to maintain their own traditions. A pluralistic philosophy acknowledges more than one ultimate principle. A text is not a container for one deep meaning: it is a site for a plurality of readings. A pluralistic artist works in a number of styles and media, without assuming that one is essentially better than the other.

polysemy   The existence of many meanings in (or obtainable from) a *text.* All texts are arguably polysemic to some degree, but for postmodernist theory and practice polysemy is an important principle. The literary critic who acknowledges polysemy can no longer argue that his/her interpretation of a piece is the correct one. 'Multivalency' means much the same thing.

postcolonialism This term refers to literature and criticism produced in the wake of colonialism (e.g. the end of the British Empire), and is concerned with the impact of imperialism on culture. Debates about identity, subjectivity, gender and 'race' are central. 'Western' projects of modernity and enlightenment are often *deconstructed*, as is the notion of the 'margin' (e.g. 'marginal' voices, identities, etc.). Language and representation are often the focus of analysis. Some postcolonial theorists (e.g. Edward Said) examine the *discourses* through which dominant cultures represent the foreign 'Other'. The *hybrid* identity of the postcolonial *subject* is often discussed. Postcolonial critics join in postmodernism's refusal of global *metanarratives*: local identities (or struggles over identity) replace the idea of universal 'Man', particular histories replace the idea of universal 'History'.

post-feminism This can be seen as a meeting of feminist concerns (e.g. gender equality) and postmodernist attitudes (e.g. *relativism*, anti-*essentialism*). A key figure has been Madonna, for her ability to combine apparent equality in a 'man's world' (the music business) with a possibly ironic performance of female sexuality. 'Girl Power' was arguably the 1990s version of this. The television programme *Sex and the City* could perhaps be read as a post-feminist text. Post-feminism rejects what it sees as feminism's hostility to pleasure. To simplify a complicated debate: where a '1970s feminist' might see the fashion system as a form of domination (dressing up for the male gaze), a post-feminist will see it in terms of women's skilful self-creation. The less optimistic, however, argue that post-feminism plays into the hands of an unequal system.

pragmatism Treating matters only in terms of their practical consequences. Postmodern thought is often pragmatic in that it focuses on local effects and conditions rather than on grand narratives or supposedly timeless ideals. Reflected in the political realm by the emphasis, not on great ideological schemes (e.g Marxism), but on 'what works', this is sometimes seen as a product of *anomie* or disillusionment. The American pragmatist philosopher Richard Rorty suggests philosophy should worry less about what is 'true' and more about what is useful. Against Lyotard, for example, he argues that it is useful and possible for different cultures to agree with each other about some things. This can be done without assuming the existence of universal values (he agrees with Lyotard that these do not exist). Essential human nature is irrelevant – all that matters is what serves a particular purpose at a particular time.

relativism The belief that knowledge, values etc. are relative rather than absolute. A claim of any kind is 'true' only in relation to something else (e.g. a context, a culture, or a specific point of view). This means that no claim can be universally valid. This is an old idea. It is also commonplace (to say that beauty is in the eyes of the beholder is to assert a relativist view of aesthetics). So-called 'political correctness' sometimes involves relativism about 'cultural values'. Postmodern theory is often said to be relativist, or to lead to relativism. Enemies of this position say that relativists can't believe in anything, and that they are therefore morally and politically paralysed (they have no grounds on which to criticize anything). Relativists argue that you can believe something is right without assuming that it is absolutely or universally so (they must believe, after all, in the rightness of relativism).

rhizomatic A rhizome is a disordered underground stem bearing roots and shoots which look like individual plants but belong to the same system (e.g. tubers). Gilles Deleuze uses this as a metaphor for the networks of language and meaning in postmodernism; it is a desirable model because it is horizontal, democratic and has no real centre – connections can be made anywhere. It is a useful model for social systems in that it suggests people/activities/representations grouping in unpredictable ways, making unforeseen connections. The Internet is the most obvious example of a rhizomatic system, but the circulation of *signs* in general can be looked at in the same way.

semiotics The study of how *signs* work in society. A 'science', based on linguistics, which examines the processes by which *texts* become meaningful. Semiotics studies languages as systems or structures: anything from cinema to interior design to cuisine can be read as a language, according to semiotics. Although it is no longer very fashionable as a discipline, semiotic ideas remain extremely influential.

sign/signifier All communication is based on signs. In *semiotics* a sign is a unit of meaning with two elements: a physical form (i.e. a signifier, such as the sound of a word) and a reference to something (i.e. a signified, such as the meaning of a word). A sign can be anything that a community recognizes and uses as meaningful. Roland Barthes shows that everything from the Eiffel Tower to a hairstyle can be a sign. The linguist Ferdinand de Saussure argued early in the twentieth century that signs are meaningful only because they belong to a language system; meaning therefore comes from relationships (and, crucially, differences) between signs, rather than from reality or nature.

Others have focussed on identifying different types of sign. The American philosopher C. S. Peirce famously named three:

Icons (signs which resemble their signifieds, e.g. a photograph)

Indexes (signs with causal connections to their signifieds, e.g. smoke as an indication of fire)

Symbols (signs with a purely conventional meaning, e.g. words)

While these ideas are important to postmodernism, thinkers like Derrida and Baudrillard tend to emphasize the fluid and dynamic nature of signs. Poststructuralists note that signs don't get meaning from language alone; they need *discourses* and contexts. The word 'icon', for example, has a different meaning for semiotics than it does for art history. Baudrillard suggests that there is no experience free of signs. He also refers to 'free floating signifiers'. By this he means signifiers which, not being grounded in 'reality', take on new values as they are transferred to new situations. An example of this might be the *rhizomatic* travels of the image of a child in a red hooded coat (endless versions of 'Little Red Riding Hood', *Don't Look Now*, *Schindler's List*, numerous adverts etc.).

simulation A term used by Baudrillard in the 1970s and popularised in the early 1980s, but still informing the way people look at media representations, digital imagery, cloning, artificial intelligence, etc. A simulation (or a simulacrum) is sometimes defined as an image of an image – not a copy of an original, or a fake, but a free-floating *sign* produced by endlessly self-generating systems. We might say that music files or vintage arcade games downloaded from the Internet are simulations in this sense. Simulations are not unreal; they close the gap between the real and the 'artificial'. For Baudrillard society has become a simulation of itself.

spectacle According to Guy Debord (*The Society of the Spectacle*, 1967) mass media and *commodification* have turned us into passive spectators of life: a spectacle is something we watch rather than actively participate in. Capitalism seduces us by turning everything, including social relations, into spectacle – as the entire world becomes fodder for consumption, we become less willing to change it. It is time to *appropriate* the spectacle and reclaim its signs. Many aspects of cultural studies would challenge this negative view of spectacle (e.g. in what sense is consumption 'passive'?). Nevertheless, Debord's theories are still attractive to activists, certain music critics and others who position themselves against the 'mainstream'.

subject/subjectivity The notion of the subject has different meanings according to context. It sometimes refers to the individual person, conceived as a unified being with a private consciousness and a unique 'self' or identity. This model of the subject has been central to Western thought, and remains popular in everything from soap operas and love songs to liberal political thought. Most thinkers in the field of postmodernism (or at least those with some sympathy towards it) question this view of the subject, arguing instead that we have no 'essence': we are 'in process' and we are defined through *discourse*. The term 'subjectivity' can refer to the way the self is structured by specific social situations; watching a film, for example, might offer us a voyeuristic subjectivity (a film theorist might say it positions us as voyeuristic subjects). 'Subject' is often seen as a better word than self because it hints at the notion of being subject *to* something.

text/textuality This can be a surprisingly complex term, depending on who uses it and what they contrast it with. For semiotics, a text is an enclosed structure whose meanings come from internal relationships between the signs that it uses. Roland Barthes opposes it to the idea of a 'work'. To see something as a 'work' (e.g. a novel) is to see it as a unified, organic product with a deep meaning intended by its author. To see it as a text is to see it as a resource for endless interpretations. Postmodern theories tend to regard everything as text. In other words, nothing is outside of language; everything is composed of *signs, codes* and *discourses* and is therefore open to many different readings. To call a scientific treatise or a work of history a text is to say it is writing; it uses certain devices, belongs to a certain *language game* and is vulnerable to *deconstruction*. 'Textuality' refers to the condition of being a text; it sometimes means nothing more than the effects produced by the way a text is put together.

taking it further

Books

A complete bibliography of texts on postmodernism would contain thousands of entries. What follows is a rather shorter list of works that are either particularly useful, or have been influential (as demonstrated by the number of other books that refer to them). They should be reasonably easy to find in good bookshops and/or libraries. Thinkers around this subject rarely respect traditional boundaries between academic disciplines, and postmodernism blurs distinctions between the cultural and the social; therefore the way I have clustered these books is far from rigid (Jameson, for example, could fit into most of the groups). Dates in square brackets indicate original year of publication.

For more on postmodernism's questioning of the relationship between reality and representation, including ideas about 'mediation' and 'spectacle':

Baudrillard, Jean *Simulations* (Semiotext(e), 1983)

In the 1980s this was the book to be seen with for artists who fancied themselves intellectual. Still a touchstone for recent explorations of 'digital culture', and the most compact statement of Baudrillard's 'social science fiction'.

Baudrillard, Jean *America* (Verso, 1988 [1986])

In this collection of musings on his experience of America Baudrillard comes across as a dotty professor on holiday. Unafraid of cultural stereotypes and sweeping generalizations, this is a provocative but entertaining exploration of hyperreality.

Best, Steven and Kellner, Douglas *The Postmodern Turn* (Guilford Press 1997)

An excellent overview of postmodern thought which links the philosophical, the technological and the artistic in thought-provoking ways.

Debord, Guy *The Society of the Spectacle* (Black and Red, 1970)

The most important statement of situationist thinking. A major influence on Baudrillard, and still informing contemporary accounts of the role of spectacle in everyday life.

Kellner, Douglas *Jean Baudrillard: From Marxism to post-modernism and beyond* (Polity Press, 1989)

A detailed, critical examination of Baudrillard's thinking, from the Marxist structuralism of the 1960s to the hyperreality of the 1980s. Discusses many of the connections between Baudrillard and other thinkers.

Norris, Christopher *What's Wrong With Postmodernism: Critical theory and the ends of philosophy* (Harvester Wheatsheaf, 1990)

A highy critical account of postmodernism, taking particular issue with Baudrillard's 'irrational' (apparent) rejection of notions like 'truth' and 'the real'.

For more on poststructuralism, including deconstruction:

Belsey, Catherine *Critical Practice* (Routledge,1980)

An excellent introduction to poststructuralist literary theory. Strong on Barthes, Derrida and Lacan.

Barthes, Roland *Image-Music-Text* (Fontana, 1977)

A collection of essays by Barthes from various sources. Includes the important pieces 'The Death of the Author' and 'The Third Meaning'.

Derrida, Jacques *Of Grammatology* (John Hopkins University Press, 1976 [1967])

For a long time Derrida's most well-known book, this concerns the 'privileging' of speech over writing in much Western thought (the main targets are the linguist Saussure and the philosopher Rousseau).

Derrida, Jacques *Writing and Difference* (University of Chicago Press, 1978 [1967])

Contains the landmark essay 'Structure, Sign and Play in the Discourse of the Human Sciences'. Derrida subjects structuralism

(Saussure again, as well as Levi-Strauss) to rigorous critique, and finds that it suppresses its own radical implications about the play of 'difference' in language. Saussure sees speech as 'authentic' language and writing as its poor relation; Derrida sees speech as another form of writing, no closer to thought than any other kind of sign.

Derrida, Jacques *Positions* (Athlone Press, 1981 [1972])

Three interviews with Derrida, including a quite accessible account of deconstruction. Probably the best place to start trying to read him 'in person'.

Foucault, Michel *The Archeology of Knowledge* (Tavistock,1974 [1969])

An analysis of how 'discourses' are formed, transformed, legitimated and regulated.

Foucault, Michel *The Order of Things: An archaeology of the human sciences* (Random House, 1974)

Influential for its examination of the emergence (and imminent death) of 'Man'.

Norris, Christopher *Derrida* (Fontana, 1987)

A solid introduction to Derrida's work, emphasizing its place within Western philosophy more than its contribution to critical theory.

For more on postmodernism in the arts, including popular culture and debates about cultural hierarchies:

Docherty, Thomas, ed. *Postmodernism: A reader* (Harvester Wheatsheaf, 1993)

Contains many important essays and extracts from various perspectives, and covers a range of different art forms. Also includes some useful essays on postmodern politics.

Foster, Hal, ed. *Postmodern Culture* (Pluto Press, 1985)

First published in America as *The Anti-Aesthetic*, this much reprinted collection of essays has become something of a 'classic'. Contains influential pieces by Jurgen Habermas, Fredric Jameson and Jean Baudrillard. An attempt to define the radical or resistant potential of postmodernism at a time when it was generally seen as a conservative or reactionary tendency.

Hutcheon, Linda *The Politics of Postmodernism* (Routledge, 1989)

In this lucid book Hutcheon sees postmodernist art as a political practice which criticizes representation from within. Particularly good on straegies of irony, intertextuality and metafiction. Hutcheon has written a number of very interesting books on this area.

Huyssen, Andreas *After the Great Divide: Modernism, mass culture, postmodernism* (Indiana University Press, 1986)

Postmodernism for Huyssen signals the end of the great (modernist, elitist) divide between high art and mass culture.

Jencks, Charles *The Language of Post-Modern Architecture*, 4th Revised Edition (Academy Editions, 1984 [1975])

Jencks' landmark definition of a postmodernist architecture that combines different styles and creates 'decentred', irrational spaces.

McRobbie, Angela *Postmodernism and Popular Culture* (Routledge, 1994)

McRobbie sees postmodernism as the emergence of diverse, previously marginalized voices. It should therefore be embraced. Modernism is a patriarchal, imperialist metanarrative, which suppresses diversity.

Venturi, Robert *Learning from Las Vegas* (MIT Press, 1977 [1972])

Venturi celebrates the way that, in the buildings of Las Vegas, 'the sign is more important than the architecture'. In doing so, he rejects modernism for 'an architecture of bold communication', playfulness and 'disjunctive variety'.

Waugh, Patricia *Metafiction: The theory and practice of self-conscious fiction* (Methuen, 1984)

Looks in detail at strategies of self-deconstruction in postmodernist novels, and at how they examine the complex relationships between fiction and reality.

Wallis, Brian, ed. *Art After Modernism: Rethinking representation* (David R. Godine, 1984)

A collection of essays which demonstrates the impact of postmodernism on art. Famous essays by Walter Benjamin, Roland Barthes, Michel Foucault and others give extra context and weight to the selection.

For more on questions of identity, subjectivity and the body:

Butler, Judith *Gender Trouble: Feminism and the subversion of identity* (Routledge, 1990)

Remains probably the most influential statement about the 'performance' of gender. An 'anti-essentialist' argument that gender differences, far from being 'natural', are a fiction create by society to regulate sexuality.

Deleuze, Gilles and Guattari, Felix *Anti-Oedipus: Capitalism and schizophrenia* (The Athlone Press, 1984 [1972])

A vast, difficult book written by a philosopher and a psychoanalyst. Seen as a founding text of poststructuralism, it attempts a political analysis of desire and its repression. Contains important critiques of psychoanalysis and Freudian notions of the unconscious.

Foucault, Michel *The History of Sexuality: An introduction* (Penguin, 1981 [1976])

Harraway, Donna *Simians, Cyborgs and Women* (Free Association Books, 1991)

A highly influential book arguing like Judith Butler for an 'anti-essentialist' feminism that is informed by postmodernist theory. A central text in recent cyber- and techno-theory, it looks at the (potential) effects of technology on subjectivity and gender.

For more on the political implications and social conditions of the postmodern:

Anderson, Perry *The Origins of Postmodernity* (Verso, 1998)

This begins with a short yet thorough history of the idea of the postmodern. It then becomes a detailed review of Fredric Jameson, whom it regards as postmodernism's most important and convincing theorist. Like many thinkers, Anderson sees postmodernism as the failure of culture to oppose consumer capitalism.

Callinicos, Alex *Against Postmodernism: A Marxist perspective* (Polity Press, 1990)

Callinicos has little time for postmodernism. He sees it as a combination of rampant consumerism and political disillusionment. It is a symptom of capitalism ('late' or otherwise), and needs to be analyzed as such (exploitation and class war have not gone away, they have just been better hidden).

Connor, Steven *Postmodernist Culture: An introduction to theories of the contemporary* (Basil Blackwell, 1989. Revised edition, 1996)

This book was invaluable to me when I was a student. Covering a lot of ground, it is particularly strong on literature and theory, perhaps less so on popular culture. The revised edition expands on cultural politics and explores debates around postcolonialism.

Derrida, Jacques *Specters of Marx: The state of the debt, the work of mourning, and the New International* (Routledge, 1994 [1993])

Derrida criticizes Fukuyama (see below). Surprises many by arguing rationally and using evidence from the real world.

Eaglestone, Robert *Postmodernism and Holocaust Denial* (Icon Books, 2001)

A highly readable, concise essay on a challenging subject. This is part of Icon Books' excellent *Postmodern Encounters* series, each of which focuses on a specific problem within the area. Other titles include *Derrida and the End of History* by Stuart Sim and *Nietzsche and Postmodernism* by Dave Robinson.

Fukuyama, Francis *The End of History and the Last Man* (The Free Press, 1992)

This controversial book argues that the consumer economy and liberal democracy have 'won' all the political arguments and will soon rule the world. Fukuyama sees this as good news because he believes the free market creates political freedom. Human history has been completed by the triumph of capitalism.

Harvey, David *The Condition of Postmodernity* (Blackwell, 1989)

Harvey provides a detailed theory of the economic conditions referred to by Jameson and others.

Jameson, Fredric *Postmodernism, or, The Cultural Logic of Late Capitalism* (Duke University Press, 1991)

A mammoth volume, ranging freely and flashily over many aspects of contemporary life. Since many of the case studies it uses (from architecture, film, poetry etc.) are read as symptoms of the same set of social/historical conditions, the book doesn't have to be read from cover to cover. Though Jameson often writes in a lively, excited style about postmodernism, he doesn't approve of it. In my experience readers sometimes find Jameson's analyzes of specific examples (e.g. the art of Warhol, the novels of Doctorow) dazzling yet superficial.

Lyotard, Jean-Francois *The Postmodern Condition: A report on knowledge* (Manchester University Press, 1984 [1979])

This book was central to the spread of the word 'post-modernism' throughout academia in the 1980s. But it has to be said that it is not as useful as either its title or its standing would suggest. Lyotard himself didn't seem to regard it particularly highly. The main body of the text concerns the status of knowledge in contemporary science. The most widely read section, 'Answering the question: What is postmodernism?', was appended later, but is not clearly connected to the rest of the book. Contains well-known quotes about postmodernism being 'incredulity toward metanarratives', knowledge being 'a matter for TV games' and so on. Worth reading to see such quotes in their proper context.

Soja, Edward *Postmodern Geographies: The reassertion of space in critical social theory* (Verso, 1989)

Arguing in part that cultural theorists need to give more consideration to geography, Soja shows the impact of postmodernity on the organization of physical space. Capitalism 'spatializes' society as a means of discipline and control. Like many other thinkers on urban space, he takes Los Angeles as the central example, and is influenced by Lefebvre and Foucault. His more recent book *Postmetropolis:critical studies of cities and regions* (Blackwell, 2000) explores these themes further.

Squires, Judith, ed. *Principled Positions: Postmodernism and the rediscovery of value* (Lawrence and Wishart, 1993)

A collection of essays (by Kate Soper, David Harvey and others) which attempts to find a sense of value within postmodernism: Does postmodernism have to lead to the rejection of ideas like quality, evaluation or worth? Can the need for 'principled positions' be reconciled with postmodernism's 'relativist' distrust of absolutes? Most of the contributors here want to take aspects of postmodernism on board, but are anxious about the ethical and political implications of so doing.

Websites

Sifting through the Internet for good material on postmodernism can be a long and fruitless task. The following sites are useful though, and contain good links:

Erratic Impact philosophy research base:
http://www.erraticimpact.com

Popcultures:
http://www.popcultures.com

Contemporary Philosophy, Critical Theory and Postmodern Thought:
http://carbon.cudenver.edu/~mryder/itc_data/postmodern.htm

Cultural Studies Central:
http://www.culturalstudies.net

Illuminations:
http://uta.edu/huma/illuminations

Cultural Studies and Critical Theory:
http://eserver.org/theory/action/lasso

Everything Postmodern:
http://www.ebbflux.com/postmodern

Panic Encyclopedia:
http://www.freedonia.com/panic/

Critical Theory:
http://www.crasis.com

index